I0142172

The Vine Bleeds

Published by Brolga Publishing Pty Ltd
ABN 46 063 962 443
PO Box 12544
A'Beckett St
Melbourne, VIC, 8006
Australia

email: markzocchi@brolgapublishing.com.au

All rights reserved. No part of this publication may be reproduced, stored in a retrieval system or transmitted in any form or by any means electronic, mechanical, photocopying, recording or otherwise without prior permission from the publisher.

Copyright © 2015 J M Yates

National Library of Australia Cataloguing-in-Publication entry
        Yates, J. M.
        The vine bleeds : the impact of domestic violence:
        a woman's journey of spirit and strength
        9781925367003 (paperback)
        Subjects: Family violence, Victoria, Melbourne, Fiction
        Abused women, Victoria, Fiction.
        A823.4

Printed in Australia
Cover design by Working Type Studio
            www.workingtype.com.au
Typeset by Wanissa Somsuphangsri

BE PUBLISHED

Publish Through a Successful Publisher. National Distribution, Macmillan & International Distribution to the United Kingdom, North America. Sales Representation to South East Asia
Email: markzocchi@brolgapublishing.com.au

The Vine Bleeds

The impact of domestic violence.
A woman's journey of spirit and strength.

J M Yates

In memory of my mother who was the glue
that bound our family together.

Acknowledgements

I would like to thank my family for their continual support during the writing of this, my story. My gratitude is also extended to Stu Hatton, my meticulous editor and Josephine Scicluna, for her assessment of the memoir. My appreciation is also extended to Tara Wyllie, Mark Zocchi and Wanissa Somsuphangsri at Brolga Publishing. I am indebted to Sue Ogilvie and my fellow students and tutors at Deakin University for their insightful workshopping.

1

Clutching my boarding pass, I step onto the moving walkway. Splashes of colour disappear as people steadily pass in the other direction. At the gate-lounge, lost in their own thoughts, others wait to board. A small child sits at his mother's feet grizzling, pulling a dummy in and out of his mouth, vying for her attention. Businessmen tap the keys of their laptops, and the occasional mobile phone rings.

I join the queue, automatically moving forward as the dark-haired flight attendant, in a navy skirt and spotted shirt, ushers passengers onto the plane. I settle into my window seat hoping I'll be alone, but soon a smartly dressed, middle-aged woman joins me. Another hour and a bit and I'll be in Melbourne. As the plane taxis onto the tarmac I think, *Then what?*

My chest feels tight, my stomach is in knots; I feel helpless, guilty.

Why did I agree to continue the Call Processor training? I should have stayed in Melbourne these last few weeks.

The plane climbs steadily. With bright blue sky above and thick, fluffy clouds below, I ponder death and what, if anything, comes after. I frame questions about the God I was taught exists but whom I have begun to doubt. I've been called home from working interstate; my mother, diagnosed with liver cancer two months ago, is dying. The specialist was hopeful treatment would give her another year or two, but Mum has not responded well. I've been commuting interstate every week, and it's been difficult leaving her each time.

What will happen to her when she dies, I wonder?

I look out the window at the peaceful view, and a feeling of calm envelopes me.

It was different this morning. I woke suddenly with my stomach churning and a sense of foreboding. Had I been dreaming? I couldn't remember. The sun's rays creeping through the thin drapes of the hotel room warmed me and although it was early, I rose, opening the drapes to the vista of Coogee Beach. I watched the waves break across the sand and rush out again. Just like figures passing on a carousel, joggers in shorts and people dressed for work moved along the promenade. I set about getting ready for work, but my apprehension remained.

After a successful training session, quite a few participants remained to ask questions. I noticed Karen, my site contact, lingering in the background, but thought nothing of it. She quietly spoke to each attendee, and one by one, they disappeared.

She turned to me. 'Your husband just rang. He thinks you should return home immediately. Your mother's deteriorated.'

Karen paused to allow the news to sink in.

'We've organised a seat on the next flight to Melbourne and I'll drive you to the airport.' Putting her hand on my arm, Karen added, 'We're getting your luggage from the hotel, don't worry about anything—are you okay?'

I nodded. Karen gently manoeuvred me into a chair and handed me a glass of water.

I knew this was inevitable but I hadn't expected it to come so soon. I'd called the hospital the previous afternoon, but couldn't speak to Mum. I'd wanted to hear her voice, talk to her—something felt wrong. The previous night when I rang home, my husband Mark and daughter Vanessa had reassured me everything was fine.

*

The view of soft white clouds reminds me of the thick lamb's wool rug in front of the fireplace in my childhood home. I loved lying on the floor beside this rug, chattering to Pellie, my imaginary friend who lived in it.

I never lay on top, even though it was so soft—if I had, I might have hurt my friend. Whether I was happy, lonely or frightened, he always listened. Lassie my collie dog was special too, wagging her tail whenever she saw me. I smile, remembering how appalled my mother was to find me, on my hands and knees, sharing the dog's dinner.

I close my eyes. More memories materialise.

It's dark and someone is screaming. Only four years old and terrified, I put my hands to my ears to block out the horrific noise. I feel a sticky substance down the front of my pyjamas. *I've been sick; I want Mummy.* I climb out of bed and stand in the doorway; fear-stricken, I watch my father storm past dragging my mother by her hair along the floor. She is clad only in bra and corset.

'Ray, please ... you're hurting ...' she yells.

'Shut up, whore!'

'Ray ... my hair ... stop it!' she screams as she tries to hold her hair at the scalp.

'I haven't finished with you yet.'

He continues dragging her by her hair.

'You need to learn a lesson.'

I run back to bed and put my head under the pillow, trying to block out the awful sound.

*

The next morning, I threw my pyjamas in the laundry basket, dressed in the clothes my mother had put out the previous night, and wandered out to the kitchen. My mother was stirring porridge on the gas stove under the brick chimney. The wooden table in the centre of the room was covered with a green checked plastic cloth. The green meat safe and ice-chest were on the opposite wall. Through the window above the green porcelain sink, I saw the large nectarine tree laden with fruit that would be ripe and luscious after Christmas.

'Hello, Mummy.'

My mother turned around; she looked different. 'Sit up and have your brekkie. Then we're going shopping.'

I noticed her brush her cheek as she turned back to the stove. I was confused. Her eyes looked really strange.

After breakfast I ran out to the verandah that extended across the back of the house. The verandah was effectively my playroom. A large wooden box, made by my father, sat near the window. Inside the box were my toys, including my favourite golliwog.

Rather than play with the toys, I decided to find Lassie. Reaching up on my toes, I opened the door and ran down the ramp of the fernery, which was covered with a grape vine. On the left of the backyard was the vegetable garden. Last weekend when my father returned from the country, I had helped him in the garden.

'What about we plant some radishes, Jenny?' he had said while we were having breakfast.

He prepared the vegetable patch by digging a trench and putting a layer of torn-up newspaper in it. Then he covered the newspaper with dirt from the next trench he dug. 'Newspaper's good for composting, Jenny—really breaks up the ground.' Once the trenches had been completed, he went to the shed and brought back a packet of seeds. 'See this packet Jenny? It says "Wilding & West Seeds"; they're special, you know.'

This meant nothing to me.

'Although you can't read this word, it says "Wilding", and that's your grandpa who lives in Sydney—this is his business,' my father told me. I still did not know what he was talking about.

'Daddy, can we plant them?'

'Of course. We'll make a nice straight row with the rake so we can sprinkle the seeds and then we will cover them lightly with soil. Okay?'

I smiled. I loved gardening with my dad because he was always in a good mood while working in the garden.

Once the radishes were planted, I sat on the lawn, watching him prune the hedge along the fence.

'Are you going to cut the grape vine too?' I asked.

'This is not the right time, Jenny. If you prune it when it's growing, it will bleed,' he explained as he continued snipping the hedge. 'It only thrives and has lots of grapes if it is nurtured and treated well.'

The next weekend I checked the radishes we'd planted and found they had two small, round leaves on them. Lassie bounded up from the back fence and I patted her, thinking that my father must have gone to the country again this morning, because I hadn't seen him. *It's nice when he's away, because Mummy and I have fun.*

My father was an insurance agent and travelled to the country most weeks, selling life insurance to the farmers.

Lassie was by my side as I got my small trike from the shed. My mother called out, 'It's time to go to the shops.'

'Can I take my bike, Mummy?'

'I guess so … hurry up.'

As we walked down Anthony Street I noticed she was wearing sunglasses, yet it wasn't sunny. Lassie sat outside while we entered the shop. We bought butter, sugar and tea. Because it was war-time all these items were rationed.

'Thanks Mrs Wilding … did you realise you've reached your quota?' the shopkeeper asked, tearing the coupons from the ration books.

'Yes, half a pound of tea every five weeks is impossible. We always run out. I'm using dripping on the sandwiches to make the butter last the fortnight,' my mother replied.

'Yes, it's hard; the missus says it's not so bad with the sugar though.' The shopkeeper placed the articles in paper bags on the counter.

'The two pounds of sugar is more than adequate for us. I just wish they would allow more tea.' My mother placed the bags in her shopping bag.

I rode beside her as we headed home and asked, 'When's Nanna and Pop coming?'

'They're catching the train in Sydney on Friday. We'll pick them up Saturday morning,' my mother replied.

My grandparents came to Melbourne every Christmas for about six weeks and it was an exciting time for me. My pop was special. I adored sitting next to him while he smoked his long brown cigars. I loved the smell.

'Will I sleep in the lounge when they come?'

'Yes, we'll pin your stocking up on the mantle shelf. Seeing I've just got some more butter, perhaps we'll make some biscuits when we get home. Then on Christmas Eve we'll leave Santa biscuits and cordial. Will that be good?'

'Yep!' I replied.

*

The train rolled slowly into the station, steam rising from its funnel. I jumped up and down on the platform, chattering all the time. My mother was strangely quiet while my father stood rigidly, hands in his pockets. He appeared tall to me, even though he was medium height, and his moustached lips bore a smile that lit his small bespectacled face. His hat was set securely on his sparse black hair, his tie was straight and his coat buttoned as he looked up and down the carriages.

'There they are,' he said, pointing to the second carriage from the end. A distinguished, silver-haired man alighted, dressed in a dark suit. He pulled out a watch attached to a chain hanging across his waistcoat, looked at it, and returned it to his pocket. A tall, thin woman in a silky dress with a fur wrapped around her shoulders followed him, a wide-brimmed hat perched on the side of her head. A huge smile lit up the man's face when he saw the welcoming party, but the thin-lipped woman's facial expression did not change.

I wrenched my hand from my mother's and ran to my pop, who lifted me up high in the air, whizzed me around and then gave me a big hug. Nanna offered the side of her cheek. My mother stood in the background while my dad greeted his father with a slap on the back and hugged and kissed his mother.

My pop looked across at my mother and smiled. 'Nice to see you, Sophie.'

Soon we were driving home in the big black Buick.

*

Excitement mounted as Christmas Day drew near. In the lounge, the Christmas tree held pride of place in front of the high stained-glass window that was next to the fireplace. My mother carried in a big box of decorations and I ran over to open it.

'Can we put the decorations on the tree now, Mummy?'

'Of course.'

'I'd better put the star on first, it'll be easier,' my father slurred, a glass of whisky in his hand.

Pop set his whisky glass down, placed his cigar in the ashtray, looked inside the box and picked up a brightly painted wooden reindeer. He handed it to me, saying, 'Here, you must put on the first decoration.'

I beamed.

Everyone helped—or nearly everyone. Nanna put a bauble on the tree, then with whisky in hand, sat down and watched, her thin lips set.

After decorating the tree was completed my mother said, 'I've got a few things to do in the kitchen.' She picked up the box and quietly left.

Nobody noticed.

'What about another drink, Dad?'

'Sure, Ray. Your mother's glass is empty too.'

The whisky decanter was soon drained.

I enjoyed being with Pop; he made me happy. Sometimes I wandered to the kitchen to see what my mother was doing.

Mum's not much fun anymore, she's always cooking or something. She seems sad, I thought.

My father always seemed to be telling my mother to do this or that for Nanna and Pop—like a servant. I loved having my grandparents stay. The days were bright and happy but often at night, after I went to bed, there would be raised voices and the sound of my mother crying.

I woke on Christmas morning to find Santa had consumed the biscuits and cordial and left wonderful presents. I ran to my parents' room. 'Mummy, Daddy, Santa's given me a pram and a bride doll and a pillowcase full of things. Come and see!'

My father groaned, turned towards the wall and pulled the sheet over his head.

'My, you're a lucky girl!' My mother cuddled the doll that I pushed into her arms.

'Daddy, look!'

'Go back to bed,' he mumbled.

'Leave your father. He'll look later when he wakes up,' she sighed as she hopped out of bed. Smiling, she took my hand. 'Mummy wants to see what else Santa brought.'

*

Everyone at the table was talking at once.

Pop handed me a bonbon. 'Pull, Jenny, pull! Good girl, you got it! Put the hat on,' laughed Pop.

My mother was busy dishing up chicken and loads of vegetables. Chicken was special; we only had it at Christmas. Pop chatted to my father, while Nanna sat very straight, hands folded together on top of the serviette in her lap. She said little. On the table decorated with tinsel were chocolates and lollies. The plum pudding with money in it, everyone's favourite, was soon consumed. The whisky decanter was refilled.

After lunch everyone adjourned to the lounge to open the pile of presents around the tree. I watched Nanna while she waited for the presents to be distributed. Tall and slim, she wore elegant clothes and beautiful jewellery: long dangling earrings, and multiple rows of beads. My mother, handing out the presents, was much shorter and a little plump. She dressed simply and didn't have any jewellery. I thought Nanna looked like a queen. I was afraid of her, yet I looked forward to her special presents.

*

The six weeks disappeared quickly and I was soon saying goodbye to my grandparents.

My father was still working in the country selling insurance during the week and returning home for the weekends. I missed Pop now he had returned to Sydney, but I was happy my father was away.

While I was eating my breakfast one morning, my mother sat down at the table with a cup of tea.

'Darling, do you sometimes feel lonely?'

'No. I play with Pellie and Lassie and with Elaine next door.'

'Well soon you will have a baby brother or sister to play with.'

I wasn't sure about this. I enjoyed having my mother to myself. I kept eating my toast. 'Where will it sleep?'

'We'll put a cot in your room. You'll have someone to talk to, and you won't be afraid of the dark anymore,' continued my mother.

'I don't want a cot in my room.'

Over the succeeding weeks my mother kept talking about the new baby and at the weekends while we were gardening, my father kept telling me I would soon have someone to play with all the time. I started to get excited. They wouldn't tell me if I would have a brother or a sister, they just kept saying I would have to wait and see.

'When it's time to collect the baby from the hospital I'll need your help, Jenny,' my father said, trying to make me feel important.

'Do you have to pay for it?' I asked as we were planting onion seeds. I scattered the small brown seeds in the row my father had made with the rake. I gently sprinkled them with rich brown earth. I liked the feel of it falling through my hands.

'Well I guess so. Would you like to save for the baby? If you do some chores I'll pay you, and we'll put the money in a large bottle and keep it in my wardrobe. What do you think?'

'Oh Daddy, yes please.'

I did my chores and I thought I was paid handsomely. Sometimes my father gave threepence or sixpence, and if I did an extra good job I received one shilling. As the months rolled by, the bottle in the wardrobe became quite full. I was occasionally allowed to empty the bottle and count the money, and then I'd tell Pellie how much I had.

One morning as I was relaying the state of the bottle to Pellie, my mother, now quite large, lumbered in.

'Hurry up, Jenny, we're going down the street. Something very exciting has happened.'

Mystified, I collected my shoes and Lassie's lead.

Today, the usually quiet Anthony Street in Ormond was alive. Every house seemed to have someone in the front garden. As we passed, the neighbours excitedly called out and waved. 'Wonderful news, Mrs Wilding!'

'It's marvellous! So glad it's over!' My mother laughed, smiled and waved back.

I didn't understand what all the commotion was about.

We reached North Road. What a sight. Colourful flags were flying from every shop verandah. People were standing in the streets, shouting and jumping up and down. Shopkeepers stood outside their shops chatting. Spontaneity and laughter was the theme, and in the distance, I heard the sound of beating drums. Soon a band appeared. The players with drums, trumpets and saxophones marched briskly down the centre of the main road and people followed behind, singing and laughing.

'Mummy, this is fun. Why are all the flags up on the roofs?' I didn't understand what was going on.

'This is the most wonderful day. Even when you're grown up, today, the 8th of May 1945, will be remembered. The war has ended.'

'What's a war?'

'Oh darling, it's hard to explain. But it's when different countries fight each other. It's cruel and it's sad.'

'I don't know what you mean.'

'Well, Jenny, a long, long way from here a lot of very brave men from Australia have fought to protect countries that are our friends. Lots of people have been killed so we could be safe. But now that the war is over, our brave men can come home. That's why everyone is happy. Come on, let's dance to the music too,' said my mother.

After a short time, a little puffed, she sat on the bus stop bench next to an elderly gentleman. He was bent over, his arms leaning on his walking stick. 'Wonderful news, hey?' he said.

'Yes, it's been an amazing few weeks,' my mother answered.

'Yeah … quite eventful. Thought it was marvellous when I heard of Hitler's suicide.' The man looked at my mother and smiled. 'Then the German forces in Italy surrendered … it didn't stop there … the surrender in Holland and Denmark followed.'

'And now Britain has declared an end to the war … it's just wonderful. My baby will now come into a world free of war.' My mother leaned back and smiled. She sat for such a long time. She looked tired yet happy. I played with Lassie, danced to the music, and watched the people who were rushing up and down the street with their colourful streamers and flags.

*

'Mummy, can I get up now?'

It was a month or so after Victory Day, and I didn't dare get out of my new bed until Mummy came. There was no answer. I kept calling, but eventually clambered down from the high bed and put on my slippers and dressing gown. I started up the hall to my parents' room. Daddy met me in the hall, smiling as he picked me up. Yuck, his breath smelt horrible. I was surprised I didn't get into trouble for getting out of bed.

'Jenny, your little baby brother's arrived.' He put me down.

'Where is he?' I ran up to the bedroom. 'Where's Mummy?'

'She's in the hospital with the baby. We'll go to see them after breakfast.'

'I don't want breakfast. I've got to take the money to pay for him.'

'We're not going till you're dressed and have eaten your cornflakes. We'll pick the baby up in a few days and we'll take the money then.' Daddy patted my head. 'Off you go and get dressed. Mummy put your clothes on the end of the bed.'

*

My mother was in a huge white bed. She looked small and she had a bundle in her arms. 'Ray, he's all head and no body,' she announced with a smile.

'Where's his body, Daddy?' I asked, anxiously.

He laughed, picked me up and sat me on the bed next to my mother. I studied this fair-haired, big-headed baby. His hands were so tiny. I looked at mummy who was concentrating on the baby—I wanted her to talk to me. She looked up and smiled at me.

*

The day the baby was due home, I just couldn't wait. Daddy seemed so slow getting himself ready. He read the paper and drank many cups of tea. Eventually we were on our way. At the main entrance of the hospital I started crying.

'For goodness sake, what's the problem?' Daddy brushed his brow with his hand. 'Stop your screaming, I've got a headache.'

'Daddy, the money—it's at home. I can't pay for the baby.'

'It's okay. I've got money in my pocket. I'll pay and you can pay me back.'

My stern father picked me up and gave me a hug.

'But Daddy, I wanted to. Let's go home and get it.'

'Not a chance. Be a big girl and stop crying,' my father said in an exasperated tone as he put me down.

*

Things changed. My mother was always busy bathing, feeding or nursing this thing that made so much noise. She kept asking me to help, but I felt left out.

The following year I commenced school. Mum, with my baby brother David in the pram, walked me to school on my first day. As we reached the gate she put her arms around me. 'At lunch time I'll pick you up here and we'll go home for lunch.

Wait for me if I'm not here, won't you? Don't forget: wait. Now let's find your classroom.'

In the classroom, the teacher told me where to sit. Mum bent down and gave me a kiss. 'Now wait at the gate Jenny … don't forget.'

'Mummy, can't you come here?'

'Jenny, the teacher doesn't like all the parents coming to the classroom. Mummy was told she had to pick you up at the gate. So just wait there. Okay?' With a wave, my mother left the room.

I was a little nervous and also excited, but as I watched my mother leave I suddenly felt lonely and scared. I wanted to cry. Other children were crying, but I wasn't going to be a cry-baby.

The teacher read a story and we played a game. At recess we were marched outside into a huge asphalted area. In the centre was a tree with a large leafed canopy, and underneath in the shade were crates of bottled milk. We were all handed a bottle. I only liked the vanilla-flavoured milk that my mother made, but the teacher told me to hurry up when she noticed I wasn't drinking. I put the bottle to my lips. The milk was warm and yuck, but I drank it up so I wouldn't get into trouble.

At lunch time, we were shown the shelter shed where we could eat our lunch. I was going home for lunch, so the teacher walked me to the gate to meet Mummy. I waited. After a long time I decided to walk a little way down the street. I walked and walked and finally, tired and distraught, found myself at the beach. I was lost. Nobody was around; I sat on the wall separating the sand from the path and cried.

'Are you lost?'

I peeked through my fingers and saw a man dressed in a dark suit. He knelt down in front of me, but not too close, and smiled. I said nothing and rubbed my tear-stained face and started to swing my legs.

'Where's your mother?'

'She was supposed to meet me. She didn't come,' I sobbed.

'What's your name?'

'Jenny.'

'Oh, Jenny Wilding?'

I nodded.

'Don't cry. I think you live in Anthony Street ... don't you?'

I nodded again.

'I thought so. I collect your mother's insurance premium each month. Come on, stop crying, you'll be home in no time.'

The man gently took my hand and led me to his car.

*

The doorbell rang. My distressed mother opened the door.

'Jenny, Jenny, where have you been?' She scooped me into her arms. 'Where did you find her?' She looked up at the man.

'At the beach. She'd walked a long way. Said she was waiting for you at the school gate.'

'The baby was asleep and I was late to pick her up. The teacher took her to the wrong gate.' My mother brushed my hair out of my eyes. 'I can't thank you enough. It's so lucky you found her. I didn't know what to do. I came back here from school thinking she'd be here. My neighbour went one way, I went the other. I've notified the police. It's been horrendous the last three hours. Oh, please come in. Have a cup of tea.'

'Thanks all the same but I've still got calls to make. Glad it's all sorted now. Bye, Jenny.'

Mum closed the door, looked at me, then picked me up in her arms and hugged me tight. She carried me to the kitchen, sat down and nursed me for a long time but didn't say anything. Then she put me down.

'Into the bathroom. Get undressed while I run your bath. Tomorrow I'll come to the classroom to pick you up; the teacher will just have to understand.'

*

My father arrived home from the country unexpectedly. He stormed angrily into the house and yelled, 'Where's my tea? The least a man can expect is for his tea to be on the table.'

Mum said nothing but quickly prepared some food.

I was scared. We sat at the table—Dad with his glass of whisky, Mum with a strained expression. In the centre of the table was a plate of cream-puffs, a very special treat. I'd never tasted one. I eyed those puffs during dinner, while my parents argued. I concentrated on eating every morsel, even the cabbage; I knew to have a cream puff I must empty my plate.

My father was accusing my mother of being a whore when all of a sudden, she stood up, reached over, picked up a cream puff and threw it, hitting him on the shoulder. The cream spilled down the front of his suit. Then she picked up a second and threw again. I watched the centre of the table. *Mummy, please leave at least one.* But quickly the plate was empty. Cautiously, I looked at my father. His face was white with cream and red with fury. His clothes were covered in cream and pastry.

He jumped up and grabbed my mother by the hair.

'You bitch! You're nothing but a prostitute. I'll fix you, you little slut!' My father dragged her towards him and I heard the resounding thud as his hand met Mum's face.

'Stop it! What about the child?'

'You should have thought about that before. You'll pay for this—by God you'll pay!'

He forced her into the bathroom and closed the door.

I looked at the closed door then sat down cross-legged on the floor and rocked backwards and forwards, whimpering as I listened to the piercing screams and dreadful thumping noises.

Outside the rain had eased, but a bitter wind lashed around the house.

I stood and went to David, who was standing in his cot crying. I put my hand through the bars and stroked him as I'd seen my mother do. The bathroom door opened.

'I'll fix you, bitch!' Dad pushed Mum, her pretty cotton dress now ripped, up to the bedroom. The door closed, but the raised voices continued for a very long time. Then I heard the slam of the front door.

'Ray, let me in! Please Ray, it's freezing!'

'Shut up, bitch! Shut up or you'll get more!'

My father sat in a lounge room chair, lit a cigarette and sipped his whisky. My mother continued banging on the door, begging to be let in. He turned on the wireless, which stood in a dark wooden cabinet in the corner of the room. The stations were marked on the glass dial that occupied the top section of the cabinet. Below the dial were several knobs to adjust the volume and tone and to change the station. My father turned the volume knob as far as it would go to block out my mother's piercing screams.

'Daddy, Daddy, let Mummy in. It's windy and it's raining and it's cold. Please let her in!'

'Shut up or you'll get a belting!'

'Please Daddy, please!' I started to open the door. He

bounded out of his chair, grabbed me, picked me up and threw me into my bedroom.

'I'll teach you to interfere! Don't move.' He tore to the laundry.

I started down the hall towards the front, but my father rushed back and grabbed me.

'Don't you touch the front door, do you understand?'

He started to belt me around the legs with a solid bicycle pump. As the pump connected with my legs, the pain was excruciating. However, the sting when the metal-tipped hose on the end of the pump connected and wound around my legs was worse.

I screamed.

He jolted upright, pump in hand, and picked me up and tossed me into my bedroom, shutting the door. 'Stay there and don't you dare come out, do you hear?'

I climbed up onto my bed, crying quietly. The swollen red welts on my legs hurt, and outside I could hear the howling wind, but no longer could I hear my mother.

Mummy will be so cold.

2

'Jenny, come and I'll do your hair.'

Norma, our next-door neighbour, bustled into the playroom. I was sitting on the toybox, holding my golliwog. Elaine, Norma's daughter, knelt on the floor, placing a blanket over my favourite doll in its cot.

'Come on, dear. Let's get those rags out of your hair,' Norma said.

She had earlier wound rags around sections of my hair to make long sausage curls, just as my mother often did.

'Your grandma will be here any minute. Elaine, tidy up. We'll be off home once Jenny's grandma arrives.'

Gently, Norma took my hand and led me to the kitchen, where she sat me on the table, and set about fixing my hair.

'It'll be good once Grandma's here, dear. You'll see.' Norma gently combed the curls.

At the sound of the key in the front door, she set me down from the table.

'There she is. Off you go and say hello.'

I didn't move. She gently pushed me up the hall. Next to my father was a short, plump little lady, with a round face and shiny skin. Her hair was caught up at the nape of her neck, but fine wispy bits escaped. Her navy coat was open, revealing a dark green box-pleated skirt and a navy woollen jumper. Her thick stockinged legs disappeared into sensible black shoes.

'Norma, this is Lillian, my wife's mother.' My father turned to the little lady, saying, 'And this is our next-door neighbour, she's been looking after the children.'

I snuggled into Norma's side, holding her hand tightly.

'Hello, Jenny.' The lady I would come to know as Grandma Stenhouse knelt down. 'I've been so excited knowing I was finally going to meet you for the first time. Where I live … it's such a long way away. What a big girl you are … such pretty curls. You must be five now. Is that right?'

I nodded.

Norma said, 'I'm sure you'd like a cup of tea after your long train trip. I'll make one before I go.' She closed the door and walked down the hall, with me trailing after her.

'Ray, where's my daughter? I want to see her straight away.' My grandma deftly removed her coat and hung it on the hallstand.

'In there.' He pointed to the bedroom.

Grandma called to me and extended her hand. 'Let's go and see Mummy.'

I turned around and stood still, but Norma gently pushed me towards her. She took my hand and we went into the bedroom. Grandma closed the door.

My mother was bedridden after the violent beating the night she was locked out in the bitter cold. The doctors were unsure when she would walk again, and my grandmother had agreed to look after David and me until alternative plans could be made.

She bent and kissed her daughter. 'Oh Sophie, look at you!' My grandma turned away and wiped her eyes.

'Oh Mum, I'm so glad to see you. It's been so long.'

'It certainly has—must be six years. I wish it was under better circumstances.'

'You've no idea what it's been like. I'm scared of him. He's kind when sober, but once the drink gets a hold, he's a monster. I never know who is coming home.' My mother winced as she tried to move.

'The drink's no excuse. What do the neighbours think of him locking you out? Couldn't you have gone to them for help?'

'Norma's marvellous. She's been helping me every day. I couldn't go to them… it was the middle of the night … so embarrassing.'

'Well if you had, you might not be in this predicament. What do the doctors say?'

'Not a lot. Just keep telling me I need to rest and that hopefully the medication will do its work.'

'Well you're not to worry. I'm here now. It's amazing what rest will do for the body. We'll work it all out. Is there anything I can get you?' Grandma was still holding Mum's hand.

'No, I'm fine … Norma brought me a cup of tea just before you came.'

Grandma stood up. 'I'll let you rest. I'll go and meet the baby and of course get to know my little granddaughter.' She looked down at me and smiled. 'There's one consolation: at last I'm meeting my two grandchildren.' She held out her hand. 'Come on Jenny, you can show me the way to the kitchen. Norma's making me a cup of tea.'

We walked down the hall to the kitchen. My father was nowhere to be seen. I clambered up onto the chair at the table and sat quietly, eating a biscuit and drinking a glass of milk. Grandma sat sipping her tea and talking to Norma, and then she asked, 'Where's David, Jenny? Perhaps you can show me?' She smiled and glanced at Norma, who nodded her head.

'Go on, Jenny. Grandma can bring David out here. It'll soon be time for his bottle.'

I shyly climbed off the chair and walked past her to the bedroom.

'So this is where you sleep, Jenny. What a big bed!'

Grandma eyed the high three-quarter bed in the corner of the room. The cot was opposite. She picked up the baby and sat on the bed, quietly talking to me.

Grandma Stenhouse is so different from my Nanna Wilding, who's tall and slim. She doesn't look like a grandma; she's short and sort of fat. But she's nice; she smiles and talks to me; Nanna Wilding doesn't.

Grandma Stenhouse settled in. Each day, she walked me to and from school, pushing the pram. She told me about my cousins who lived near her in Maitland, and she said she hoped one day I would meet them.

'Grandma, why doesn't Mummy get better?' I asked one day.

'Sometimes my dear, it takes a long time,' Grandma replied. 'But Mummy will get better.'

'But why can't she get out of bed? If I was a doctor I'd make her better. I think I'll be a doctor when I grow up.'

'That's a good idea, Jenny.' She smiled.

While I was at school, Grandma looked after David and my mother and did the housework. When I returned from school and had finished the snack Grandma always had waiting for me, I would climb on my mother's bed and stay there until tea time. She listened to me while I read my school reader. Each time I had difficulty in pronouncing a word, my mother would say, 'Sound your words, sound your words, Jenny.'

My father continued to work in the country and spent his

weekends at home, gardening. He was fertilising the lemon tree a couple of months after my grandmother arrived.

'How's Sophie?' Our neighbour Murray's head appeared over the fence.

'Not bad, improving every day.'

'It's good her mother's here, I guess.' Murray wiped the perspiration from his face.

'She won't be able to stay indefinitely—my father-in-law is not a particularly patient man. Not sure what I'll do. Sophie'll need help with the children and the house for quite a while.'

'I'm sure Norma would help,' Murray boomed.

'Thanks, but I've decided I'll have to give the country work away.'

'Well just remember we'll help where we can. Got a lot of time for Sophie.' Murray's head disappeared.

My father, with his love of flowers and shrubs, ended up buying a florist shop. He was following in the footsteps of his father, who from humble beginnings as a miner in Western Australia became a seedsman, with his own business and florist shop. Dad's father also wrote gardening books and hosted a regular radio segment on gardening. My father worked in the mines when he was twelve, and by the time he was eighteen owned and operated a bus route from Carnegie to St Kilda. So another business was the obvious choice for him. He worked hard building the business in Glenferrie Road, Malvern, and he obtained a weekly spot on 3AK, a Melbourne radio station, providing gardening advice, as his father had done on 2UW in Sydney. He often worked late at the shop, with the obligatory bottle of whisky as a companion.

To give Grandma a break he occasionally took me to the shop, which was exciting. The front section was clean and tidy, with flowers tumbling out of big buckets of water. At the back was a small counter with a cash register and a pile of brown paper to wrap the flowers. I watched the customers wandering from bucket to bucket trying to decide whether to buy stocks, snapdragons, carnations or gladioli. In contrast, the back section of the shop was quite messy, especially when the two girls working for my father were busy making wreaths. Sometimes they let me put some flowers into a wreath, a round circle made with intertwining wire covered with green florist paper. Each flower was wired along the length of the stem and then green florist paper was wound around the upper section, leaving some wire exposed to push into the wreath. It required large amounts of flowers and greenery to complete one wreath, and usually many wreaths were ordered for each funeral. I would sit on the bench helping until the girls sent me to play with the two shop cats: Gwenny, a black Persian; and Winny, a striped ginger cat.

One night at dinner, Dad was in a sombre mood.

'Good shepherd's pie, Lillian.' He took a mouthful.

'Glad you're enjoying it,' Grandma commented coolly, and continued eating.

'Had a bit of an unpleasant day today.'

'What happened?' Lillian put her knife and fork together.

'Found Gwenny up the lane, skinned. She was a beautiful cat. What bloody idiot would do that? Had to bury her … it nearly made me sick.'

I screamed and ran from the room.

'Ray, what possessed you to say that in front of the child? She adored that cat!' With a menacing look, Lillian left the room and went to console me. My father continued eating.

Mum slowly improved and with Grandma's continual support and encouragement, she started to take a few steps. It was a slow progression, but after several months she started to resume some of the tasks around the house and helped to look after us.

The time came for Grandma to leave. I wished she could stay; with Grandma in the house, everything was peaceful.

*

I was excited on my sixth birthday and wondered if my father would be home for my birthday tea. For some reason he had gone to hospital the day before. However, when I returned from school, my mother said Daddy wouldn't miss my birthday for anything. Auntie would be coming too.

I thought the dress with puffed sleeves that my parents gave me was very pretty. Auntie Nita arrived with Snakes and Ladders, and Nanna Wilding sent a pretty necklace. My father didn't appear, so we started dinner. Everyone wore party hats. David, a bright blue hat on his head, sat in his high chair banging his spoon on the tray, to let everyone know he was there. In the centre of the table was a bowl of lollies—a special treat.

My father arrived.

'They took my eye out, turned it around and put it back in again,' he commented loudly as he lurched into the room.

I looked in awe at the big white pad covering his eye. *How could they take Daddy's eye out and put it back in?*

My mother fetched his meal. Silence engulfed the table.

'Having a good birthday, Jenny?' he boomed.

I nodded and kept eating.

'How's school?'

'The doctors are coming. Mummy's signing a form.'

'What form?'

'Just the annual medical check, Ray. Need a bit of history, that's all.' My mother started to cut her meat.

'Go get the form, Jenny. I want to see it,' he roared.

I looked at my mother, who nodded, so I slipped off my chair and went to the kitchen. Returning, I gave the form to my father, who quickly glanced at it and immediately tore it into small pieces.

'No daughter of mine will be examined by school doctors. You tell them that, Jenny.'

I started to cry and David followed suit. *The teacher said I must return the signed form tomorrow. I'll be in trouble.*

'Stop snivelling. Eat your tea.'

A tense atmosphere settled on the table. Everyone quietly continued to eat. Later, my mother lit the candles on the birthday cake and without a smile I blew them out. Everyone sang 'Happy Birthday'—my father in a very loud voice.

Curled up in bed, I wondered what the teacher would say. I straightened my legs and began to roll backward and forward, singing quietly. I often rocked myself to sleep, especially when I felt unhappy or scared.

Tomorrow I'll read the book Elaine lent me, I thought dreamingly as I rocked. *What's it called? The Tale of ... The Tale of Town Mouse ... Johnny Town-Mouse ...*

*

I'm sitting on my toybox, turning the pages. There is Johnny Town-Mouse, eating scraps from the table, then sheltering from the rain under a leaf.

Suddenly Mickey Mouse, my favourite toy, is standing menacingly in front of me. He becomes bigger and bigger until his head reaches the ceiling. Towering over me, he bends down and grabs

my book, pushing me. I fall into a sea of large creepy, crawling bugs.
He rips the cover off the book, tears the pages into little bits, and
throws them amongst the bugs. The bugs chew them all up. Mickey
moves to the doll's cot. He grabs my new bride doll, punching it in
the face. The doll's face disappears. He snatches Golliwog and shakes
him. Golliwog's stuffing falls out. The bugs eat it. 'Good, he's dead,'
says Mickey.

I woke crying loudly.

My mother rushed in.

'Mickey's hurt my doll … and Golliwog,' I sobbed.

'It's just a nasty dream, darling.' She hugged me. 'Tonight
you can sleep with me.'

She carried me back to her bed, where I snuggled in and
felt safe.

After breakfast the next morning, I went to the playroom
and soon returned to the kitchen.

'I've put Mickey in the bottom of the toybox. He's horrible
and I'm never playing with him again. My doll is okay and I've
put Golliwog in my bed.'

'Jenny, remember it was only a bad dream; it didn't really
happen.' My mother bent down and hugged me. 'Come on now,
let's get ready for school. I'm taking you today.'

At school, my mother spoke to the teacher and signed
another medical form.

*

My father spent two years building the florist shop into a
successful enterprise, and it became well known throughout
Melbourne. His staff increased to six, and now not only did
they make the wreaths and wedding bouquets, but they also
organised floral arrangements for many business and corporate

functions. Now that the business was a success, he no longer found it a challenge, so sold it and bought a run-down General Store in Moorabbin.

The shop was located on Nepean Highway, opposite the council chambers and a chemist shop. Next door was a large double-fronted poultry auction room. A fruit and vegetable shop was situated a few doors towards South Road, while further along stood a lone house. On one corner of the South Road and Nepean Highway intersection, there was a hotel, while on another there was a newsagent. Several more houses were dotted amongst paddocks of long grass that lined the highway.

There was a storeroom and three cold, damp rooms behind the shop, all old and in a state of disrepair. In the storeroom was a heavy cast-iron, floor-mounted set of scales used to weigh flour, sugar, tea and oats. A counter ran down the centre of the shop. Behind this were shelves stocked with canned food, large biscuit tins and brown paper bags filled with weighed produce. My parents spent long hours running the business, so I was transferred to the local school, but we continued to live in Ormond.

Each day I walked to school on my own, along an unmade path at the side of Nepean Highway and past Gilbey's Gin Distillery. My new school seemed much bigger and the desks were different, with two children sitting together. We shared an inkwell in the centre of each desk, and I began using a pen with a nib. I would dip the nib deeply into the inkwell as I wrote, resulting in large ink stains on my first two fingers.

The hours after school were lonely, as my mother was always busy, but I sometimes helped out in the storeroom. I put sugar or flour into a brown paper bag that I rested on one side of the scales. Then I placed a one-pound weight on the other side, and when the crossbar was perfectly straight, I knew the flour or sugar was the correct weight. I folded the brown paper bag so it would remain closed, ready to stock the shelves in the shop. Sometimes I went for a walk in the paddocks behind the shop, or wandered into the auction rooms and watched the cages of hens, chickens, ducks and roosters being sold. After closing the shop, my parents stocked the shelves before returning home for tea, so I played with David. It was a pretty boring time for a nine-year-old. Each day was more or less the same, but one day when I was exploring the paddocks at the back of the shop, someone called out.

'Hello.'

I turned. A skinny, dark-haired boy loped towards me.

'You're from the grocer's shop, aren't you?'

'Yes.'

'Do your parents own it?'

'Yes. Why?'

'Aw, just wondered. My dad owns the fruit shop. What's your name?'

'Jenny.'

'Mine's George. Like some fruit? I just help myself. Come on; let's get a banana, then we could climb the quince trees.'

'Quince trees, where?'

'Ah just down the road a bit.'

'I've never seen them.'

'They're old knobbly trees, but I love climbing them. The fruit makes your mouth feel funny, but it's still good to eat. But let's get some fruit from me dad's first.'

'Are you sure you're allowed?'

'Of course I am.'

We wandered back up the track and into the back of the fruit shop. George's parents were busy serving. He boldly grabbed a couple of bananas, shoved them in his pocket, then picked up a couple of apples and rushed out of the shop. We set off down the track again and walked further than I had ever been. Then I saw the old gnarled quince trees, all in a row, probably the last of an old orchard. Nearby, in the high-grassed paddock, was a dugout area.

'Let's eat our bananas first.' George jumped into the dugout. 'I come here often. Just lie and look at the clouds. Jenny, what do you think that one looks like?' George pointed skywards.

I looked up. 'I don't know … perhaps an elephant.' I could imagine a trunk, big head, four legs and a little tail.

George passed a banana and I squatted next to him. After a while I lay back, hands behind my head, as he was doing, and watched the clouds roll by. Together we imagined all kinds of images. Bananas eaten, we jumped up and ran to the trees, and George scaled one quickly and looked down.

'Come on, come up here.'

I looked up. I had no idea how to climb the tree. 'I don't know how.'

'It's easy. Put your foot on the branch, there on the left. That's right. Now hold on to the trunk, pull yourself up. See, you can do it. Put your other foot on the next branch. Good!'

George pulled out an apple and took a bite. I kept clambering, and finally reached him.

'Just lean back in the fork of the trunk. Don't be frightened.' George passed me an apple.

When I felt more at ease, I looked around. *Wow, it all looks different.*

It started to get dark, so we set off home and found the shops had closed. My mother was up the ladder stacking shelves and my father was bringing in stock from the outside storeroom. My little brother sat astride his trike in the centre of the store.

'Where've you been, Jenny? I've looked everywhere for you,' my mother said crossly. 'After this morning this is just too much!' She glared down.

'What happen this morning?' I asked.

She proceeded to tell me that she had told David he could ride his trike up and down the footpath in front of the shop. When she went to get him for kindergarten, she couldn't find him. She'd rushed back inside, asking, 'Ray, where's David?'

'I saw him through the window a few minutes ago,' he had replied, handing Mrs Briggs her change.

'Well he's nowhere to be seen now.'

My mother had rushed back outside, but there was no little boy or trike in sight. She'd run down the highway to the hotel, then back the other way to the railway line. She had wondered what on earth could have happened to him. Where could he have gone? He was only four years old. The alarm was raised and the whole neighbourhood was looking for my brother. Hours went by with no sign of him.

Mum continued the story, telling me that early in the afternoon, the local bus had been travelling along its normal route when a passenger called out.

'I think that little boy on the trike is from the grocer's. I was in the shop earlier. They're frantic. He's been missing since first thing this morning. I'm sure it's him.'

The driver had stopped and the woman alighted.

'David!'

The youngster turned and smiled.

'Where are you going, young man?'

He didn't answer.

'Mummy and Daddy are missing you. I think you'd better come home with me. You can have a ride on the bus.'

Apparently David was unconcerned. He'd been having fun riding his trike. On the bus, he had sat quietly next to this complete stranger, looking out the window. Later, reunited with his parents, he'd asked his mother, 'Why are you crying, Mummy?'

Now I understood why she was so cross. I looked up at her on the ladder. 'I'm sorry Mum; David getting lost was just like me when I started school. Today I met the boy from the fruit shop. His name's George. We've been climbing trees. I brought a quince for you.'

'Jenny, I've told you before, you need to let me know where you're going. There's no excuse. You don't even know this boy. It could have been anyone.'

'Mum, I knew it was alright 'cause he took me into his shop to get some fruit.'

'Pass those cans to me. The sooner this shelf's packed, the sooner we can go home.'

My mother stretched up and reached to the shelf. 'Mr Baker mentioned today that you've been taking biscuits from the tins without asking. Have you?'

'Sometimes … when I'm hungry. George is allowed to help himself to fruit.'

'Just ask, Jenny. Then everyone will be happy.'

Mean old Mr Baker, telling Mummy. I don't like him. Yesterday when I stood in the doorway and reached around the corner to open the biscuit tin on the shelf, he walked past and shut it, jamming my fingers. Why's he so nasty?

Mr Baker worked for my father and was popular with the

customers. Always neat in his white grocer's jacket and apron, nothing was a trouble. If customers asked for an assortment of biscuits, a quarter pound of this and a quarter pound of the other, he would cheerfully oblige. He smiled and chatted while he put the biscuits into a brown paper bag and weighed them before handing them to the customer. He cleverly made himself invaluable to the customers, displaying an attitude that gave the impression he was the owner. Mr Baker's popularity far outweighed my father's, because my father was often bad-tempered when he was behind the counter, especially if he had been drinking. My mother tolerated Mr Baker because she needed him when my father was absent—at the pub or out the back sleeping off a drinking bout. Mr Baker secretly enjoyed his position of power.

As usual, it was late when we arrived home from the shop. My mother carried my sleeping brother inside and then prepared dinner. Dad went to the garage. He had shouted at her all the way home, saying she was nothing but an idiot for the way she had handled the bloke who had delivered the cheeses. 'You don't just pay him!' he had yelled. He just never let up and I had no idea what it was about, but knew my mother was very upset. While I was having my bath, I wondered if I would see Elaine this weekend. I hardly saw her anymore. Now David was bigger, I played with him a bit at the shop, but it was not the same as spending time with Elaine.

After dinner I went to bed and straight to sleep.

Sometimes I went to sleep in the playground at school. I didn't have any friends in my new school, and ate lunch on my own. While everyone played together, I would lie beneath the big gum tree, and trying to be inconspicuous, I would pretend to be asleep. Sometimes I did go to sleep and wouldn't hear the bell ringing. The teacher would wake me when she realised I was missing. Then I felt important. Someone had taken notice. However, eventually the teacher decided to make an example of me. She stood me on the platform in front of the class and hit me several times around the legs with the strap. It hurt, but the humiliation was worse. I didn't cry.

*

The next morning I found my mother in the laundry off the verandah.

'Morning, dear.' She was stirring the clothes in the gas copper, with a thick wooden stick. 'Your breakfast is on the table. Is David awake?'

'No.' I wandered towards my doll's cot at the other end of the verandah.

'Once I've put these clothes through the wringer, you can help me peg them on the line.'

'Mm,' I said without interest.

'I need to go to the shops. We'll take Lassie.'

'I want to play with Elaine.'

'You can, when we get back.'

'Can't I stay with Daddy?'

'No, Daddy's busy. He wants to concentrate on his books.'

Why do we have a shop? My parents are always too busy for anything.

I skipped into the kitchen. There stood my father, stirring a glass of orange juice, with the castor oil bottle in his other hand. I stopped in my tracks, took one look, then rushed to my bedroom and crawled under the bed. I pushed myself against the far wall.

'Come here! Where are you?' he called from the kitchen.

I didn't answer.

'Jenny, there's a drink here for you.'

I still didn't answer.

He walked in, knelt down and peered under the bed. From my dark corner, I saw my father, his straight black hair balding at the top. He was looking vicious. He enjoyed giving me this horrible stuff.

'Come on, Jenny. It's for your own good. You won't have trouble going to the toilet.'

He put the glass down beside him and stretched his arm under the bed, but couldn't reach. Once more, he cajoled and I cowered in my corner. Then his mood changed.

'Get out now or it'll be the worse for you.'

I knew what would be in store if I didn't. I started to cry.

'Get out of there now. If I move this heavy bed, you'll know about it.'

I crawled out and he handed me the glass. I took one sip and screwed up my face.

'Drink it straight down, then you won't taste it.' He looked menacingly at me.

Softening, he said, 'When you're finished, you can have a glass of Mummy's homemade lemon drink. You'll like that.'

Between sobs, I drank. *I'm glad I'm not staying home with him.*

*

'Jenny, I'm ready. Get the dog's lead.'

Lassie pulled at the lead as we walked down Anthony Street. David, riding his small trike, arrived at the corner and stopped.

He pointed. 'Look, Mummy, look!'

On the opposite corner was a huge white tent with ropes attached to the ground with pegs. An elephant was tethered by a chain around its foot. Nearby was a cage containing lions, and next to that were two camels tied by a rope through their nose-rings.

'Mummy, it's a circus! Oh I want to go,' I said.

'I don't think we can, love. I'm not sure Daddy would want to go.'

'Please, Mummy!' I pleaded.

'Please, Mummy!' David chorused.

'Jenny, I said I don't think so. Let's leave it at that.'

'Can we go and look at the animals?'

'I guess so.' She guided us across the road.

'David, look at the elephant's feet. They're so big!'

David held grimly onto Mum's hand. The man with the elephant let me give it a piece of apple. He showed me how to hold the apple flat, in the palm of my hand. The elephant's trunk slowly rose up. I was scared, but I kept my hand out. The tip of his trunk gently ran across my hand, tickling it, as he took the piece of apple. I laughed.

'Look David, he took the apple. He took the apple!' I excitedly jumped up and down.

We did the shopping, and on the way home I wanted to return to see the animals, but my mother said we didn't have time.

I put Lassie's lead away and rushed next door to tell Elaine about the circus. She already knew about it, because her family had gone the previous night. She told me all about it. I desperately wanted my family to go, but I was beginning to realise that my family was different from Elaine's. The members of her family were always laughing and messing around together, whereas in my family there was more yelling than laughter. I was scared of my father, except when we were gardening, and seeing my mother assaulted terrorised me. I was feeling quite miserable as I walked home.

My mother was smiling broadly when I arrived.

'Jenny, Daddy's taking us to the circus tonight. He has tickets.'

This was a huge surprise, and showed the other side of my father. The loving father, rarely seen.

*

We entered the big tent, and my father bought David and me a packet of fairy floss. I didn't know what it was; it looked like coloured cottonwool. My mother explained it was something yummy to eat. Inside the tent were rows of tiered seats; we found ours and sat on the hard planks of wood. Two clowns were fooling around in the ring, in the centre of the tent. I laughed and excitedly looked up and saw lots of ropes and a swing thing. *I wonder what that's for.*

Once the show started it was dusty, as the animals churned up the dirt in the ring. There was so much going on. Music played from the gramophone, while brightly decorated horses with ladies in ballet dresses on their backs trotted around the outside of the ring. In the centre stood the lion's cage, where the trainer was persuading the animals to do tricks. The elephant and the camel did tricks too. Overhead, trapeze artists flew through the air, and clowns were everywhere, acting the fool. I had never seen anything so exciting. It was magical.

I didn't want it to end. David sat clapping and swinging his legs back and forth while my parents were laughing and holding hands.

3

'Stop whining, David, I'm warning you!' slurred my father, turning the car sharply into the driveway.

'He's tired, Ray … he's hungry. This is no fun for the kids … we need to leave the shop earlier … it's so late when they get their tea.' Hands clenched, Mum sneaked a sideways look.

'The little bastard's always whinging!' He braked hard, lurched out of the car and staggered to the front door. I was sprawled across the back seat playing possum, so Mum tapped me on the shoulder while David climbed out.

'David, Daddy's tired. We'll miss bath … there's a good boy, and I'll cook you an egg.'

David, still moaning he was hungry, wandered up the front path and under the verandah's bricked archway. As he entered the house, my father lunged.

'You whinging bloody kid!' he yelled, dragging my brother down the hallway to the bathroom. He closed the door.

We heard David's screams as we walked up the path, and once inside, the terrifying sound of the nauseating thud of David's head repeatedly hitting the wall reached us. Mum dropped the box in her hands and rushed down the hall.

She banged on the door yelling, 'Ray, stop it! You'll hurt him. He's just a little boy. Ray, please…'

Scared, I stood rocking from side to side. The door opened and my father leapt out. He grabbed my mother by her hair, dragging her into the kitchen.

'Don't tell me what to do with my own kids. He needs to learn.'

My mother pulled herself free and edged around the table, trying to avoid my father, but he caught her again, flung her to the ground, and kicked her in the back. Then he shoved the meat safe in her direction and it fell on top of her. He walked into the dining room and poured a drink.

I put my arms around David and led him to our bedroom. We were both crying.

'Shut up! All of you shut up, you hear?' My father stormed into the bedroom. 'Get to bed, both of you … not another peep from you!'

Instantly our crying ceased. The door slammed and in the dark, we undressed, put on our pyjamas and clambered into bed. After a while a small voice said, 'I'm hungry.'

The next morning, Mum's eyes were black again. I was now in the fifth grade, and acutely conscious of the aftermath of these regular episodes. I wondered what the customers thought when they saw my bruised and battered mother in the shop. I also wondered what my father thought in his sober moments.

The commute to and from the shop each day put a strain on the family, and the business was growing, so my father decided to acquire the shop next door. He knocked down the adjoining wall and installed a delicatessen. Mum looked after it while he continued to manage the grocery section. My parents became even busier. There were three old storerooms attached to the grocer's shop, and my father organised for two to be cleaned and painted. These became bedrooms. Behind the new shop, he built a kitchen, bathroom, dining room, and lounge room. The bedrooms were entirely separate from this section, so a covered walkway was built. Once our new home was completed, we moved in. David and I shared a room next to our parents.

This home was very different from the comfort of the only home I had ever known before. However, there was one consolation: I now had a place where I could read, which meant I wasn't so bored after school. *The Magic Faraway Tree* was my favourite book. I dreamed of visiting the lands at the top of the tree like Jo and Bessie.

One afternoon, soon after we moved, I skipped happily home from school along the back lane and into the dusty backyard. After dropping my bag in the hallway, I made a jam sandwich, and thought I'd better let Mum know I was home.

I climbed the steps into the lounge and saw my father lying on the settee.

'Jenny. Jenny, come here,' he whispered. 'Sit by your old dad, that's the girl.'

I walked towards him. He grabbed my arm, pulled me down on the couch and held me tight.

'You know Jenny, Daddy's dying. Won't be long now. I'll be gone before the night is out.'

I began to cry. I tried to get up but he held onto me.

'Don't cry. It's for the best, love. No-one'll miss me. I'm finished.'

I managed to pull myself free from his grasp, and rushed into the shop.

'Mummy, Daddy's dying. He's on the lounge. Mummy, come quickly.'

'Quiet, love.' My mother continued speaking to the customer.

'Mummy, you've got to come!' I yelled, terrified.

'Jenny, not now. Your father's fine. Go and play.'

I couldn't understand. *She doesn't care. Why won't she come?*

I rushed back. His eyes were shut and he was quite pale. I ran back to my mother, grabbing her arm.

'Mummy, you've got to come!' I implored.

'Jenny, go outside. Leave your father. He's okay.'

Mystified, I watched her walk to the cash register as Mr Baker strode past.

He grinned and whispered to himself, 'Drunk again.'

With a tear trickling down my face, I wandered out the front door. It was then I remembered what happened the previous week, when I was walking home alone from school. I had been passing Gilbey's Gin Distillery when I saw a group of kids ahead, fooling around in the long grass at the side of the highway.

One of the boys had yelled, 'My Mum says your father's a drunk. Your father's a drunk.'

Some of the other boys took up the chant. 'Your father's a drunk! Your father's a drunk!'

The ringleader staggered out of the grass zigzagging in front of me, impersonating him.

Each afternoon, my father, with his white grocer's apron on, walked along the main road to the hotel. He spent a couple of hours there before returning to the shop.

I ignored the boy and kept walking.

'Jenny's father's a drunkie,' he taunted, swaggering along.

The others sniggered. I tried to pass but they moved around me. The ringleader poked at me and the others followed suit, then he turned around, put his foot out and tripped me.

'Ha, ha, ha,' he laughed, standing over me.

I jumped up, dodging back and forwards until one girl took

pity on me and let me through. I ran down the road without looking back, the taunting words 'your father's a drunk' ringing in my ears. I didn't stop until I was inside the shop.

'Jenny, what's up? Why the tears?' My mother looked at her grubby red-eyed daughter.

'Jenny!'

I ignored her and rushed out of the shop, through the house and out the back to the paddocks, not stopping until I reached the dugout, where I flopped down and sobbed. Eventually, I looked up. A vivid light radiated from a cloud in the sky and, coupled with the stillness of the paddock, it calmed me.

*

On my eleventh birthday, my father bought me a two-wheeler bicycle. Although I was eager to ride it, I had to wait until he was ready to help me. On Sunday, with the shop closed, he took me and the bike out to the road. He patiently explained the mechanics of riding, and then demonstrated. I'd never seen him ride a bike, and thought he looked really funny. He always seemed so serious, but today was different—he was laughing and we were having fun.

He showed me how to use the pedals, and the trick of pushing my feet back on them when I needed to brake. However hard I tried, I couldn't get my balance. He patiently stood behind me while I positioned myself on the seat. Then we slowly started to move down the road, wobbling all over the place, with my father holding the back of the seat to balance me. Suddenly, I took off and left him flat on the roadway, where he gained a skinned nose and brow. Mum, watching from the footpath, tried not to laugh at the comical scene: me soaring, and her husband flat on his face.

The following week I was desperate to go to the pictures. For a while now I had been allowed to go to the Saturday matinee—and now, with a bike, I could ride there. Last week the serial had ended with Batman trapped in a small room with two walls closing in on him, and I was anxious to see what would happen. However, the previous night, my brother and I had been fighting at bedtime. Exasperated, Mum had banned the pictures. I thought perhaps Mum might change her mind if I made her a cup of tea.

I carried the tray with the pot of tea and plate of biscuits into the shop. In the delicatessen, Mum was stripping cloth from a large round cheese. She inserted the sharp knife into the side of the cheese and cut the coarse woven cloth covering it, then grabbed the piece of cut cloth, and pulled sharply. The cloth came away, displaying a beautiful golden cheese with a crumbly texture. She continued tearing the cloth away until the whole cheese was exposed.

'Mum, I've made a cup of tea.'

'Thanks, Jenny. That's nice.'

I stood rubbing one foot along my other leg. 'Is the tea okay, Mum?'

'Yes, lovely and hot.'

'Mummm, I'm sorry about last night. I won't do it again. Could I … could I please go to the pictures, please … ?'

'Ah, now I see. Jenny, you and David were very naughty last night. You know lights out means go to sleep. I know sharing a room is hard, but you're four years older.'

I said nothing, but watched her feet intently.

'Alright. I'll let you go this time. Here's a shilling. Nine pence for the show and thruppence for an ice-cream. Now out of here, I'm busy!'

I skipped out the back, made myself a sandwich, and rode to the local Mechanics Hall, where I parked my bike and bought a ticket.

The lights dimmed and everyone sang the club song: "*We are members of the CCC ...*" The news clips appeared first on the screen, then the serial. The walls kept coming, closing in on Batman, then the horrible churning noise ceased. Robin had overpowered Penguin and his gangsters, and turned off the wheels that had been pushing the walls together. Batman was free.

I bought an ice-cream at interval, then watched the main feature and rode home.

My brother met me at the gate.

'Sis, I've found six kittens. Four black and two striped!' he excitedly exclaimed.

'Where?'

'The auction yard.'

'You're not supposed to go there when it's closed. You'll get into trouble.'

'Shut up. Come and see.'

'I'm not going in there, David. Anyway, how did you get in?'

'I found a hole in the fence. Come on Sis, you've got to see them.'

I followed him through the fence, and he led me to an open section under the auction yards.

'Look!' David picked up one of the kittens and brandished it in front of me.

'David, something's wrong with its eyes. They're full of muck. All the kittens' eyes are the same ... put them back.'

'But Sis, there's no-one to look after them.'

'What about the mother?'

'I've been here all afternoon. She hasn't come. Let's take them home and show Mum.'

'No. We'll tell her they're here. See what she says.'

We wandered home and explained our find. Mum said that on Monday she would contact the animal inspector, who would take care of them and have their eyes fixed. David spent all of the next day just sitting watching the kittens. He'd been told he mustn't touch them. His affinity with animals had begun to show itself.

During the following week, I didn't see much of David after school and wondered what he was up to. The animal inspector had removed the kittens, so David wasn't with them. On Friday while I was peeling potatoes, I looked out the window and saw David emerging from the staff toilet, which was located in the backyard. He shoved something into his pocket and went out the back gate. I wondered what he was up to; he seemed quite sad since the kittens went. I thought nothing more about it.

That night at dinner, everyone was quiet. My parents were uncommunicative, and we knew better than to break the silence. After sweets were eaten, my father leaned back in his chair and slowly crossed his legs, as he was in the habit of doing. Casually, he took a packet of cigarettes from his pocket and placed them on the table. Mum started clearing the dishes, and I rose to help her.

'Stay where you are, both of you.' My father pointed to Mum's chair.

She slithered back, an anxious look appearing on her face. I sat, the familiar knotted feeling returning. Dad swung around and faced David.

'Well, young man, how about a smoke? Care to join me, eh?'

'No, thank you.' David looked intently at his empty dessert plate.

'Come now, son, I hear you enjoy a smoke.'

I bet Mr Baker's been telling tales again, I thought, jiggling my leg. It dawned on me what my brother had been putting in his pocket that afternoon.

'Here, take it.' My father took a cigarette out of the pack and poked it in front of David.

My father looked at me. 'And you … stop jiggling.'

David kept his eyes down and didn't take the extended cigarette.

My father thundered, 'I said take it! Don't ignore me!'

David extended his hand and my father handed him the cigarette, placing a box of matches on the table.

'Now son, light it up. Show us how grown up you are.'

David just looked, a tear collecting in the corner of his eye.

'Light up, now,' my father boomed.

My little brother slowly put the cigarette in his mouth, the tears freely running down his cheek. He looked at Mum, hoping she would intervene. The look on my father's face warned her to keep quiet.

'Come on, son.'

My father lit a match and held it at the tip of David's cigarette. My brother drew in his breath a little. The cigarette glowed. My father lit a cigarette for himself and then blew out the match.

'Now, son, show us what you can do. Let's start with the drawback.'

David rested the cigarette between his lips.

'I said, do the drawback! Take a puff. Then breathe in more.' My father demonstrated. 'That's right. That's how it's done.'

David, spluttering, took the cigarette out of his mouth; he began coughing as the smoke rose above him.

'Now son, again. Anyone that smokes does the drawback. Again. That's right.'

David's coughing increased and he was enveloped in a cloud of smoke.

'Once again, son.'

'Ray, stop this, he'll be sick.'

He turned to Mum, arm raised.

'Who asked your opinion? You're here to watch, so shut up.' My father turned back to David. 'Again, David. Still enjoying smoking, eh? Going to pinch any more smokes, eh? Answer me.'

'No.'

'No, who?'

'No, Daddy,' gasped David.

'Learned your lesson?'

'Yes, Daddy. I'll not take any more, I promise.'

'Good. Off to bed.'

David, deathly white and still coughing and choking, slid off his chair and left the room.

'That'll teach him. He'll think twice before he tries that again.'

Mum picked up the dishes and walked out. She dumped them in the kitchen sink and went to the bedroom to comfort David. The next day he was too sick to go to school.

My father was not drunk that night but his sadistic streak and need to control was paramount. He could be brutal, and delighted in creating issues out of nothing. It was then that the beast emerged. I will never understand how he could be so cruel to his young son. How my mother coped with her hell of a life,

I don't know. Always trying to keep the peace, all her energy went into protecting us and herself physically, so she had little left emotionally.

*

I arrived home from Sunday school to find my parents stacking shelves. I read for a while but, feeling bored, I went searching for my brother.

'David, let's go and get some specimens for school.'

Other kids brought stuff for the nature table at school all the time, but I never had.

Seven-year-old David was idly kicking a toy football and was equally bored, so he agreed to come. We walked out the gate and down the unmade track, passing the dirty and untidy backyards of the local shops. On the right were paddocks of long green grass swaying in the wind, and the row of quince trees that George and I had climbed. I watched the cottonwool clouds moving silently across the brilliant blue sky as I skipped down the path.

'Sure you know where you're going, Sis?' Trudging across the paddocks, David continued, 'We'll get into trouble if we go too far.'

'It's not far.' I wasn't sure where I was going.

We found a track and as we started walking along it, in the distance a boy appeared on a bicycle.

'Do you know where the creek is?' I called to him as he rode past.

The tall, muscular teenager with blonde hair stopped.

'Sure!' Parking his bike by the side of the track, he said, 'I'll take ya there if ya like.'

He was friendly, but I knew my mother wouldn't approve.

Desperate to find some specimens to gain the teacher's approval, I grabbed David's small hand for support.

'Would you?' I shyly looked at the teenage boy.

'Let's play a game first.' He moved away from the track and through the grass, towards some thick bushes. 'Pick a letter of the alphabet and we will play that game.'

'I don't know.' I wondered what this game was.

'Just pick a letter.'

'Ah, B, I suppose.'

'Oh, that's a good one. It's the kissing game,' he said with a smirk on his face.

I looked at my brother. My tummy felt funny. 'I'm not playing that!' I held my small brother's hand tighter.

'Okay then, pick another letter.' He threw his head back and laughed deeply in short spurts.

'N.' I knew this wasn't right.

'Great. The fucking game.' He lunged forward and made a grab at me. 'Come on, it's fun. You'll enjoy it.'

I fell to the ground as I tried to run, and started to cry. My Sunday best—cream pleated skirt with straps over my shoulders and my pastel striped knitted jumper—were now covered in dirt and grass stains. *I'll be in trouble when I get home*, I thought.

'Get away!' I screamed, scrambling and crawling on my knees. The boy pounced, pinning me to the ground. At that moment I felt a searing sharp pain on the inside of my thigh.

As the boy sprawled across my back, my brother started hitting him. My face was pushed into the ground and I tasted dirt.

'Get offa my sister! Get off! Leave her alone!' David screamed, continuing to hit the boy.

The large boy turned me over and I saw the clear blue sky

above. I was sobbing uncontrollably.

He held my shoulders firmly and grinned, 'We're just playing a game. Having some fun. So stop crying.'

As his hand moved down he saw my bloodstained skirt. Instantly he sprung up, ran across the paddock, and rode off without a word.

I lay there wondering what on earth had happened. Everything was a blur. My crying brother put his small arms around me.

'Sis … You're okay.'

I started to get up, picking at the grass seeds on my jumper. I looked down and saw my bloodstained skirt, and remembered the pain I'd felt when I fell to the ground. What would happen when my parents saw the mess? No longer warmed by the sun, I felt cold. I was scared.

Hand in hand, we arrived home and stood in the barren backyard, trying to find the courage to go inside. My leg was hurting as I slowly walked through the lounge room and up the two steps into the storeroom. It was empty, but raised voices were coming from the shop. I entered, trying to be inconspicuous. Here I was, a forlorn young girl, dirty, with grass seeds in my hair, bloodstained clothes and a pain high up in my leg.

My mother looked around and with an anguished cry rushed over. 'What happened?'

'I fell on a tin, it cut my leg.'

'A boy hurt her. He had her on the ground. I kept hitting him.' David was still holding my hand.

I couldn't understand what was going on. One minute my mother was cuddling me and the next she was angrily asking why I talked to the boy. My father strode across and grabbed me.

'I'm taking her to the doctor … you look after David.'
Holding me by the arm, he walked me to the car.

*

Chairs lined the walls of the waiting room. Through the window
I could see tall gum trees in the adjoining park, and blue sky.
My father rang the bell on the desk. I sat feeling miserable;
I was afraid of him and unsure of what was happening. The
surgery door opened. My father whispered to the doctor, and
then beckoned to me. I knew the doctor, but today he seem
taller and his face was serious—not the usual smile. He helped
me onto the high white bed. My father sat by the desk while the
doctor examined my leg. The doctor cleaned the wound, then
gave me an injection to dull the pain while he stitched the deep
gash in my thigh. He said I needed a tetanus injection because
the gash was caused by tin. Could have been rusty, he said.

Then, to my horror, he lifted my dirty skirt higher and
removed my pants. *What's he doing?* I was acutely embarrassed,
and his examination made me feel uncomfortable and scared.
He then put my pants back and helped me to get down. I was
sent to the waiting room.

Later that week my mother gave me a book to read. It
described the reproduction of animals, plants and humans. It
didn't mention how the small human being got into the womb
in the first place.

4

The new year brought change: secondary school for me; and later on, a new home for us all.

On my first day at Mordialloc and Chelsea High, dressed in my new uniform (green checked dress, bottle-green blazer, long grey socks, and straw hat), I caught the train to school with my mother. My second-class term ticket had already been bought; first class, with its padded leather seats, was not for the Wildings. We forgot to look for a non-smoking carriage, and the smoke haze in the crowded compartment created an eerie atmosphere—I felt I couldn't breathe. The trains, known as 'red rattlers', were brought into service from the Flinders Street railway yards, where they sat in the boiling hot sun. They had no air-conditioning, and when they reached our station, the crowded carriages were still extremely hot.

Five stops later, a stream of green left the station and moved *en masse* down the highway. Surrounded by students and parents, we crossed the bridge and walked apprehensively through the park. I was oblivious to the creek framed by gum trees, and the picturesque wooden boats of various shapes and sizes moored at its banks. I wondered what this school would be like, and then sighted an impressive double-storied brick building, with its grounds bordered by a large green hedge. The school looked massive.

The new students at Mordialloc and Chelsea High were asked to congregate in the quadrangle, where they were welcomed by Mr Tippett, the headmaster. He appeared short and slight standing on the dais, but I thought he had a kind face. Once I was allocated to a form, my mother left. I looked around and saw a sea of strange faces.

In primary school I was in one classroom; now I moved from room to room, with different teachers for each subject. It was confusing and plain scary trying to find my way around in a place that seemed so vast. I found myself in Red House, and at the first house meeting, the house captain emphasised that we needed to work at getting individual points for our house. House points were only awarded in competitive sports, and as I was not the least bit sports-minded, I wondered how I would achieve these confounded points.

In form one most subjects were compulsory; however, there were choices with the language and craft subjects. Without direction from my parents, because as usual they were busy with the business, I decided on Latin in preference to French. I knew it was a compulsory subject to enter the medical faculty at university, and my dream was to be a doctor. I chose needlework as my craft subject. My mother knitted and made all her clothes, so it seemed a natural choice.

Science fascinated me; using a Bunsen burner and experimenting with different formulas was exciting. Pity about the teacher. He delighted in punishing students, especially the boys, who would be called to the front of the room for the most minor offences. Obviously enjoying the experience, he made them bend over, and using the T-ruler, hit them several times on the buttocks. Girls were told to produce 1000 lines of 'I must not talk in class' by the next morning.

A few months after I commenced high school, my father told us the shop had been sold and we would be moving. He was extremely pleased with the tidy profit he had made. The new pink-brick home on Nepean Highway in Cheltenham had big rooms with wall-to-wall carpet, and a bedroom each for David and me. Along the wall facing my bedroom door were two built-in robes and a dressing table. The window looked out to the big backyard that contained several fruit trees. Rather than get out of bed to turn off the light after I had been reading, I just pulled a cord that hung from the ceiling above. Even better, the house was much closer to my school, and to get there I could catch a bus outside my front gate.

Dad returned to the insurance business and we all settled into suburban life. Milk was delivered at night by horse and cart, the paperboy riding his bicycle made early-morning deliveries, the baker brought the bread during the day, and ice was delivered twice a week for the ice-chest where all the perishable food was kept. Each morning my father rose early, collected the paper, and read in the toilet that adjoined the house. He spent an inordinate amount of time out there, even in the winter. I couldn't fathom why, when it was so cold. The first ritual of the day completed, he made tea, took a cup to Mum, who would still be in bed, and then for the next hour sat at the kitchen table reading and re-reading the paper. Each morning, tea was taken to my mother's bedside, no matter the mood of the household.

Each afternoon after school, David would rush into the house. 'Mum, Mum, where are you?' He would go through the kitchen and down the hall, glancing into each room, then if he didn't find her, out into the backyard, where she would be gardening or bringing clothes in from the line.

With a 'Hello Mum!' and reassured by the sight of her, he would happily wander off and amuse himself.

My father skilfully transformed the garden from a wilderness into a delightful and restful place. He built a fernery and a guinea pig cage for David, whose love of animals continued to know no bounds. Two guinea pigs were purchased and it was David's responsibility to look after them. They rapidly multiplied.

One night Mum heard my father's car drive into the garage. He didn't come in, so after a while she walked outside, but found the garage in darkness. She called. There was no answer. She thought he must have walked up to the local shop, so went back into the house, but an hour later he still hadn't arrived. She collected a torch from the laundry and went down the path towards the garage. As she passed the guinea pig cage, she heard something scuttling. Shining the torch, she saw her husband lying full length in the cage, asleep among the guinea pigs. Disgusted, she returned inside.

Sometime during the night, my father came to bed, smelling foul from a combination of the guinea pig cage and stale alcohol.

*

The garden completed, my father decided to paint the house. A fashionable colour, lipstick pink, was chosen for the lounge ceiling, while a neutral colour was chosen for the walls. Mum took David and me to the beach while my father painted. He mixed the paint for the ceiling and put the can on top of the ladder. The job was coming along nicely, so being on his own, he decided he needed a drink.

It didn't stop there. At regular intervals, he climbed down

the ladder, went to the garage and took a swig from his concealed bottle.

The day progressed. My father deteriorated. On one trip down the ladder, he stumbled. The ladder went one way, lipstick paint the other. What did my father do? He walked through the paint, down the hall, across the kitchen and outside to get another drink, leaving a trail of pink footprints on the beige floral carpet. He returned, walked through the paint again, picked up the empty paint tin and took it out to the garage. He made a futile attempt at cleaning up, but gave up and went to bed. On her return, my devastated mother, unable to rouse him, shooed us outside and mopped up as much surplus paint as she could.

She succeeded in cleaning up the kitchen linoleum, but when David and I came inside she said to me, 'The carpets in the lounge room and hall are ruined.' She looked miserable.

Early the next day my father left the house without a word. He returned with a large roll of cheesecloth and four gallons of turpentine. He started in the hall, soaking the carpet with turpentine and then mopping it up with the cheesecloth. After David and I left for school, Mum joined my father on hands and knees. For the rest of the day not a word was spoken between them, but the result was incredible. From an unholy mess that both of them thought could never be rectified, the carpet was left with only a slight pink tinge that could have been a reflection of the ceiling.

Although the painting was a disaster, Dad's garden was not. The harvest was abundant. His tomatoes fed the family and our neighbours, and when the season finished, Mum made pickles with the green tomatoes left on the vines. The Saturday after the carpet resurrection, Mum cut tomatoes, mixed them with other ingredients, and boiled them up. Then she bottled and labelled the finished product. I enjoyed helping her, although I detested cutting the onions. The lid had just been put on the last bottle when there was a knock on the front door. Mum opened it, and to her surprise, two policemen stood there.

'Mrs Wilding?' one asked.

'Yes.'

'We'd like to speak to your husband. Is he home?'

'Yes. Is everything alright?'

'We need to speak to him.'

Mum went out to the garage.

'Ray, there're two policemen at the front door. What's it all about?'

'I don't know.' He pushed past her and went inside. She followed but found the front door was shut, so she stood in the hall, a hollow feeling in her stomach. The door opened; my father looked at her, but said nothing. He sent David and me to our rooms, and then gently told Mum that her mother had died that afternoon. She had been washing the kitchen floor in her home in Maitland in the Hunter Valley, and had had a heart attack.

I heard a hollow scream, followed by more cries, and then the sound of my parents' bedroom door shutting. I stayed in my room. Used to hearing similar sounds, I felt the familiar gripping feeling in the pit of my stomach. It wasn't until the next morning that I discovered my Grandma had died. I had not seen her since she had looked after us when my mother was sick. The house had been peaceful when Grandma stayed with us, and I had come to love her dearly. I went to my bedroom, threw myself on the bed and sobbed.

*

Mum left to go to Maitland the next day. Since she married and even before that, she had spent little time with her mother. Mum had trained as a nurse, and opportunities arose that took her away from Maitland; then after she married she came to Melbourne. Now she was returning to attend her mother's funeral. She kissed David and me goodbye—her eyes were clouded and her smile was absent.

My father decided to make soup for tea. He put split peas, barley, bacon bones, and diced vegetables into the pressure cooker, set it on the stove, and then went outside. Shortly afterwards, I heard a loud hissing sound and ran to the kitchen. The soup was shooting up to the ceiling because my father had forgotten to put the pressure valve on the cooker. The ceiling near the stove was covered in soup, and it was oozing down the walls. He cleaned up the mess, threw the leftover soup in the bin and decided to cook steak, sipping whisky as he cooked. Eventually tea was ready. He put a plate in front of me, another in front of David. The vegetables were swimming in the blood oozing from the steak.

I looked up. 'Daddy, the steak's not cooked.'

'Just eat. That's the way it should be cooked. You too, David. Eat up.'

Neither of us touched the food.

'Eat up, both of you!' he yelled.

I cut the meat, brown on the outside, but completely raw inside. Screwing up my nose, I put a piece on my fork, lifted it to my mouth and then put it down.

'I'm warning you, eat it!' my father slurred.

'Daddy, I can't,' I whimpered.

'Off to bed, both of you. Ungrateful little wretches! Go!'

We quickly clambered from the table and rushed down

the hall, our father screaming obscenities.

The next morning, I helped David get ready for school. We were both hungry. I put Weet-Bix in bowls and made toast. My father ignored us and read his paper. David walked to the primary school and I caught the bus at the corner of our street. My father was not the same when he drank. I missed Mum, and after what had happened the night before, I felt squeamish. I didn't want to be at school.

I looked at the timetable on the inside of my locker door while I organised my books. *First period, History. That's upstairs*, I thought. I settled into a desk, as a grim Mrs Drake walked in. She spent most of the lesson shouting at the class. As I looked up after scribing lines and lines of uninteresting stuff from the blackboard, the teacher swung around and aimed. There was an ominous thud, then complete silence. The blackboard duster had hit its mark: Ann Hackett, the class talker. Anne's look of amazement generated a burst of laughter from Mrs Drake. I kept my head down. I didn't want to be next.

On a previous occasion, Mrs Drake had sent me out of the room for talking. Students sent from a classroom were expected to go to the headmaster's office immediately, where their name was recorded in the nuisance book. Three times in the book and a student could be expelled.

Too terrified to go to the headmaster, I had hidden in the downstairs cloakroom. Not a good idea. A student found in the cloakroom during class could be suspected of stealing. Sitting on the floor, I heard teachers and students' voices at the sports cupboard located just outside the cloakroom. I didn't know what to do. I stood up, but if they looked through the open doorway, my feet would be visible. Down the middle of the room ran two raised panels that were covered in clothes hooks. I climbed onto the lower hooks, feet spreadeagled, and held on to the top row of hooks with my hands. There I stayed for the whole period, while teachers and students organised the softball equipment for the afternoon's match.

My heart raced and I prayed no-one would come in because if found, I would be in deep trouble. Cloakrooms were out of bounds. *Why am I doing this? I'm always in some sort of trouble.* I kept quiet, in my exceedingly uncomfortable position.

Eventually the door to the sports cupboard was closed, and they moved away. The bell rang and, stiff and sore, I climbed down from the pegs and went looking for my friends.

At primary school I had been friendless, but here I established bonds with several girls. I felt uncomfortable with boys, and this was something that stayed with me throughout my life. Boys sat on the left side of the classroom, girls on the right. I avoided sitting in the centre aisle so I wouldn't be next to a boy. During class one boy sometimes sent notes asking me to meet him at the creek after school—forbidden territory for girls. Walking to school from the station or bus stop, the girls, once across the bridge over Mordialloc creek, had to walk through the park by the highway, while the boys went along the creek. Any girl found near the creek was under threat of expulsion. Anyway, I didn't have any urge to meet Peter. His face was a festered mess. Imagine kissing him!

I didn't live near any of the girls at school, so it was hard work cementing relationships. Nevertheless I did become particularly close to Barbara, a quiet, unassuming girl. I was a good scholar, but Barbara struggled, so we helped each other when studying for exams. Her results improved dramatically once we started working together. I despaired of my fair skin and so envied Barbara's olive skin and her long, beautifully groomed hair. Her clothes looked freshly pressed and the seams of her grey stockings were always straight. Hard as I tried, my appearance was usually scruffy.

Out of the blue my leg became painful and I started to limp. My parents took me to doctors, then specialists, and eventually the ligaments in the ankle area were diagnosed as the problem. My leg was put in plaster and I needed crutches.

The first time I climbed the steps of the school bus, I was greeted with, 'Now she's on crutches, she'll lose her leg next.' The school kids laughed at the prefect's caustic comments.

At school, I found it difficult getting my books from the top locker while kids scrounged in the lower lockers. Climbing the stairs to the first floor was like going on an overnight hike, and I missed playing netball. Once again, I felt isolated from everyone—except for Barbara, who supported me. We became even closer.

Eventually the plaster was removed, and my specialist prescribed a boot with an iron rod down one side and a leather cross-piece over the ankle. I found walking quite awkward. On the second day, when changing rooms between periods, I started to walk up the stairs behind a group of kids. I reached the second stair above the first landing when the boy at the top yelled, 'Guess what, we're in the science room!'

As one body we all turned; I stumbled forward, putting my arm out in an effort to regain my balance. It connected with Mrs Greene's face as she stepped onto the landing. The cookery teacher refused to believe it was an accident, and banned me from her classes. The rest of term found me in the art class I hated, missing the cookery class I loved.

I didn't mention my school problems to my parents, I was afraid of my father's reaction, as it didn't take much to set him off. I hadn't forgotten the medical form incident when I was in primary school. I concluded it was probably wise to say nothing, because he would either go up to the school and make a horrible fuss, or he would decide it was all my fault and that I deserved what was happening.

Just the other Saturday morning, David had come into my room annoying me and fooling around with a cutthroat razor.

'David, put it back in the bathroom. If Dad finds out you're mucking around with his razor, you'll be in trouble.'

David ignored me and I tried to push him out the door. He shoved me back, crawling under my bed. I knelt down and tried to push him out, yelling, 'Get out, get out, you little idiot! Get out of my room!'

'I'll go when I feel like it. Ha ha, you can't reach me!' He brandished the razor blade at me.

Then he let out a yell. 'Aaah, I've cut myself!'

I ignored him. 'Just get out, I hate you!'

He crawled out, flesh hanging from a deep gash in his thigh, with blood everywhere.

'Mum, Mum, quick! David's cut himself!' I yelled.

Mum ran into the room and immediately grabbed a towel from the bathroom, winding it around David's leg, pushing the sagging flesh together. My father rushed him to hospital, where the nasty wound was stitched.

My father blamed me for the whole incident. He wouldn't listen to me or acknowledge that David shouldn't have been in my room, or shouldn't have had the razor blade. I wanted some privacy, but he didn't or wouldn't understand. My leg started to jiggle—I knew it annoyed him, but did it unconsciously. He lashed out and slapped me sharply across the face.

'You're big enough, old enough and ugly enough to know

better. David's younger, you should set the example.'

My father's temper episodes were on the increase. Recently he had wheeled the Victa lawnmower out of the garage and wound the rope around the flywheel to start it. He pulled hard, but nothing happened. After a few attempts, he picked up the mower and threw it over the fence. Fortunately, no-one was walking along the path. He stormed into the garage and drank for the rest of the afternoon. When he came inside, everyone knew to steer clear. Mum quietly put his meal in front of him; we silently ate our tea and then asked to leave the table.

My father's drinking not only affected the family, but also his work. As Manager of New Business for a large insurance company, he headed a team of about twenty men who travelled country Victoria, selling insurance to graziers and dairy farmers. It was a lucrative livelihood. His base salary was excellent, and it was supplemented by commissions from the business the men in his team brought in. During the week, he travelled Victoria to meet with the men. His drinking continued to increase, and its effect on his behaviour meant he started treating his staff in a similar fashion to his family. Some moved on. For a time he successfully made plausible explanations to his superiors, but they eventually realised he was the problem, and warned him to change his ways.

He stubbornly continued drinking. However, he suffered chest pains while staying at a country hotel, and the publican took him to the local hospital, where it was confirmed he had suffered a heart attack. The doctors warned him to reduce his drinking or there would probably be a recurrence. This jolted him, and once out of hospital and back home, he ceased drinking.

Family life changed. No yelling and fighting—my parents

spoke quietly to each other. Mealtimes became a pleasure; David and I were able to speak at the table—we had previously been told that children should be seen but not heard. The family went for drives and picnics at the weekends, and my father became involved in his children's hobbies. It was a happy and peaceful time, especially Sundays. Mum cooked roast lamb or beef and Yorkshire pudding for lunch, and we all sat at the dining table, lingering over the meal. After lunch, Mum would make coffee with Bushells Coffee and Chicory Essence in a pot, and pour it into tiny cups that had a border of dainty blue flowers painted on the outside. I loved drinking from these cups; it was always very special. Sunday evenings, we sat around the fire eating the cold leftover meat with salad, and bread, or homemade scones. After dinner, we played gin rummy. My father peeled apples for everyone, sprinkling them with salt, and this became a special favourite of mine. These Sunday evenings gave me the false sense that we were a normal family. For three months peace reigned, then after an upset at my father's work, which he wouldn't discuss, he returned to the drink with a vengeance.

One evening, after David and I had gone to bed, an awful argument erupted between my parents. David and I remained in our rooms, listening to my father's cruel words and insinuations. He said he had proof of his accusations and he knew what my mother was doing behind his back. I knew from my mother's piercing screams that she was being beaten, but feared going to help her.

The next morning, I walked down the hall, picking up large handfuls of hair. My mother had taken to collecting pulled-out hair and storing it in a hatbox. My father usually chose to take to my mother's hair when she had it permed or something special done. He had left for the country; she was not well, and still in bed.

My parents ceased talking. During the next six months, when they needed to converse they spoke through us.

'Tell your mother I won't be home until Thursday.'

'Ask your father for ten shillings to buy your books for school. I don't have enough money.'

Nevertheless, each morning, Mum's early cup of tea was by her bedside.

5

My father arrived home late after another week in central Victoria. Business was slow. Times were tough for the farmers, and committing to years of paying insurance premiums was not a priority for them. Yet Dad's management expected new business to increase.

My mother silently placed the stewed meal from the oven in front of him. They were still not on speaking terms.

'I'm not eating this shit!' He jumped up, knocking the plate to the floor, and staggered to the bedroom, collapsing on the bed.

The next morning, he disappeared into the garage, where he tinkered with his car and drank. At about five o'clock, while preparing tea, Mum heard the car start up. Then she heard it revving loudly at the front of the house, so she walked to the window. The car was parked on the grass median strip between the main highway and the unmade service road. As she watched, my father stepped out of the car, went to the boot and took out a rubber hose. He bent down, slowly connected it to the car's exhaust and then walked to the driver's door, placing the rubber hose through the window as he sat in the driver's seat. He closed the door.

David and I were playing knuckles on the grass out the

back when Dad drove out of the garage. We thought nothing of it, then a few minutes later Mum rushed through the connecting gate in the fence we shared with our neighbours. Wondering why she was in such a rush, we followed her. She was distraught.

'Cliff, Alice, look!' She pointed towards the road. 'What in God's name is he doing?'

'Come inside.' Alice gently guided Mum through the house. David and I followed.

'He's been in the garage all day … drinking I suppose.' Mum was shaking.

'You can't deal with this. We'll need to get help … Cliff, call the police.'

'Please, no!' Mum pleaded. 'What will everyone think?'

'Sophie, there isn't an alternative.' Cliff picked up the phone. 'Ray can't be reasoned with when he's like this.'

Mum nodded and Alice handed her a handkerchief.

Mum felt blessed having Cliff and Alice as neighbours. Sympathetic and understanding, they never complained about the constant shouting and disturbances emanating from our house, but many in the neighbourhood did. Mum kept to herself, finding it impossible to face those around her.

I looked over their heads towards the window, and was totally freaked out by the vision of our big, black, shining Chevrolet with a hose extending out of the driver's window to the exhaust. In the driver's seat was my father, who seemed quite small. Cars were rushing past on Nepean Highway, but nobody stopped. Nobody was doing anything. David sat in one of the lounge chairs and was totally absorbed playing with the jacks in his hands.

'I'll stop him!' I yelled, and rushed towards the front door.

'No, Jenny. Come back!' Mum made a grab for me, but I moved quickly away.

Cliff came up behind me, holding me gently, but firmly. 'Jenny, your dad's not rational. We need to let the right people look after him. I know it's scary, but it'll be alright.'

I started to cry.

Mum, Cliff and Alice continued to watch from the lounge window. Mum was wringing the hanky in her hand, and Alice was comforting her. I was agitated and angry. I felt they should be doing something, not just sitting in this room. *Cliff should go and stop my father; no-one seems to care.*

'I've got to talk to him.' Mum rushed from the house, down the drive and across the road.

She banged on the window. 'Ray, Ray, stop! Open the door, Ray!'

He kept looking straight ahead, ignoring her. His neck and shoulder twitched, as it did when he was aggravated. She banged on the window again, but my father stared resolutely ahead. She realised he hadn't started the car and somewhat relieved, she returned inside.

The moment my father saw the police arrive, he staggered from the car, across the service road and through his front gate. There he stood, arms folded across his chest, glaring at the policeman who stood outside the gate. My father knew that without a warrant or a complaint from his wife, the police couldn't enter private property.

'Mr Wilding, we'd just like to talk to you.'

'Stay out, don't come through that gate. Everything's alright, isn't it Sophie?' he slurred.

Mum didn't answer.

'Mrs Wilding, I think you need help. Do you wish to make a complaint?'

'No she doesn't; everything's okay. Sorting a few things out, aren't we?' He looked over at Mum.

Mum still didn't say anything.

'Mrs Wilding, I urge you to talk to us.'

'It's alright, Constable, I think we can look after it all now. Thank you for coming,' my ever-courteous mother answered.

They tried again to convince her, but it was to no avail. I was standing near the house, feeling very scared. Why would he want to do such a thing; why would he want to leave us? Would my father, now safe, be taken away by the police? Or if not, would he once again abuse Mum for calling them? It seemed to me nothing good would come out of this. Was it manipulation or was it real?

In hindsight, I realise my father was not only an alcoholic, but he was also acutely depressed, and a man who believed he was a total failure.

The police left and the car stayed where it was, the hose still connected. My father wandered to bed. He returned the car to the garage the next morning, and then pruned the fruit trees as if nothing had ever happened.

I noticed one difference, though: my parents were speaking.

*

Towards the end of my third year at high school, we were asked to select our subjects for the senior years. The form teacher said in our selection, we should consider the requirements for the job we hoped to have when we left school. She suggested if we were thinking of working in an office, shorthand and typing would be suitable, while science or language stream might suit others, depending on their career choice. Still keen to be a doctor, I knew I needed my parents' support, because without it the expensive university fees would be prohibitive.

I was sitting in the kitchen drinking Milo and eating a piece of cake after school when the back door opened. Goldie, our golden cocker spaniel, had pushed past the wire door and was perched on the kitchen step. Although not allowed into the house, everything except her tail was in the kitchen. She knew this was the limit. Excited by the smells emerging, Goldie's front paws danced. The wire door closed behind her as her tail entered the kitchen.

'Outside!' Mum instructed. The dog backed out several inches, the tail once again hidden. She looked expectantly. We both laughed. Goldie knew just how much she could get away with.

'Mum, we have to pick next year's subjects.' I looked at her.

'Do you, dear? Any ideas?'

I took a deep breath. 'You know I've always wanted to be a doctor.' I paused.

'Mm, you did love playing doctors and nurses when you were little. You've mentioned it, but I didn't think you were really serious.' Mum sat down opposite me.

'Mum, I've always been serious. I really can't remember ever wanting to be anything else. I like helping people. It was awful when you were so sick and when Grandma died. You were so unhappy. I want to stop people from dying.' I looked pleadingly at my mother.

'Grandma died very suddenly. She had a heart attack. Doctors couldn't help her, love.'

'Well I want to help people who were sick like you, and find cures for things like heart attacks … I don't want to work in an office or a shop. That would be the pits. My dream is to be a doctor, so I've picked the science stream. Anyway, I love science,' I said passionately.

Mum saw my serious expression, but she knew my father would never agree.

'Jenny, you're an excellent student, but going to university … there's so much study … not many girls go, and even fewer are doctors.'

'I can do it … I know I can.'

'You'll be there for years, Jenny.'

'I don't care. There's nothing else I'm even remotely interested in. It's all I've ever wanted to do.'

'Well let's think about it. I've got an idea; we'll talk to Dr Chamberlain. He can tell you what it's like to be a doctor, and about the university course and all that.'

'It won't change how I feel, Mum.'

Mum made an appointment with our family doctor, who gave me the impression that he believed medicine was a male-oriented profession.

He certainly didn't encourage me. He spoke of years of study and, after graduation, the long hours and dedication. He explained medicine was a career that interfered with family life. He believed, for a girl, it would be next to impossible to have a family and be a successful doctor. He suggested with my keen interest in science, I would be an excellent chemist. I could have my own business and yet still have a family.

I was fourteen and thought the life of a chemist would be dreadful. I had hated living in the grocer's shop, and my memories of my mother slaving in the delicatessen told me that this was not what I wanted. The doctor said being a chemist would allow me to have a family. Well I didn't want any children of mine growing up as lonely shop kids with parents who were always too busy! The shop sure interfered with our family life.

As we walked home I told Mum how I felt.

Mum suggested nursing. She had been a nurse. 'It's rewarding ... you're helping people and that's what you want to do ... and Jenny, it can lead to other things.'

I didn't answer.

At dinner my father appeared in a good mood, so I nervously decided to broach the subject.

'I'm choosing my subjects for next year,' I said to no-one in particular. 'Miss McLeod said we should think about what we want to do when we leave school before we decide.'

'What subjects are you interested in?' my father asked.

'Science, and I want to continue with Latin.'

'Why on earth do you want to do that? Science isn't for girls. You're good at dressmaking. Take dressmaking subjects.' He smiled. 'I'll help you start your own business.'

'Not dressmaking, Dad. I don't want to sit at a sewing machine all day.'

'Well, go into an office. You don't need science subjects for that. Do they have shorthand and typing classes?'

'Yes, but Dad, I don't want to work in an office.' I took a deep breath. 'I want to be a doctor.'

'Don't be ridiculous! No daughter of mine is going to be a doctor. Medicine's no career for a woman. Anyway, you'd never cope. You have a choice: dressmaker or working in an office. Pick the subjects relevant to both. Then you can choose one or the other when you leave school. By then you'll know better what you want to do.'

I tried to explain that being a doctor was something I'd wanted ever since I could remember. All that came out was,

'Dad, please, I've always wanted to be a doctor, haven't I Mum?'

Mum nodded.

'No more discussion. I want to see the subjects you've chosen. Is that clear?'

'Ray, I took Jenny to see Dr Chamberlain today to talk about being a doctor,' Mum nervously spoke up. 'He suggested, as she's keen on science, she might consider being a chemist.'

'She can forget her stupid ideas! She's not going to be a doctor or a chemist, and you needn't suggest nursing. She's not living away from home. What possessed you to take her to the idiot doctor?'

The discussion ended, and nobody spoke for the rest of the meal. I left the table and went to my room, where I slumped on the bed. I was so angry. *If I'd said I wanted to go into an office, he'd demand I do something else.*

David knocked, came in and sat on the bed. He didn't really understand the depth of my despair; nevertheless, he felt sorry for me. 'Don't worry, Sis; it'll work out, you'll see. Mum and I are going down to watch the television. Come with us. It'll make you feel better.'

Television was new, and was introduced to coincide with the 1956 Melbourne Olympic Games. They were called the Friendly Games, and it was an exciting time for Melbournians. The opening ceremony was simple, with schools performing the maypole dance. My school took part, but I wasn't chosen to be one of the ribbon holders. I was bitterly disappointed, but my form went to the athletic events at the Melbourne Cricket Ground (MCG). I loved the noise, the colour, the crowds— and watching the sprinting, hurdles, shot put, long jump and high jump. It was a fabulous day. The comradeship between the athletes and the rapport with the crowd was memorable. Use of drugs was unheard-of, and the price of tickets was within the reach of most. Even Mum was able to scrape together enough to go. Security was minimal; so much so that a ticket holder, once through the MCG gates, was able to pass her ticket through the cyclone fence to a friend.

My father would not consider buying a television set—he wasn't going to have one of those newfangled things in his house. I suspect he couldn't afford it. Mum, David and I often went down the street after tea to watch TV in the radio shop window. Shopkeepers placed televisions in the window to allow the public to watch, and to encourage them to buy the new technology. It became a neighbourhood social event, attracting a large crowd. I loved going.

The next morning I had a bright idea. I loved my grandfather deeply and thought he understood me. When he came at Christmas, he always listened. I enjoyed being with him and felt it was reciprocated. Although I only saw him once a year, I could clearly visualise him sitting in the lounge armchair. Such a distinguished man, his right elbow leaning on the wide arm of the chair; in his hand the fat brown cigar that he took such a long time to prepare. I loved watching this preparation. He would slowly remove the cellophane packaging, and slip the coloured foil ring from the cigar. Then he would take a small tool from his waistcoat (where he kept his gold watch), puncture one end of the cigar, then put it to his nose and slowly—ever so slowly—smell its aroma. Next, he would gently stroke the cigar before putting it in his mouth, lighting a match and inhaling to ignite the tip. I felt my grandfather could solve all problems, or at least intercede with my father on my behalf. *He might help me go to University. With his business in Sydney, I'm sure he can afford it.*

I decided to write to him.

1351 Nepean Highway
Cheltenham

15th November 1956

Dear Grandpa,
I hope you will be able to help me. At school we are choosing our subjects for the next year. The teacher has said we should choose carefully, considering what career we are thinking about.
As I have told you many times, I desperately want to be a doctor. You have always said I should follow my dream. Well my dream is to help sick people and make them better. I want to find ways to cure things like the heart attack that Grandma had. To be a doctor I need to choose the science stream. When I told Dad he said medicine was not for women and girls don't go to university. He said I should work in an office or become a dressmaker.
Grandpa, I would die if I had to do either of those things for the rest of my life. I know you understand. Please could you help me go to university? Once I become a doctor I will be able to pay you back everything. Please Grandpa, I hope you will help me.
Your very loving granddaughter,
Jenny

I sent the letter with great expectations, and was confident the problem would be resolved. I still had a couple of weeks before the final decision regarding my subjects had to be made.

At dinner, a week or so later, Dad was in a foul temper and the atmosphere was tense. David and I kept quiet. My father pushed his empty plate forward, folded his arms, put his elbows on the table, and looked menacingly at me.

'Didn't we discuss what you are going to do when you leave school, Jenny?' I looked at my plate and said nothing.

'Look at me.'

I looked at him, still not answering.

'Don't ignore me. What are you doing when you leave school?'

'Dressmaker, or work in an office.'

'So why did you write a letter to my father telling him I don't support you? Oh, and that I said girls don't need an education and they certainly shouldn't be doctors.'

I said nothing.

He rose from his chair, swung his arm, hitting me hard across the face.

'Answer me.'

I raised my arm up to protect myself, covering the imprint of my father's hand on my face. 'I don't know.'

'Ray, stop it. She didn't mean any harm.'

'Didn't mean any harm? Running to my father, whinging and whining about me and my decisions. You'll never do that again, will you?' He stood over me, his arm raised high above his head.

'Ray, leave her alone.'

My father sprung around and instead connected with the back of Mum's head. 'Whore, you want it instead, do you? You've been encouraging her. You're trying to make her like yourself.' He grabbed Mum by her hair, dragged her to the bedroom and slammed the door.

I crossed my arms on the table, put my head down and sobbed. *It's no use. It's no use. I hate him. I hate him.* I put my fingers in my ears, trying to block my mother's screams. *Why did Grandpa talk to Dad instead of me? I trusted him. Mum's the only one I can trust, but she's so scared of Dad.*

I wonder what my father thought the next morning, as he lay in bed, his head throbbing and his wife with two black eyes beside him. Did he regret doing it? She didn't have affairs. She was a good woman, not like his first wife who gave him three girls and then had a boy by another man.

*

I commenced fourth form resigned to never being a doctor. During the year the opportunity arose to apply for either a nursing or teaching bursary, which meant I would be bonded to the public hospital system or the Education Department for three years. When the headmaster announced the nursing bursaries applications, I rushed to get a form, only to find my parents must sign it.

Apprehensively I took the form home. My rationale was that if my father did not have to pay for my training, he might allow me to apply for the bursary. I told Mum, but secretly I felt I had little chance of convincing my father.

'A student nurse must stay in the nurses' home. No daughter of mine is going to live there. Everyone knows what goes on. Your mother lived in a nurses' home and look what she got up to!'

Mum had told me of one instance when she and several other nurses sneaked out to meet boys. They had a car accident, Mum suffered a leg injury, and of course they were found out.

When teaching bursaries became available, the excuse of

not living at home, or the cost, did not apply, but I was still not allowed to register. My father had made up his mind. I was to have only the minimum education and I would follow the career he chose.

*

I looked forward to weekends. I went to the pictures on Saturdays at the local theatre with my friends from the church youth group, while Sundays were days of freedom. My father didn't mind me going to church, and this allowed me to get away from the house. After the early morning service, I usually wandered down to the local shops to enjoy a milkshake, and then back to the church to teach Sunday school. I went home for lunch then returned for youth group. We all attended the evening service, so I would arrive home around nine o'clock.

I wanted to wear slacks on the youth group's annual snow trip like all the others.

'No Jenny, pants are not ladylike,' my father said when I broached the subject. 'No lipstick either,' he warned.

Recently when my girlfriend Janet visited, my father had growled, 'Get that horrible red muck off your face!' I had wanted to slip through the floor, I was so embarrassed.

Unbeknownst to Dad, Mum bought slacks and a lipstick for me. I rolled the slacks up under my coat, and called out goodbye to my father. I applied the lipstick while walking up the street.

One sunny Saturday I set off for the pictures, walking along the highway. Everyone had been in a good mood at home; usually there was always a drama before I left.

At the picture theatre, I joined the church group congregated outside. Among them were a couple of boys and several girls I didn't know. We sat together and I discovered myself next to one of the new boys. I was struck dumb. Everyone was talking, but I looked straight ahead. The lights dimmed and the serial commenced. I became engrossed and then I felt pressure on my knee. My stomach lurched. *I should push his hand off.* It stayed there until interval. The lights came on. I looked straight ahead. The hand was no longer there.

'Hello. My name's Greg; what's yours?'

'Ahh, Jenny,' I whispered.

'Like lemonade or an ice-cream?'

I looked up and saw a round face with a crooked smile that displayed two slightly crossed front teeth. Several strands of straight dark hair fell across his face. He wore dark trousers, a polo-neck jumper and a black lumber jacket.

I said nothing.

'Come on, let's get an ice-cream.'

He gently grabbed my hand, lifting me out of the seat. My stomach churned and my face burned. This had never happened before. No-one took notice of me. He seemed nice. *It won't hurt to have an ice-cream.*

Back in our seats after the interval, Greg took my hand and held it throughout the film. My arm got pins and needles, but I didn't move. My heart thumped and I started to perspire.

The film ended and the theatre lit up. I grabbed my cardigan from my lap and jumped up.

Greg smiled. 'Are you coming next week?' I nodded. 'Well I'll see you then.'

We met each week and I grew to like him more each time. Greg was eighteen and four years older; he seemed so grown up and he made me feel special. Soon he suggested meeting during the week. How could I explain I wasn't allowed out, except to the Saturday pictures and church?'

'Ah, I've a lot of homework and can't sort of meet you during the week.'

'I can't wait a week to talk to you, Jenny. Give me your phone number and I'll call.'

'I'd rather ring you. How about you give me your number?' I gulped. My father would be furious if a boy called.

'No worries, but I'd like your number too.'

'I don't have a phone,' I lied.

'Oh, I thought everyone had a phone these days,' he answered.

'When will you ring me?' He scribbled his number on a scrap of paper and handed it to me.

'What about Tuesday after school?'

'I finish work around four thirty and usually get home about five. Could you ring then? I work for my brother. He has an earthmoving business, but the yard's just over the road from my house. If I know you'll be ringing, I'll be there.'

'Okay, Tuesday.' I waved and rushed down the street. *He really likes me.* I was ecstatic and was busting to tell someone. *I can't wait for Monday so I can tell Barbara.* I had already told her about Greg, but I'd said he was just a member of the group that went to the pictures. I hadn't said he was interested in me.

When I arrived home from school on Tuesday, I kept looking at the time while I sat in the kitchen eating a snack. Mum was preparing tea. I wasn't sure how I was going to get to the telephone box. It would have been much easier if I could have rung Greg on my way home.

'Mum, I've left my coloured pencils at school. I need them for homework … have to draw a map of China. I'll have to buy some.'

'Jenny, I haven't got money to burn. Borrow David's.'

'His are not home either; I've asked.' I crossed my fingers behind my back. 'Mum, I'll buy them out of my pocket money.'

'No, here's two shillings; that should be enough.'

I felt guilty. I knew Mum was short of money, and I had plenty of coloured pencils.

I rushed out the front gate still in my school uniform, and crossed the highway, following the path by the side of the railway line until I reached the shopping centre. There was someone in the phone box outside the station, so I waited, my stomach knotting up as time dragged. Eventually, the woman came out and I squeezed into the box and closed the door. I dialled the number and a woman's voice answered. I'd expected Greg. *Of course, it's his mother.*

'Hello Mrs Johnson, could I speak to Greg please?'

'And who's speaking?'

'Jenny.'

'Jenny who?'

'Jenny Wilding.'

'Is he expecting you to call?'

'I think so.'

I heard the phone clank and then an excited 'Hi, Jenny. I wondered if you'd ring.'

We talked for ages, until an angry woman tapped loudly on the door of the phone box. I told Greg I'd better go, but promised to ring on Thursday. The woman scowled as I left.

I wandered past the dairy, thinking about our conversation, when I realised I hadn't bought the pencils. I rushed back to the newsagents and was walking out of the shop as a prefect passed.

'Hold on there, where's your hat?'

I kept walking.

Miss Carpenter, the headmistress, was extremely strict about students wearing their full uniform in public. This included hat and gloves. She also enforced the length of students' dresses with a vengeance.

The prefect rushed up. 'Where's your hat?'

'At home.'

'That's a thousand lines—"I must wear my hat at all times." Get them to me, before school tomorrow, in the prefects' room. Is that clear? You know when you wear your uniform, you wear your hat.'

My heart sank. One thousand lines! It would take all night, and I had homework. I'd been feeling great too; I wouldn't have missed talking to Greg for anything. On Thursday I'd remember to wear my hat, or change out of my uniform.

6

I became adept at finding ways to see Greg without my parents' knowledge. I saw him at youth group each Sunday, rang during the week when I could, and continued meeting him at the pictures. The intrigue of our secret rendezvous was exciting. When things were not good at home, I always had something to look forward to—our next meeting.

Sometimes we went to his house rather than the pictures. The first time we did this, Greg met me at the railway station, where we caught a bus. I was quiet, nervous at the prospect of meeting Mrs Johnson, whereas Greg was bubbling. He was excited and proud to be taking his girlfriend to meet his family.

We hopped off at Bernard Street and I was surprised to find it was quite different from where I lived. I was surrounded by a mixture of market gardens, orchards and industrial businesses. The earthmoving business run by John, Greg's brother, was in the same street. We walked until we came to a large, rambling house, encompassed by a verandah. Old, densely canopied trees surrounded the cream and green weatherboard house, which was quite different from the brick house I lived in. We went around the back and walked up the verandah steps into the kitchen, where Greg's mother greeted us. The oven door was open and a delicious aroma was filling the room.

'Mum, this is Jenny.' Greg proudly put his arm around me.

'Hello Jenny, it's good to meet you at last. Greg never stops talking about you.'

'Hello, Mrs Johnson.' I bowed my head.

I didn't know what else to say. Mrs Johnson seemed nearly as wide as she was tall—and she was not very tall. Her sandy permed hair spilled across her wrinkled forehead. *Gee, she's short ... wish Greg was taller ... then I could wear high heels.*

'Greg, take Jenny into the lounge. I'll bring in drinks and scones in a jiffy.'

Mrs Johnson bustled around, shuffling her feet, which were immersed in oversized slippers.

Greg took my hand and led me into a large, cold room. The tree's canopy at the front of the house made the room dark, and the old black leather lounge suite added to the gloom. I was embarrassed. This was the first time I had visited a boy's home, and Mrs Johnson was treating me as someone special.

I looked around. Dark stained shelves covered with books occupied one wall. A curved glass cabinet full of crystal stood in the corner next to the couch and opposite two large black leather chairs. Magazines were strewn around the room and also on the coffee table that separated the couch and chairs. Although dark, it had a comfortable feel.

Mum would never leave magazines lying around like this.

Mrs Johnson sailed in with a tray.

'Enjoy! Greg tells me you two find it difficult to have time alone, so I'll leave you to it,' she said, closing the door firmly behind her.

'Is she for real? My mum wouldn't do that.'

'Mum's a good sport. She knows we can't go to your place.'

I leaned forward and put a spoonful of sugar in my tea and

stirred. I was acutely aware of Greg sitting beside me, and that we were alone.

'Where's your dad?' Looking straight ahead, I busily put jam and then cream onto a scone.

'Ah, he'll be down the backyard somewhere, mucking around with some motor or other. He might come up later.'

We ate the scones and gradually Greg moved closer, putting his arm around me. And then he kissed me. His mouth was insistent, pushing my lips open, his tongue probing. It hadn't been like this when we had kissed in the lane on the way home from church. I pushed him away.

'What's wrong?'

'Nothing.'

He moved closer and lifted my face to his and gently kissed me.

'Is that better?'

I relaxed and laid my head on his shoulder.

He kissed me again, his hand slipping under my shirt, searching. I stiffened. I didn't know what to do. The petting became more insistent. I was embarrassed and my first instinct was to push him away again, but I didn't.

Before we realised, it was dark. I jumped up. 'What'll I tell Mum? It's so late!'

'We'll think of something. I'll borrow John's ute. Have you home in a jiffy.'

Mrs Johnson looked up from the sink, where she was scraping carrots.

'Off now are you, dear? Come whenever you like. You're always welcome.'

I smiled. 'Goodbye, Mrs Johnson. The scones were lovely.'

I rushed out and hopped into the ute. 'Tell your mum you

went to Janet's after the pictures and didn't realise it was so late,' Greg said as we drove down the drive.

'Do you think she'll buy that?'

'Yeah, you often go to her place.'

He stopped up the road from my house and leant over and gave me a quick kiss. 'It's been a wonderful afternoon. Happy?'

'Very.'

I ran down the highway and into the house. My parents were in the middle of an argument and didn't notice me. I went to my room, closed the door to lessen the sound of the yelling, and flopped onto the bed. I lay with my knees up, looking at the ceiling, where the streetlights were creating patterns and lighting up the darkened room. *What a brilliant day … sort of awkward. When he kissed, that fluttering feeling … never felt like that before. Wasn't sure … but I kind of liked it. I didn't know loving someone could feel so good. He's kind … he understands me … wish I could bring him home … wish Mum and Dad were different … there'd only be an argument.*

The following Saturday, I arranged to stay at Janet's because Greg was scheduled to sing and play the piano accordion at a local dance. I sat on my own, without anyone to dance with, but I didn't care. He stood on the stage, playing, singing and displaying his infectious crooked grin. It was lonely but I was so proud, and I knew I would have him to myself after the dance.

We continued to secretly meet. I attended functions where he was performing, then I would stay the night at Janet's. Her parents were often out until very late and didn't realise that Janet and I had not gone out together. They worked most weekends in their business, so we took advantage and met at their house. Janet would leave us alone, but eventually she got tired of the situation and grew to resent us taking advantage. She asked

Greg not to come—I was welcome but he was not.

*

On their way to church, some of the youth group would meet at Dawn and Heather's in Wallingford Street. Then, as they passed my house, they would all call in to pick me up. This particular Sunday, I opened the door and gulped. Greg's infectious grin greeted me. Lost for words, I didn't see the others standing there. He thought it was a buzz to be at my front door with my parents unaware of who he was.

I yelled goodbye, slammed the door and tore down the drive before anyone gave the game away.

'Just what do you think you're doing? You know it'll cause heaps of trouble if they find out. It was a bloody crazy thing to do.'

Greg laughed. 'They'll never know. I wanted to see where you lived.'

'It's not funny.' I stormed ahead.

Greg raced up and put his arm around me. 'Jenny, I'm sorry. I didn't mean to upset you. I was at Heather's and I always hate walking ahead while they pick you up. I guess I didn't think.'

I was silent. The others caught up and moved ahead. 'I guess no harm's done.' I put my arm around him. 'It'd spoil everything if they found out.'

Greg took the plate of food I had in my hand and we continued walking. Because the Rosebud youth group were visiting, we were all bringing something for tea.

We took our guests on an orienteering bushwalk of sorts in the Cheltenham Park, along the tracks that wandered through the large trees, and then returned to the church, where we adjourned to the adjacent playground. I was watching Greg swinging from the monkey bars and laughing at his antics when I looked up to see my mother, stone-faced, watching me. She beckoned.

I walked slowly to her.

'Who's that boy?' My mother looked towards Greg.

'Which boy?'

'You know which boy. The one on the bars.'

'Oh, he's just one of the boys in our group.'

'How well do you know him, Jenny?'

'Oh, hardly at all. He hasn't been coming long.'

'If you know him "hardly at all", why did he have his arm around you today?'

'He didn't.'

'You're lying.'

'No, I'm not. I rarely speak to him.'

'Don't make things worse. I saw you today.' My mother's voice was getting louder.

I felt a familiar burning sensation as blood rushed to my head.

'You're coming home this minute, do you hear?'

'Please, Mum …'

'Get your coat.'

Humiliated, I collected my coat and slowly returned to where I had left her. She was not there. I looked across to Greg, praying silently. But yes, there she was, pointing her finger and angrily talking to him. My mother turned heel, grabbed me by the arm and walked me down the street.

'I don't know what your father will say. I trusted you, girl. You're too young. How long has this been going on'?

'How long has what being going on?'

'This boy, how long have you been seeing him?'

'I only see him at church.'

'Can't even trust you at church!' Mum strode ahead.

Dad was weeding the front garden as we walked through the front gate.

'I caught her walking arm in arm with some boy.'

'You what! Jenny, what's this?'

'He's just a boy in the youth group.'

'Get inside,' Dad said. 'We'll talk about this later.'

I rushed to my bedroom and crashed on my bed. Tears dribbled down. *They'll probably bar me from going out … I won't be able to see him.*

Darkness fell. I went to the kitchen for a drink. Mum and Dad were sitting at the table and it was obvious I'd interrupted their conversation.

'Well my girl, what do you have to say for yourself?'

I put the glass under the tap but didn't answer.

'I'm speaking to you.' Dad was surprisingly articulate for a Sunday night.

I turned towards him. 'I don't know.'

'Where'd you meet this boy?'

'Youth group. He's no-one special.'

'So you walk arm in arm with "no-one special", eh?'

I didn't answer.

'How long have you been seeing this boy?'

'I'm not seeing him,' I whispered.

'It's obvious you can't tell the truth and therefore can't be trusted.' My father spoke quietly and slowly. 'You're grounded; no youth group, no dancing or anything else. Is that clear?'

'That's not fair.' I banged the glass on the table, spilling water.

'Until you can convince me otherwise, that's the way it is.'

I glanced at Mum. Her look convinced me that I could expect no sympathy.

Picking up the glass, I went to my room.

On the way home from school the next day, I rang Greg. He wasn't there, so I asked Mrs Johnson to tell him I could only telephone after school tomorrow. She said she would pass the message on. The following day, I hopped off the train, intending to ring Greg, but as I passed through the platform barrier, there he was. He put his arms around me and held me tight. We walked down the lane next to the railway line and turned into another overgrown lane running parallel with some houses. This isolated spot was one of our favourite places; here we had privacy.

I told him I was barred from all social functions. 'They'll watch everything I do. I won't be able to see you.'

'I'll meet you after school when I can. You can ring me. I'll start work earlier; my brother doesn't mind. Jenny, I'm really sorry. If I hadn't been so stupid and picked you up, this wouldn't have happened.'

'They'd probably have caught us some time, I guess.'

He met me after school whenever he could, but I couldn't stay long because I had to get home. I used excuses (that my class had been kept back after school, or I'd missed my train), but even so, our time together was limited. Eventually Janet took pity on us and let us resume meeting at her place.

Finally after several months, my parents allowed me to return to youth group, on the understanding that I had nothing to do with the boy. I promised.

We realised we must be extremely careful, and we became expert at the art of deception.

*

My interest in school waned. At fifteen, with my career choices barred, I saw no reason to stay, so with my parent's agreement, I left at the end of fourth form. Maths was my best subject and I enjoyed working with figures, so Mum took me to see a friend of hers who was a comptometrist. A comptometer was a manual calculating machine, a forerunner of the computer. It was a complex mechanical device, which bridged the gap between adding machines and today's electronic calculators. But there was nothing automatic about it. The operator needed agile fingers to press as many as ten buttons simultaneously. Intelligence and a good memory were required to mentally convert pounds, shillings and pence, as well as tons, hundredweight, quarters and pound weights into a decimal equivalent to do the calculation. Mum's friend encouraged me to complete a course at Burroughs Business College. The morning course left afternoons free, so an afternoon job was found, through another of my mother's friends, in the office of International Combustion. My father's wish that I work in an office was fulfilled.

At college, I spent most of my time learning rows and rows of conversion tables. I practised improving my speed and accuracy on the comptometer, because this was what employers looked for.

Wendy, another student, went dancing at Caulfield Town Hall every Saturday, and asked me to come along. Soon it became a regular thing.

I loved Glen Miller's music—'In the Mood' was one of my favourites. I felt free while flying around the floor during the quickstep, and pivoting again and again at the corners of the dancefloor was exhilarating. Dancing became a regular and important activity. If I wasn't meeting Greg on a Saturday afternoon, it became a ritual to make a new dress for the evening dance.

My afternoon job was located at the business end of Collins Street. Each day I travelled to the city by train, then walked to Burroughs. After college, I caught the tram down Collins Street; its wheels clacked on the steel tracks in the road. The office was close to the renowned Hardie Brothers jewellery store, which in those days was the Tiffany's of Melbourne. Close by, on the corner of Russell Street, was Russell Collins, a popular restaurant frequented by the businessmen of the city. It was the first establishment in Melbourne to have revolving doors. My father worked nearby at Southern Cross Insurance, and he occasionally took me to lunch as a special treat.

We would meet outside the T & G Building and walk downstairs to the basement through Russell Collins's revolving doors, into the most fabulous, sophisticated place—or so I thought. During these lunches I felt close to Dad, who made me feel special and important. We talked freely, but only about everyday things, and never about what was happening at home. He encouraged me to have whatever I wanted on the menu, and cost was never an issue, yet I knew Mum never had any money. My father was friendly, talkative and polite to the waiters—very different to when he was at home. I knew his drinking created much of the unhappiness, but I also suspected he was unhappy too. But I didn't know why and I wished I did. I couldn't fathom why he was so cruel, and why he said such horrible things to Mum, and sometimes to David and me. With only an hour for lunch, these special times were soon over, and I would return to the office.

I shared the outer office with Miss Macdonald, an older single woman who was secretary to the manager. Miss

Macdonald, the manager and I were the only staff in the Melbourne office. As junior clerk, I did odd jobs, collected the mail from the post office, ran errands, did the filing and typed letters. My salary was three pounds per week and I gave Mum one pound for board. My train fare was eleven shillings and nine pence; I banked one pound, and the rest was spending money. A pound was the equivalent of two dollars, and a shilling equalled ten cents, but of course the buying power was much greater than today.

With my course completed, Mr Taylor, the manager, offered me full-time work on the condition I went to night school to learn typing and shorthand. This meant the skill I'd just spent months obtaining at college would not be used. With my love for figures, I preferred the idea of working as a comptometrist because, to me, typing was boring. Nevertheless, my parents felt 'an extra string to my bow' would be useful, so it was decided I should stay and gain extra skills and experience. The company paid for night school, and my salary was increased to five pounds and five shillings per week.

I continued doing the same tasks as before, but now Miss Macdonald gave me extra, infinitely boring jobs such as checking letters and doing the filing. Oh how I hated the mountains of filing! Twice a week, I cooked my tea—an egg or something similar—in the office's makeshift kitchen and went to night school. I detested shorthand. Typing on the manual forerunner of electric typewriters and word processors was tedious and slow. It was difficult pressing the stiff keys, especially with my little finger that was not particularly strong, but I persevered.

I had never felt comfortable in the office, and this did not change. Miss Macdonald spent much of her time in with the manager with the door shut. They whispered together, which made me feel decidedly awkward. Once when there was an urgent call for Mr Taylor, I knocked and opened the door of his office. Miss Macdonald hurriedly dropped her skirt. She had been warming her posterior by the gas heater.

Not long after I commenced work, Greg bought his first car: an old Austin A40. It was his pride and joy. Meeting each other and getting around became easier, with privacy no longer a problem. Instead of attending youth group, the pictures or other functions, we took to necking in the parking area at Mentone or Beaumaris beach.

Greg didn't dance, and with him singing at functions on a Saturday night, I continued to go dancing with Wendy. I enjoyed it immensely, especially the attention I received from the boys. Often, a boy brought me home, gave me a kiss goodnight and that was it—I might see him at the dance the following week. When the boy's car pulled up in front of my house, I knew my mother was watching. She had smoked since the beginning of her nursing career, and the glowing cigarette moving impatiently backwards and forwards in the window looked like some sort of demented firefly.

One night I was dancing with a chap I did not know and we won the lucky spot—two tickets to another dance held during the week. Keith took me home and asked if he could take me to the midweek dance. I told him I would think about it and to ring me on Monday. I really didn't think my parents would let me go.

They surprised me and said yes, but my father insisted he meet the boy. When Keith arrived, I invited him in to meet my parents. Dad asked him to come outside and led the boy to the garage.

I wondered what on earth was going on, but eventually

they returned. Once in the car I asked, 'What did Dad want?'

'Just gave me a lecture on treating you right,' said Keith.

'Oh, I'm sorry.' I blushed.

Keith, a marvellous dancer, made me feel as if I were flying. Once home, he wanted to pash. With arms tightly around me, he kissed me. It was like kissing a duck's bum—so different from Greg. Keith's lips were jammed together. I jumped out of the car. *Yuck, I'm not seeing him again!*

*

A salesman named Adrian joined the company nine months after I did. We were introduced on his first day, but then I didn't see him much because he was visiting clients. Stocktake time arrived and Miss Macdonald sent me with Adrian to the warehouse to count stock. We spent the first day counting large engineering parts. Adrian climbed the ladder, while I entered the figures he called out on the stocktake sheet. He talked about his little boy and what the family had done during the weekend. He was interested in hearing about my activities, and I felt at ease and enjoyed his company.

After morning tea the next day, I walked down one of the aisles and started counting screws. Suddenly, I was grabbed from behind; Adrian swung me around and attempted to kiss me, grabbing for my breasts and trying to lift my skirt. I hit at him, pulled myself away and ran out of the warehouse, caught a bus and returned to the office. Miss Macdonald asked why I was not with Adrian. I blurted out, 'He … he tried to kiss me … he touched me.'

'You probably led him on,' she snapped. 'We'll need to hear Adrian's story.' The secretary went into Mr Taylor's office and closed the door. *She doesn't believe me*, I said to myself.

Adrian arrived in the mid-afternoon. 'Hi, Jenny.' He smiled brightly, walked to the closed door, gave a sharp knock and entered.

Adrian left an hour later with a cheerful goodbye. I continued working.

'Jenny, in here please,' Miss Macdonald called.

A serious Mr Taylor sat behind his large desk.

'What's this nonsense, Jenny? It appears you've been letting your imagination run away with you. You come here to work, not romanticise.'

'But ...'

Mr Taylor raised his hand. 'No excuses. We'll say no more about it. We'll forget it ever happened. Is that clear?'

'Yes, Mr Taylor.'

'You can go now. See you tomorrow.'

'Goodnight, Jenny.' Miss Macdonald smiled.

On the train, I weighed up whether to tell Mum. I hadn't led Adrian on, even though Mr Taylor thought I had. *I don't want to go back. I've never liked working there*, I thought to myself. I arrived home and relayed what had happened to Mum; I didn't like keeping things from her. She mentioned it to my father.

The next morning, I walked apprehensively into the office, feeling more uncomfortable than usual. Miss Macdonald greeted me with a smile and Mr Taylor called out good morning. I started on the pile of filing.

Around mid-morning, through the door came my father.

'Good morning, Mr Wilding. Mr Taylor's expecting you.' Miss Macdonald guided him to the inner office. The door closed behind the three of them. I stewed. What the hell was he doing here? I could guess.

Eventually, the door opened and Miss Macdonald beckoned.

Mr Taylor looked up. 'Jenny, your father and I have had a long talk about yesterday.' He continued, 'We think you'll be happier in another job. We'd like you to continue here until you find something else. You can take time off for interviews. We'll be sorry to lose you, but your father and I both agree that after what's happened you'd feel uncomfortable. Your father felt you'd be happy to stay if Adrian moved on, but Adrian's staying.'

I was silent.

'Jenny, go and make a cup of tea for us, please,' Miss Macdonald said gently.

I was glad to make an exit. *I bet Dad demanded that Adrian get the sack.*

Miss Macdonald took me under her wing, helping me look in the paper for positions, and offering pointers on interview technique. She seemed to care. Adrian continued to rush loudly into the office with a bright smile. As Dad said, typical salesman.

I looked for a comptometrist position. If I must work in an office, I would rather work with figures than bang a typewriter. I found a position in the payroll department of the Melbourne Harbour Trust, a historic old building in Market Street with beautiful marble pillars and high ceilings. The environment was quite different. I worked in the main office, where the desks were lined up along the wall on one side and against the large windows on the opposite side, with a passage between. Although there was a large group of people in the area, it was always quiet. The typing pool was behind us in a large glass room. The work was allocated to each typist, and watching them sitting at their desk typing reminded me of fish in a bowl. I punched a time clock at the start and end of each day. Clock-off time was six minutes past five. I found it amusing that the staff queued from five o'clock so they could sign off as early as possible. I worked with three other girls in the payroll section, which meant I now had people to have lunch and go shopping with. The paymaster was a stern little man who pored over his work, but as long as we did our work accurately and in a timely fashion, he left us alone.

*

I continued dancing regularly, occasionally coming home with a boy, unbeknownst to Greg. The boys meant nothing to me—Greg was my boyfriend. It was easier to meet him now he had a car, but I wanted a normal relationship—one where I could take my boyfriend home, like my friends did. I was always made welcome within Greg's family, and I was spending more time at his home when everyone was out. The petting became heavier. We would go to the drive-in and grope throughout the picture, then go to sleep and wake up to find not a car in sight.

At seventeen I still had not lost my urge to follow a career in medicine. I knew it was impossible to become a doctor without my father's financial support, but I still considered nursing. The repetitious payroll work bored me. My mother encouraged me to apply to Prince Henry's, a major hospital in Melbourne. I passed the interview with flying colours and was accepted into the new year intake. Excitedly, I was measured for my uniform. All seemed well. I would finally be leaving home and be free to see whomever I wanted, when I wanted.

The acceptance letter with the starting date was delivered to my father's private mailbox. Mum was badly beaten once again. I notified the hospital that I would not be commencing.

7

After eighteen months, bored with the work at the Harbour Trust, I decided to move on. My job-hunting led me to Kraft Foods, where I secured a position in the costing department, preparing 800 dairy farmers' monthly accounts. The farmers sold milk, a necessary ingredient for cheesemaking, to the company's factories located at Strathmerton, Leitchville and Mil Lel. The farmers' payments were calculated based on the butterfat in the milk, and any raw materials the farmers bought, such as superphosphate, were deducted. Every section of the account had to balance exactly. I enjoyed the detailed work, I was using my comptometer skills, and it offered variety and increased responsibility. Although working with two others, I was accountable for my own area, instead of the daily allocation of work at the Harbour Trust.

I worked with Bev, who became a valued friend, but she was not the easiest person with whom to share a job; her expectation was that things must be done her way. Our boss, Norm, one of the clerks in the costing department, was young and married to the company's nurse.

I now travelled further and left home earlier. Nevertheless, I enjoyed the walk to Cheltenham station to catch the train to the city. I then crossed Prince's Bridge, the wind sweeping through my hair, to the YMCA, where I caught a bus to the large Kraft factory and general office in Port Melbourne. It was here that the cheddar cheese, Vegemite and cheese spreads were produced. Sometimes members of staff were asked to sample a new product in Kraft's test kitchen located on the premises.

I loved my job, and developed a friendship with Rita, another comptometrist who worked in the stock movement area. I admired Rita—as well as being slim and attractive, she was gentle and kind. Deeply religious, she applied her beliefs to everyday life. She was an inspiration.

Greg was keen to hear about the new job, and organised to meet me a couple of nights after I started.

'Thought you were never coming!' He smiled and grabbed my hand. 'It's pretty cold waiting in this laneway.'

I wrenched my hand away. 'I'm sick of this sneaking around, making excuses to get out. You just don't understand.' I folded my arms across my chest and slipped down onto my haunches.

'Do you think I enjoy standing on street corners for hours on end? Well I don't, but I care for you and want to see you, Jenny.'

'It's just not working.' My voice got louder. 'I'm sick of telling lies—sick of it all, Greg. The grass is wet. We don't have anywhere decent to go. If I'm caught there'll be hell to pay.'

'Shhh, don't shout. Don't you think I hate it too? I've told you before, you've got to stand up to your parents. You're not a kid … you're seventeen. It's ridiculous. We do nothing but fight now.'

'I tried standing up to them the other night. It didn't work.'

'Did you? You've just got to move out. I've had enough of meeting secretly too.'

'Good for you! Move out … easy for you to say.' I hopped up and started down the laneway.

'Jenny, what about your new job?' Greg called after me.

'What about my new job? You don't care.'

I ran down the path by the railway line. *I'm sick of the arguments; I want a normal life.*

At lunch time the next day, the girls were all chatting about their boyfriends and where they had been and what they were going to do at the weekend. I said nothing. I felt bad about the fight. Nobody knew my predicament (that I was seeing my boyfriend secretly) and I didn't want them to know. After lunch, Bev suggested I sit with her and check the accounts that were not balancing.

'You were quiet at lunch.'

'Mm.'

'Don't you have a boyfriend?'

'Yeah … sort of.'

'What do you mean, "sort of"?'

'I can't explain.'

'You've either got a boyfriend or you haven't.'

'I have … but it's all difficult.'

'What's difficult?' Bev looked at me and saw I was troubled. 'Let's go to the girls' room …'

I followed her. We sat on the lounge in the cloakroom, where each morning we all changed our high heels for flatties. High heels were banned in the office to protect the floors.

After some cajoling, I explained the situation with Greg and my parents, and that I had had a bad fight with him. 'He wants me to move out. I haven't anywhere to go and my mum gets a raw deal with Dad.'

'Sounds to me like you should get out.'

'I'd like to … but …'

'On my way to work I pass a place on the Beach Road … I

think it's called "Fortuna" … it's run by the YWCA. You could go there.'

'Maybe.'

'Think about it … We'd better get back inside now or the boss'll be on us.'

I rang Greg after work and we made up, but I didn't mention the conversation with Bev. During the next couple of months, things at home deteriorated, as did my relationship with Greg, because we kept fighting about me moving out. Finally I left home and moved to Fortuna.

Curfew at the hostel was ten o'clock weeknights and midnight on Saturdays. With dormitory style accommodation, I had little privacy, but I sat on my own in the dining room for meals. Unhappy at home, I was no happier at Fortuna. The only consolation was that Greg now visited; yet we both felt very uncomfortable in the communal lounge, with absolutely no privacy. We would sit upright making small talk; it was equally as bad as not being able to take Greg home.

I was sitting at the dressing table, staring at the sad and lonely figure in the mirror, when I heard the loudspeaker.

'Jenny Wilding, visitor.'

Who could that be this early on a Saturday? Probably Greg. I made my way downstairs.

'Hello Jenny, how are you?' My local vicar smiled, relaxing back into the sofa.

Hell, how'd he find me? 'Hello Father Cohen, I'm fine.'

'Good. You haven't been to church … thought you might be sick, so I called on your family. They told me you were here.'

I bet he didn't call. More like they've rung him, asking him to talk me into going home. Typical! They never go to church, but they'll use it when it suits them.

'What's it like here, Jenny? Close to the beach; pity it's still cold.'

'It's okay.'

'Go out much?'

'No.'

'What about getting to work?'

'A friend picks me up.'

'Does he?'

'It's not a he.' I spat the words.

'Jenny, your mother's quite sick. Your leaving home ... it's upset her.'

I looked at the floor.

'Jenny ...'

'Yes. I can't go back. It's not Mum, it's Dad.'

'I know ... all the more reason why your mother needs you.'

I didn't want to go home. 'What's wrong with Mum?'

'It's her liver. She looks awful ... quite yellow ... can't eat. At least give her a ring.' The vicar rose. 'Keep in touch. If you want to talk, call me anytime. Okay?'

'Yes. Thank you, Father.'

I returned to my room and decided not to do anything until Monday. I wanted to think about it. I had my freedom now—of a sort, anyway—and I didn't want to go back to the family home.

That night I went dancing with Liz, another friend from Kraft. Prior to leaving home, my parents had allowed me to go dancing more often. The venues had expanded: the Caulfield, St Kilda or Hawthorn town halls on Saturdays, and during the week, Leggett's in Prahran or the St Kilda Town Hall.

After the dance at Leggett's I stayed at Liz's, avoiding the Fortuna curfew.

'You danced with that Johnny guy most of the night. What'd you think of him?' Liz lit a cigarette.

'He's a good dancer, light on his feet, but boring. Never talks.'

We were tucked up in Liz's big double bed. She took a draw from her cigarette, offering me one from the packet.

'Ah Liz, I've never smoked,' I giggled, taking the cigarette. I put it in my mouth self-consciously.

'Here're the matches.' Liz took another draw and instantly exhaled a large cloud of smoke.

I tried to light the cigarette, but didn't draw back enough.

Liz laughed. 'Jenny, breathe in while you light it.'

I sputtered. Coughing and gasping, I handed the cigarette back. 'You can have your smoking. It's foul.' I slipped down snugly between the sheets, still coughing.

*

After dinner on Monday evening, I went to the public phone in the hall. I dreaded this call. David answered.

'Hi, it's Jenny. How's things?'

'Just the same.'

'Did you end up entering anything in that art festival?'

'No, first-formers weren't allowed.'

'That's a shame. Your sketchings are good … perhaps next year.'

'Yeah. You leaving's caused merry hell, Jenny, and Mum's sick,' David replied.

'I know; that's why I'm ringing. The vicar arrived here and told me. Bloody embarrassing. Can I speak to Mum?'

'She's in bed … Dad's put a phone in there. I'll go tell her. What's it like being out of this place?'

'Thanks ... pretty good.'

I heard my mother's soft voice. 'Jenny, I'm glad you've rung. Are you okay?'

'Course I am, Mum.'

'How's the job?'

'It's great, and the girl I work with is quite nice once you get to know her. We've become quite friendly.'

'That's good.'

'Mum, I heard you're not well.'

'Oh I'm okay, but I miss you ... I worry about you.' I heard a sigh.

'I can look after myself.'

'What's this place you're in? Is it clean? What about your meals?'

'I share a room with several other girls, and I have breakfast and dinner there. I'm okay.'

'Jenny, I wish you'd come home. It'll be better with Dad, I'm sure,' my mother whispered.

I didn't know what to say. Fortuna wasn't perfect, but things were good with Greg, and I felt I was leading a pretty normal life finally. But Mum needed me.

'Mum, it'll never be alright with Dad ... he won't change. I'll come home to help, but I'm only coming home for you.'

Feeling miserable, I went upstairs to my room.

*

It was several months before my mother recovered. My father's work problems continued and one day, I found her in tears. He had not only lost his job, but Mum had discovered that their 'debt-free' house was now heavily mortgaged, and the company owned their large black Chevrolet. Dad had borrowed from the company, using the car as collateral.

He tried to find another position within the insurance industry; however, news of his drinking had spread. The only alternative for him was to buy another business. He looked at milk bars, but decided more profits were to be gained in hotels. Mum was devastated. How would she cope with his drinking when he was surrounded by it twenty-four hours a day?

He found a hotel: The Vine, in Collingwood. The night he broke the news, I went to the dance at Leggett's with Wendy. I told her I was moving to Collingwood.

'Yuck, the slums of Melbourne. I'm glad it's not me!' she replied.

Our family's modern, middle-class house was sold. From a spotless home with wall-to-wall carpet, we move to a run-down hotel with old linoleum floors covered with years of built-up wax. It was in a back street of Collingwood. At that time (in the sixties) it was an extremely poor inner suburb of Melbourne, with narrow streets, and a hotel on nearly every corner. Two-up games thrived, as did sly grog houses, where people were able to buy alcohol after the hotels closed. In close proximity to the hotel there was a mixture of run-down terrace houses and small businesses; and there was an elastic factory next door. It was so different from the suburbs I had grown up in; I disliked the lack of trees, and the lewd comments of the gutter crawlers who suggested one should hop into their car.

Directly behind the counter of the hotel's large bar were three windows. One opened onto the Businessmen's Lounge, where a select group of local business owners in double-breasted suits with wide lapels and ties congregated. Another window faced the back lounge, where a wide variety of locals gathered: girls from the brothel opposite, exposing their voluptuous bosoms; Aborigines in dirty and torn clothing; prostitutes from Smith Street with bedraggled hair; and other unemployed and struggling people. The third window was located in the hallway that separated the two lounges. Women were not allowed in the bar, and patrons from the back lounge were barred from the Businessmen's Lounge.

My upstairs bedroom, previously a triple bedroom for patrons, was large, cold and unfriendly. My mother attempted to brighten it and fill it with furniture, but it still looked bare, even though it contained three single beds with bedside tables, two wardrobes and a large chest of drawers. The window overlooked the brewery's grain store, and each morning I was woken early by trucks delivering hops. The pungent smell of the hops was like stale earthy odours or badly off blue cheese. I found it nauseating. The view included the brothel's backyard, where the clothesline was usually full of small, brightly-coloured handtowels. I missed my comfortable old room.

I hated everything about The Vine with a passion. Spitting on the floor or wiping running noses on sleeves was common among the patrons, and then there was the smell of stale beer, and the mayhem as closing time approached. Privacy was non-existent; the family ate in the dining room with guests or patrons from the hotel. Licensing laws were rigid: dining areas must be open to the public at all times. Life for the whole family had changed.

Initially horrified by the patrons and the environment, I spent the majority of my time in my room—although I never felt it was 'my room'; it was just a room in a hotel. It contained my bed, but it was not my space. I couldn't comprehend why my father had considered such a place. In Cheltenham, I always felt safe, no matter where I went, but here I didn't even feel safe in my own home. Although a closed door separated the main hotel from the residence, it was never locked, due to the location of the dining area.

My mother worked in the bar from mid-afternoon to closing time, but I avoided going there. However, when I needed to speak to her, I had to walk through the back lounge and endure the comments from those sitting at the tables.

'Hi there nose-in-the-air, think you're too good for us?'

'Not bad tits; you shouldn't hide them away.'

'Ahh now's she's blushing,' they laughed.

Even a lifetime experiencing my father's drunken antics did not prepare me for the men in the hotel. When drunk, they were loud and abusive. Their language was disturbing, they urinated outside in the courtyard, and sometimes Mum found large puddles in the dark corners of the hallway of the hotel.

One of Mum's jobs was to clean the outside toilets, usually left in a disgusting state; and sometimes she removed badly soiled underwear from the ladies'. Mum rose early to prepare and cook all the counter lunches. She was little more than a slave. Each day, she cooked a roast, a stew or casserole, lamb's fry and bacon or the like, and shepherd's pie, as well as steaks and mixed grills to order. The weekends of the first year she spent on her hands and knees, scraping the built-up floor wax from the linoleum in the large dining room and bedrooms. She tried to brighten up the place and make it look respectable.

My father, on the other hand, spent most of his time socialising and drinking with the patrons, or locked away in his office with a bottle, on the pretext of doing the books.

One advantage of this new life was that I had total freedom. My tired parents stopped keeping track of me. I stayed out later at night and went pretty much where I wanted. My relationship with Greg had lasted five years, but it was all but over. He tried to persevere, but I was moving on. He continued to sing at functions on a Saturday night, while I went to the dances.

One night I danced with a tall young man whose hair and complexion were dark, and I was instantly attracted. Bart and I started dating, and when we went out I could wear high heels. I'd always worn flats when I was with Greg, because I didn't want to appear taller. I relished Bart's company and we got on well, although I wasn't as comfortable with him as I had been with Greg.

When I joined Bart's family for tea at their house, it made me realise his home life was vastly different from my own. His loving family made me feel welcome. Bart tolerated my father, although with his stable home life, he found my situation difficult to understand.

Our fondness for each other grew. We enjoyed dancing and went each Saturday, and sometimes midweek as well. Several weeks after ending the relationship with Greg, Bart and I were dancing together at the Caulfield Town Hall. The music stopped, and I felt a tap on my shoulder. I looked around and my stomach lurched.

'What're you doing here?' I asked.

'Come outside, Jenny, I have to talk to you.' Greg's lips were tightly drawn.

'Bart, I won't be long … he's someone from church.'

Greg grabbed my arm tightly and piloted me through the dancers. Outside he turned to me and, waving his clenched fist, he yelled, 'I've been ringing and ringing you at work. Why haven't you returned my calls?'

'I told you. It's over. We don't get on anymore.'

'Jenny, I love you… can't you understand that? After all

we've been through, you just want to throw it away?'

'How did you know where to find me?'

Lowering his voice, Greg said, 'I rang Liz. She told me.'

Hmm, great friend. 'Just get out of my life.' My voice was getting louder. 'You don't own me. How dare you pull me off a dancefloor?'

'Jenny, if you'd answered my calls …'

'You're getting me into trouble at work. Just leave me alone. We do nothing but fight. I'm sick of you working every Saturday night. You don't dance. I like dancing.'

'I'll stop working if that will please you. Jenny, I don't want to break up.'

'Well, I do. Just go!' I turned around and stormed back inside, leaving him on the pavement.

'So, who was that?' Bart tersely asked. 'He seems to own you …'

'He's someone I used to go out with.'

'Then why's he here?' Bart glared. We'd been dating on a casual basis for the last couple of months, and he wasn't aware there was anyone else.

'Bart, I've broken up with him. I won't be seeing him again, I promise,' I assured him.

A week later at work, Norm's phone rang. He beckoned me, suggesting I make the call quick because the section boss was annoyed at the number of private calls I was receiving. Greg had rung daily since the altercation at the dance. He begged me to meet him, so to get him off the phone, I agreed to a lunch meeting the following day. He picked me up outside Kraft and drove to Port Melbourne beach, where he begged me to reconsider.

I remained firm. 'Greg, we've had some wonderful times.

You've been very good to me. But it's not the same anymore. It's not working.'

'That fellow that you were dancing with, have you been out with him?'

'Yes.'

'So that's why you want to break up.'

'No, it's not. We've broken up so many times and then got back together. He has nothing to do with the reason. It's all finished.'

'You're not going to change your mind.'

'No. I've got to get back to work.'

Greg slammed the car into first gear and we drove back to Kraft in silence. I got out of the car and looked through the window.

'I'm sorry, Greg.'

He looked straight ahead. Without a word, he started the car and accelerated off.

*

The move to the hotel had a profound effect on the family. David, now a young teenager and in year eight, transferred to Fitzroy High School. Mum was concerned about whom he would be associating with, and spoke to a local off-duty policeman who was drinking at the hotel. On his recommendation, she sent David to the Fitzroy Police Boys' Club, where she hoped he would indeed mix with the 'right' kids. How wrong she was. The street kids of Collingwood used the police club as a front. They pinched cars and then drove brazenly up to the club, enticing other boys to go joyriding. David was at an impressionable age, and idolised several of the barmen working at the hotel. From them and the club, he learned skills and a way of life that his mother was trying to steer him away from.

One day my mother was busy serving lunches and Sheila, her helper, was delivering them to the bar, when David unexpectedly walked into the kitchen.

'Hi Mum.'

'What're you doing home from school?' She continued to dish up the lamb's fry.

'Ah, forgot some books I need this arvo. Mr Jenrue will go ape if I haven't got them. Forgot them last week too.'

'Have you eaten your sandwiches, or would you like some roast?' She looked up from the plate and smiled. Her pride and joy. David still did what he had done all his school life: each day, as soon as he arrived home from school, he searched out his mother. Once he found her, he was content to wander off and do his own thing.

'No thanks, Mum. Ate lunch on the way home. I'm going or I'll be late.' He gave her a hug and a kiss and walked out.

Sheila rushed in.

'Two steaks (one rare, one medium), one roast lamb and two stew. Gee, the bar's busy. The brewery trucks must all be in, or else the Robert Peel's cook's on strike.' Sheila scraped the dirty plates and tossed them in the sink to soak.

Sheila's life was tough. Married to a drunk who would not work, she supported her two boys. Coarse, but kind-hearted and full of humour (with a nickname for most of the regulars), she lightened my mother's day. She kept Mum, who was isolated in the kitchen, well informed of the antics in the bar. All the gossip found its way back to the kitchen. Toothless Sheila was no oil painting. She was tall and thin, with coarse, untidy hair, drawn back and tied with a crumpled-up black velvet bow;

and her grin was infectious. Her foul mouth often made Mum squirm, but nevertheless Mum had great affection for Sheila. As with all women, my father did not respect Sheila; he would curse at her in front of the customers, and would make a fool of her whenever the mood took him. At other times though, he was genuinely kind. Once, when she couldn't pay her rent and feared eviction, he gave her a loan, which she paid back little by little.

Although treated badly by my father, Sheila stayed. She needed the money and enjoyed working with Mum. The two women, from vastly different backgrounds, and poles apart in terms of personality, bonded together and supported each other.

With counter lunches finished, the large sink was full of plates soaking, and the benches were covered in dirty saucepans and other cooking utensils.

Mum looked around and sighed. 'Let's have a cuppa before we tackle this mess.'

'Sure, I'll make it; just sit yourself down, Mrs Wilding.'

'How many lunches today, Sheila?'

'A hundred and twelve.'

'No wonder I'm tired. Sit down. You've been rushing backwards and forwards. I'll just take ten minutes; Ray expects me in the bar soon.'

Mum looked out through the open back door to the tiny closed-in yard where the wood was stored for the slow combustion oven. Goldie stood there, her tail wagging.

'Poor Goldie, she never gets a walk. It's cruel keeping her here. Even David doesn't bother with her—too much else on his mind, I guess.'

She opened the door and Goldie rushed in and lay under

the table, waiting to be tickled. Mum returned to her seat and rubbed Goldie's chest with her foot.

Sheila sat on a hard wooden chair at the large vinyl-covered table that served as a workbench and eating area for the family. 'You know Mrs Wilding, I don't know how you keep going. You look so tired.'

'You two have an easy life.' My father stood in the doorway, swaying slightly and twitching. 'Obviously you've got nothing to do, Sophie; you can relieve me in the bar. I've got bookwork to do. Sheila, I don't pay you to sit on your backside, drink tea and play lady!'

Sheila jumped up and crossed to the sink, let out the soaking water, refilled the sink with hot, soapy water and began washing up.

'Ray, we did over one hundred lunches today. We're exhausted. I told Sheila to have a rest before cleaning up. Like a cup of tea?'

He nodded, pulling out a chair. 'And you think I've been doing nothing?'

The kitchen's happy atmosphere evaporated. The women cleaned up in silence. My father drank his tea and then walked out without a word.

The cleaning finished, Sheila put on her coat. 'See you tomorrow, Mrs Wilding. Try to take it easy.' She briskly walked out of the kitchen, through the dining room into the back lounge, and ordered herself a beer.

Mum wearily climbed the stairs, dragging each foot after the other, and went to her bedroom to freshen up.

*

I came home from work and walked down the hallway past the

open door of the bar. The crowded bar's counter was lined with pots. Although closing time was six o'clock, patrons had an extra half an hour to finish their drinks. This quirk of the licensing laws had given rise to the 'six o'clock swill', where most patrons lined up at least three pots to drink after 'last orders' was called. Counters were swamped with beer as the lines of glasses were filled. The stale smell of spilt beer on the floor, mixed with the grime and dirt, sickened me. I climbed the stairs to my room. Soon I'd have to help with the clean-up. I hated it every night.

I normally collected the dirty glasses stacked on the bar counter, then washed and rinsed them. My mother washed down the shelves and sticky counters and then placed the clean glasses onto the shelves, while Ken the barman cleaned the beer lines, replaced empty beer kegs and washed the bar floor. Dad counted the till. Often when he was too drunk, I did this too. The coins, picked up from the beer-sodden counter, were wet and sticky, and the foul smell of stale beer drifted from the till drawer. The odour sickened me—I detested it all.

'Where's David, Jenny? He should be helping in the cellar.' My father leaned against the door, a whisky in his hand.

'Haven't seen him,' I grumped.

An hour later, my father turned out the lights and locked up. Ken lived on the premises and ate meals with us, but tonight he was going out. He ran up the stairs, two at a time, to shower.

I sat in the dining room with a book while Mum organised dinner. Tonight she said we were having leftover roast from lunch, and fresh vegies. She was just too tired to cook. Dishing up, she yelled from the kitchen, 'Jenny, call your brother! He must be in his room.'

Disgruntled at being interrupted, I stomped to the stairs. 'David, tea's ready!' I yelled, and returned to my seat.

Mum placed dinner on the table. 'Jenny, I told you to tell David his tea was ready.'

'I did.'

'Well, where is he?'

'I don't know.' I sat at the table and put my serviette in my lap.

Mum went to the bottom of the stairs. 'David!' she called. There was no answer. 'David!' She climbed the stairs, pausing outside his closed door, and knocked, but there was still no answer. She walked in and found the room empty, and his schoolbag missing. She rushed downstairs. 'Ray, David's not in his room.'

He looked up slowly with a glazed expression.

'Where is he? It's eight o'clock!' Mum turned to me. 'Have you seen David since you came home?'

'No. Perhaps Ken has?'

'Ken's already left.'

'Well I don't know.' I continued eating.

'Sit down, Sophie, and eat,' my father slurred.

Mum slumped into her chair. 'Ray, David came home at lunch time.'

'Yeah … so what?'

'Well he acted a little strange.'

'What do you mean?' Ray snarled.

'I don't know. He kissed me goodbye … gave me a big hug … nearly squashed the wind out of me.

'Stop carrying on. Eat your tea.'

She pushed her plate away. 'Where is he? He's never done this before. School finished at half past three and it's now eight thirty,' she said to no-one in particular.

The phone rang, and when I answered I heard four

successive beeps. 'David, where are you?'

Mum jumped up and grabbed the phone. 'David, David, where are you? … What do you mean you're on your way to Sydney? … What do you mean you've left home? Where are you?'

'Mum, I heard STD beeps,' I interjected.

She turned to me and said, 'He's in a phone box.' Then into the phone she said, 'Who's with you? I can hear someone giggling … But where are you?'

As Mum would tell me later, David said he and some mates had hitched a ride. They had all gone home at lunch time to get food, clothes and things. David had grabbed some tins out of the pantry, his friend Stephen brought pots, and Jamie brought his billy cart so they could pack all their stuff in it. Then they met in Smith Street and didn't go back to school. When he rang, the kids had just finished their tea after lighting a fire and cooking baked beans. He assured Mum he could look after himself.

'David, please tell me where you are!' she pleaded.

David told Mum he didn't know where they were but they were trying to hitch another ride. He said they had to wait for the trucks because of the billy cart.

'What's going on? Give me the phone!' Dad snatched it. 'David, what do you think you're doing? Tell me right now where you are. Wait till I get my hands on you!'

The phone went dead.

Dad slammed the phone onto its cradle. 'The little bastard! Wait till I get my hands on him!' He lifted the handset and dialled.

'Hello, this is Ray Wilding from The Vine … Yeah, that's right. Look, my son didn't come home from school today. We've just had a call from him … Yeah, just now. He says he's on his way to Sydney. My daughter heard STD beeps … Yeah, it sounds like he's somewhere on the Hume Highway. Came home at lunch time … Can't have gone far. You're sending someone around? Okay. We'll wait.' He replaced the receiver.

The police put out an alert and there was nothing else anyone could do. We just had to wait. Mum sat numb, Dad went out to the back room, and I went to bed.

I woke to my mother shaking me. 'Jenny, Jenny, wake up!'

'What's up?'

'They've found David. They've taken him to the Seymour Police Station. Your father's leaving shortly. Will you to go with him? I can't. Someone has to be here to open up.'

'I don't want to go.'

'Please, Jenny. He needs company. Your chatting will keep him alert. Okay?'

'I suppose.'

I dragged myself out of bed. It was pitch black outside. 'What time is it?'

'Five o'clock. Thanks, Jenny. I can always depend on you.' Mum closed the door.

Great … bloody David! I quickly dressed and went downstairs. Mum was in her dressing gown, making sandwiches and a thermos of tea.

The drive was uneventful. Dad chatted away, asking me how my job was going, but there was no mention of David.

We found him in animated conversation with a policeman when we arrived. Another policeman took my father aside. 'We found four of them in a phone box trying to sleep. And a dog! It was the only shelter they could find. Probably rang you from there. Your son did ring you? That's right, isn't it?'

'Yes, about nine o'clock last night.'

'One of the blokes, doing his regular beat, noticed them. They had a billy cart full of bits and pieces. Making for Sydney, they thought.' He laughed. 'Nice kid you've got there, just a bit adventurous. If that's the worst thing he gets up to, you'll have no worries.'

On the drive back to Melbourne, there was silence for the first twenty minutes. David sat in the back.

'Well son, what've you got to say for yourself?' Dad looked at David in the rear vision mirror.

'Nothing.'

'Bit cold sleeping out?'

'It was alright. Anyway we didn't sleep out; we were in a phone box.'

'So I heard. Well I hope you've learned your lesson.'

'Yes, Dad.' David was starting to feel at ease. He had expected a flip over the ears at the very least, but Dad's temper was much more moderate when he was sober. He leaned forward excitedly. 'They're neat police. The one I was talking to showed me how to start a car with silver paper.'

My father whispered to me. 'Bloody cops, where's their brains?'

The rest of the trip to Melbourne was silent.

8

'Don't forget the cricket match on Sunday, Jenny.' My father rose from his chair.

'Sorry, Dad. Bart and I can't come.'

'Rubbish! The hotel's social day is only once a month. I'm depending on you. We won't have a staff team without you.'

'Dad, we're meeting some of Bart's friends.'

'I don't care what your idiot boyfriend does, but you're coming to the cricket match.' He headed for the door.

'Mum, I hate cricket. It's boring. Bart and I don't drink. I don't want to go.'

'I know, but Dad expects it.'

'I don't think Bart will go. He hates it. The men get drunk; they swear; it's just awful. Please Mum, can't you make Dad understand?'

'I'll try ... but ... he needs you both.'

'He doesn't pester David to go ... David just does his own thing.'

My mother didn't respond.

The cricket match was held at a local sports ground. On Saturday the regulars brought a nine gallon keg of beer (affectionately known as a 'niner') to drink after the hotel closed. If it wasn't emptied that night, they took it to the ground the next day. With hotels closed on Sundays, the match was really just an excuse to drink, although an effort was made to play the game. Usually the niner lasted until mid-afternoon, then the cricket match was abandoned. Everyone would retire to The Vine, congregating in the dining room for a 'social drink' provided by the licensee. Licensing laws were strict, but they allowed a publican to provide a drink on the house. In reality, as each round of drinks was ordered, my father noted what was owed, and this was paid in the bar the following week. Police raids were a common occurrence, so money never changed hands in the dining room. When police executed the raids, my father knew it was wise to offer the officers a drink on the house.

'You're up, Jenny.'

Bat in hand, I walked on to the field and stood in front of the stumps, which consisted of a twig across three sticks. Nigel—or Fatty, as he was more commonly called—bowled. The ball flew down, connected with my bat and soared upwards. Steve leapt into the air.

'Out! Good on you, Narra!' yelled Nigel to the tall, ever-so-slim Steve.

Steve and Nigel were inseparable. They frequented every hotel in Collingwood, went to the football together and often travelled to Foster in South Gippsland, where Steve had relatives. Steve had lived in Foster for a while, working at the butter factory and playing football with the Tigers, the local team. Each time I passed him in the corridor of the hotel, he always made a flirtatious remark. I didn't like him.

I tossed the bat to the ground and, red-faced, returned to sit with Bart on the rug. I took a sandwich out of the picnic basket. 'Didn't even get a run! You did well though … ten runs. Not that anyone takes it seriously. Looks like the niner's empty

… guess it's back to The Vine.'

'I'm not fussed about going back there, Jen.'

'Ah please, I don't want to be with those loudmouth horrors on my own. Look, they're finishing up … knew it wouldn't be long.'

I packed the remains of the picnic and, hand in hand, we made our way to the car. I was happy with Bart, and imagined our relationship continuing indefinitely.

*

'Push the tables back, boys, and bring the chairs to the fire. I'll take the orders once you're settled. Bart, help with the big table.' My small-framed father stood by the door, directing and twitching.

The tables back against the wall, we all settled around the fire. Narra, Fatty, Boza, Jim and several others I didn't know—along with Ken the barman, Mum, Dad, Bart and I—made up the group. David was not around, and no-one seemed to know where he was. He regularly disappeared for the day at weekends.

'Well boys, whose shout?' My father stood, pencil and paper in hand.

'Make it mine, Ray.' Narra winked at me and I quickly looked away.

Bart and I had a lemon squash. With each round of drinks, the noise level increased. Bart bought a round early in the night, but reneged on the second shout.

'You mean black bastard! Don't worry, I'll shout for you. There's nothing worse than a mean black bastard.' My father turned heel and headed for the night cupboard to refill the drinks.

The room went quiet. Bart looked straight ahead. I was devastated and felt sick. Almost immediately, the silence was replaced with voices that became louder, as the boys reverted to telling dirty jokes. We just sat.

My father had made offensive remarks about Bart to me on numerous occasions, but I never thought he would do what he had just done. Bart's complexion was one of the first things that had attracted me to him. I had always yearned to be brown, but all my fair skin did was burn in the sun.

'Jen, I'm going home,' Bart whispered.

'I'll come out with you.'

He got up. 'Goodnight fellas, see ya 'round.' He turned to Mum. 'Goodnight Mrs Wilding.'

'Bart, I'm sorry … I must apologise for Ray's rudeness,' Mum said.

We walked to Bart's car.

'I hate Dad. How dare he say that? I wish we hadn't gone to the match. I'm so sorry …'

'Jen, it's not your fault. It doesn't really worry me. I'll ring you tomorrow.' He kissed me, hopped into the car, waved, and drove away.

But Bart didn't ring on Monday, or Tuesday. I was expecting to go to the dance with him on Wednesday, so I rang his work.

'Why haven't you rung?'

'I've been very busy.'

'Are we going to the dance tonight?'

'Actually Jenny, I was about to give you a ring. I have to work back; perhaps we'll go on Saturday. What about tea at my place?'

'Okay.'

'I'll pick you up about four. Must go … pretty busy.'

'Bye.' I put down the receiver. He was not his usual self.

On Saturday afternoon, Bart walked into the residence of the hotel and called up the stairs. I rushed down, jacket in hand, a large smile on my face. I'd made a new dress and spent more time than usual on my makeup. It was the week before Christmas, and tonight was a special dance. I wanted to impress.

'Hi.' Bouncing down the stairs, I gave him a peck.

'Will we be off, Jen?' I realised Bart didn't want to catch up with my father.

'Yeah, sure. I'll just tell Mum I'm going. She's in the bar. You wait here.' I rushed into the back lounge and beckoned through the bar window.

'Bye Mum, I'm off.'

'Don't be too late.'

'I'll try not to be.'

Bart's Mum cooked roast lamb and rice pudding for tea. As always, his parents were friendly and kind, but especially so this night. Bart was quiet.

It was the same at the dance. We mixed with our usual group of friends. After several dances with Bart, I spent the rest of the evening dancing with others. I noticed he just stood at the edge of the dancefloor, looking at the ground.

Afterwards, we joined the crowd at our favourite coffee shop in St Kilda Road, and then drove home. He turned the engine off and I moved closer. He slowly put his arm around me.

'I've got something for you.' He opened the glove box and produced a small parcel wrapped in Christmas paper. 'Happy Christmas, Jenny.'

'But Bart, it's too early for Christmas presents. I'm giving you yours on Christmas Eve.'

'Open it, Jenny. I want to see what you think.'

I took the parcel, and undid the wrapping to reveal a flat black velvet box. I opened it to find a gold necklace entwined with pink stones, with earrings to match.

'Oh Bart, it's beautiful! I've never had anything like this. I love it!' I put my arms around his neck and kissed him. He didn't respond. 'What's wrong?'

'Jenny, I don't quite know how to tell you, but this isn't working out.'

My stomach lurched. 'What do you mean?'

'I really like you, but …' Bart took a deep breath, 'I don't think we should go out anymore.'

'Is this because of last Sunday?'

'No … not really … Well I suppose so … a bit.'

'Well what's this for then if you're breaking off with me?' I held up the necklace.

'Jenny, I really like you. I want you to have it.'

'Well I don't want it.'

'Please, please take it.' He pressed it into my hand.

I started crying. 'Bart, don't do this. We won't go to the blasted cricket matches anymore. You don't have to see my dad. Please!'

He looked straight ahead. 'It'll never work. I'm going; I'll ring you.'

'No, Bart please, don't go, please.' I pulled on his arm, but he pulled away and started the car.

'Goodnight, Jenny.'

'Bart, you can't do this.'

'Jenny, just get out. I'll ring you.'

I opened the door, slowly stepping onto the kerb. He pulled the door sharply closed and accelerated up Derby Street. I watched the car, my eyes brimming, then slowly turned, put the key in the lock and climbed the stairs. I sat on the bed, feeling numb. *It's all because of Dad …*

I didn't bother undressing, just climbed into bed and curled up into a foetal position.

The following day, tired after the sleepless night, I went to work. Once the opportunity arose, I rang Bart's work. I was told he was in a meeting.

That night, I was watching TV with Mum. 'Bart broke off with me last night.' My eyes filled. 'I really like him, Mum … he's good to me … his family's nice. I'd hoped …'

Mum looked at me. 'I'm so sorry, love … he's a nice boy.' She rose, put her arms around me and gave me a hug. 'Like a cup of tea, dear?'

I nodded.

Two days went by, and Bart didn't ring. My resolution weakened, so I rang. Bart spoke to me but made it very clear it was over. My anger and dislike for my father deepened.

*

I felt devastated, and during the coming weeks I kept to myself. I didn't go dancing. I went to work and then retired to my room. Occasionally, I bumped into Steve—or Narra, as his friends called him. Whenever I needed to go to the bar, he seemed to be in the corridor. Although polite, he appeared to be making fun of me. A handsome man he was not. His front teeth had been knocked out playing football years before, and the stumps remained. He was tall and thin, with a small head and a large, broad nose. His soft, curly hair was always in place, and his ruddy complexion confirmed he worked out of doors. Never still, he was the 'life' of any party, always fooling around and cracking jokes. Playing the spoons and saucepans was one of his specialities.

'Haven't seen Bart around lately.' Steve, a pot of beer in his hand, leant against the doorframe, preventing me from getting through.

I tried to manoeuvre around him, but he put his arm across the door and with a big smirk said, 'Left you in the lurch, did he?'

'Not at all. Let me pass.'

'I just wanted to ask you out, Jenny. How about it?'

'No, thanks.'

'Ah, come on, thought we might go to Chinatown for a meal and perhaps a show afterwards.'

I pushed past and started towards the bar.

'Think about it, Jenny. I'll see you tomorrow.'

I went through the lounge and headed to the bar counter. Catching my mother's eye, I told her I was going to the city to buy a pair of slacks. My father no longer objected to me wearing them.

In bed that night, my mind wandered to Bart. We were good together, we loved dancing, and his family were just how I imagined families should be. I'd hoped to become part of it one day. Bart and I didn't argue—not like Greg and I. Bart was dependable, quiet, caring, but something had been missing; I couldn't quite put my finger on it. With Greg I was always comfortable, but with Bart I wasn't completely myself. Now it appeared Steve was the only person interested in me.

I didn't really like him, although he did make me laugh when he was fooling around. Now he'd asked me out. My father would be furious if I went out with him. *Perhaps I'll just go out with him once.* I slipped off to sleep.

On Sunday, Steve knocked on the door of The Vine's residence. My father answered. 'I'm not selling, Steve. Had a visit from the police this morning … could be around the corner.' He started to close the door.

'I'm here to pick up Jenny; we're going out.'

'You're what?'

'Going to Chinatown.' Steve looked my father in the eye, with a smirk on his face.

My father didn't seem to comprehend. He turned tail and, swaying, made his way to the back room. Steve was pleased with himself—he had expected an outburst.

Mum was standing in the background. She looked shocked. 'Jenny, you never mentioned you were going out with Steve.'

'Well, I am. We're going for a meal in the city. See ya!' With that I walked out the front door, trying not to notice how miserable she now appeared.

We walked through the Fitzroy Gardens to Chinatown. Sunday evenings in Melbourne were vastly different from weeknights. On street corners, men and occasionally a woman preached 'the way to eternal life' and 'all must repent or go to hell'. As the evening progressed, each one tried to outdo the other, and their voices became louder and louder. Some in the large crowd took the speakers seriously, but most thought their message was at worst a joke, and at best, reasonable entertainment.

I hadn't been to the city on a Sunday evening before, and found it mesmerising. We walked through the Chinese Arch in Little Bourke Street, and Steve took me to his favourite restaurant, the Chun Yun. This was a new experience; I had never tasted Chinese food, but with Steve's help, I chose a dish that was delicious. He talked about his first love, football, and I discovered that he had trained in the past with the Collingwood team and went to the footy most Saturdays. He suggested I should go with him the following week.

'Footy? I don't think so ... I've never been to a match.'

'I thought as much. Your parents have wrapped you in cottonwool. I bet they've never been to the footy either. Come, it's great!'

'What sort of work do you do at Stan's?' I asked, changing the subject. I knew he worked at a car yard around the corner from The Vine, in Langridge Street.

He leaned forward, and a stale, sour smell wafted across the table. 'Steam clean the engines. Easy job. Stan's a pretty good boss—doesn't expect too much of ya.'

I drew back. *Phew ... bad breath or stale alcohol. Why did I come?*

'Thought we might go to the Tiv for a laugh. Ever been?' Steve leant back in his chair.

'Not on a Sunday. I've been during the week. I thought they were closed on Sundays.'

'Err ... Sundays is amateurs' night. The hopefuls have a chance to perform. It's a bit of a laugh. Sometimes you get a good one. Most are hopeless. It's cheap, only two bob.'

'Boy, that's heaps cheaper than when I've gone.'

'Well let's see what's on tonight.'

We cut through a side lane to Bourke Street and the Tivoli theatre. The audience were mostly deadbeats looking for cheap entertainment, and the acts were terrible, but it was a good laugh.

So I commenced a new and very different relationship. Perhaps it was because my self-esteem at that point was zero, perhaps I was grieving for Bart, perhaps it was because all my friends had serious boyfriends, or perhaps I wanted to hurt my father. I'll never know. I was not attracted to Steve. The only things I liked about him were the way he enjoyed life and his sense of humour—even though his jokes were often at someone else's expense. So instead of dancing (which I loved), our outings consisted of football, pub-hopping and an occasional picture show. Steve frequently went to Foster on drinking sprees, and he spent time with mates in pubs and sly grog shops. He also frequented an illegal SP bookie's home. SP (starting price) bookmakers provided illegal off-course betting on the races. They were an institution in Australian pubs, on street corners and in private homes during the 1960s, but they became less popular when the government-owned Totalisator Agency Board (TAB) came to prominence.

When we drank at The Vine, I couldn't help but notice my mother's face as she served Steve a pot and me a lemonade with a dash of beer.

After dinner one night as I was drying the dishes, Mum paused while washing a plate and turned to me. 'Jenny, why are you going out with Steve?'

'Because I like him.'

'Steve's a witty fellow, always looking for a laugh, and he's popular with his drinking mates ... but ... Jenny, he's an alcoholic. He sometimes drinks six pots of beer in the lunch hour, and more after work. He's many years older than you ... he's got no front teeth for God's sake! Jenny, you can do so much better. Don't throw your life away,' my mother begged.

'I'm not throwing my life away,' I scowled.

'This is on the rebound from Bart.'

'I couldn't care less about Bart!' I threw the tea towel down and made for the door. 'I'm going out with Steve whether you like it or not.'

I noticed as I came back down the stairs after freshening up that Mum was slumped in front of the television. Tired after another exhausting day cooking counter lunches, working in the bar and then preparing tea, she lit a cigarette and drew in the smoke, exhaling it almost immediately. She looked miserable.

'Jenny, where are you going?' she called from the dining room as she saw me slip by towards the front door.

'Out.' I slammed the front door behind me.

From that night on I chose to ignore my mother's feelings and refused to discuss Steve. But life was not easy. Estranged from my parents, I found it was no picnic being Steve's girlfriend. He did what he wanted, went where he wanted, and sought me out when it suited him. I'd watched my mother being treated this way, so I just accepted his behaviour. I convinced myself anything was better than the loneliness and emptiness I had experienced since Bart disappeared from my life, and I couldn't bear the thought of being rejected again.

The next day Steve came into the bar and slapped money on the counter.

'Pot, Mrs Wilding, thanks.'

She placed the pot under the tap and poured a beer with a good head, just how Steve liked it.

'Steve, I'd like a chat.'

'What about, Mrs Wilding?'

'I'm due for a break in a few minutes; I'll meet you in the hall.' My mother turned her back to serve someone through the lounge window.

Shortly afterwards, she touched Ken on the shoulder and

said, 'I'm taking my break now.' She walked into the hall and met Steve.

'What's up, Mrs Wilding?'

'Steve, it's about Jenny … she's young. I don't think it's a good idea you taking her out. I hope you understand. You're a man of the world … Jenny's led a pretty sheltered life.'

My mother was careful what she said. She didn't want to provoke Steve's temper—that would bring my father running.

'Well you know, Mrs Wilding, I kinda like your daughter and I kinda think I'll continue taking her out. She's old enough to make her own decisions. You think I'm not good enough. I'm from the other side of the tracks, eh? But guess what, it's a bit of a conquest for me—a person like her, going out with a person like me. The guys in the bar bet she wouldn't go out with old Steve. Well she did, didn't she? I won the bet, and got an innocent youngie into the bargain. I've won the lottery. Get used to it. Anything else you want to talk about?'

Mum turned tail and returned to the bar, steadfastly holding back the tears. She served until closing time.

The next morning, Mum woke to the sun streaming through the window. The bed, set in the corner of the two outside walls of the room, looked like a miniature in the huge bedroom. To prevent his feet from getting cold, Dad had put down a carpet runner to cover the linoleum from the bedroom door to the bed, because it was such a hike to turn off the light. Mum hadn't slept. She'd heard me come in very late, and spent the rest of the night tossing and turning.

She took a deep breath. 'Ray, I'm worried about Jenny.'

Groggy, he grunted, 'What about Jenny?'

'I spoke to Steve yesterday … tried to reason with him about taking Jenny out. He was so rude … really ridiculed everything

I said. He blatantly told me … he's going to continue taking her out. He said he initially asked her out just because of a bet.'

My father sat up, the mist clearing. 'I'll fix him. Who does he think he is?'

'Ray, please, no fuss … it'll make it worse. Jenny can be so determined when it suits her.'

'She'll do as I say. Leave it to me.'

Mum sighed, climbed out of bed and headed to the shower.

*

'Steve, you're hogging the snooker table; time to give others a go.' My father was filling Steve's pot.

'Yeah Ray, when Fatty and I finish our game.'

'I'm telling you … finish now … others are waiting.'

'When I'm ready.' Steve picked up his pot and made his way back to the table.

'Now … or you're barred,' my father yelled across the bar.

'Go to hell! You can't do that, you little prick.'

'That's it. Leave now, or I'll call the coppers.' Dad stood behind the bar, his clenched hands resting on the counter.

Steve picked up the cue, rubbed it with chalk, sighted along its shaft and took a shot. Three snooker balls dropped into adjacent pockets.

'Not bad eh, Fatty? I'll scoop the lot this go.' He prepared to shoot again.

'I wouldn't do that if I was you. Leave! That means now, Steve.'

Steve stood up to his full height and looked down at my frail, twitching father. 'You're talking to me?' Steve looked like he was about to punch my father. 'Well, there's plenty of other pubs, aren't there, guys? Who's coming?'

Half a dozen or so stood up, sculled their beers and started to walk to the door with Steve.

'And keep away from my daughter, I'm warning you.'

'You can bar me from your fucking dump of a hotel, but you can't stop me seeing Jenny, if that's what I want to do. Stick that up your arse!' Steve walked out with his mates.

An uneasy quiet settled on the rest of the patrons. Mum busied herself washing glasses, Dad retired to the back room and Ken kept serving. The bell rang for closing time, and the noise level rose as patrons queued at the bar to order their last drinks.

I helped clean up the bar, as usual.

After dinner, the phone rang and I jumped to answer it.

'Hi, Jenny,' said Steve. 'Have you heard what your father did today?'

'No.'

'Meet me at my place in ten minutes.'

'Okay.' I replaced the receiver.

'That was Steve … What did Dad do today?' I looked at my mother.

'He barred him from the hotel. There was a disagreement.'

'He can't do that to my boyfriend!'

'Jenny, we don't want you involved with him. He's not right for you.'

'You're just like Dad. Neither of you want me to be happy!' I stormed to the front door.

'Jenny, you're forbidden to see him and that's that.'

I slammed the door hard behind me, crossed the road and turned the corner into Langridge Street. Steve was sitting outside his single-fronted terrace house, which was situated at the end of a group of six. It was run-down, with a pathetic small garden that his elderly mother attempted to tend.

'Hi, Jenny.' He stretched on the verandah step. 'Your father barred me from the pub today, the arsehole.'

'I know, Mum told me. I guess he was drunk … Do you think he really means it?'

'Probably … Doesn't worry me; there's plenty of other pubs,' Steve declared.

I sat next to him. 'What are we going to do?'

'That's up to you. It's all up to you. Depends if you want to stand on your own two feet or be screwed by your parents.'

Haven't I heard that before? I said nothing.

We sat in silence for a while, then abruptly he rose and walked towards the front door. 'I'm going to bed. See you!'

I didn't want to return home, so I just sat.

Steve's mother opened the front door. 'Why are you still here? Steve's gone to bed. Go home. Little rescuer, aren't you? New clothes, bank account and you've organised to get his teeth fixed up. You might change the outside, you won't change the inside.' Mrs Stillwell firmly closed the front door.

A feeling of utter loneliness enveloped me. *If I go home this early, I'll have to face Mum and Dad and their questions. Damn Steve, leaving me high and dry! I'm standing up to my parents and it's not solving anything. I just feel so alone. He's not supportive, and it's obvious his mother doesn't like me.*

Slowly I got to my feet and wandered home.

*

'Jenny.' My boss gestured towards the phone in his hand.

I took the phone from him. 'Hello.'

'Hi, it's me. Sorry about last night. I was furious with your dad. I'd had a few drinks.'

'Your mother sent me home, which was the last place I wanted to be.'

'I guessed that. Look, I'm off to Foster this weekend. Come with me. We'll get the train Friday night.'

'You know they'll never let me, Steve.'

'Jenny, you either want to be with me or you don't. If you don't come, it'll be obvious to me you're not interested.'

'That's not so. I'll think about it.'

'Okay, but if you don't come, it's off, as far as I'm concerned.'

I put the phone down. The last time Steve went to Foster, I had said I would go. My parents kicked up such a stink, that to keep the peace I hadn't gone. It would be worse now. I returned to my desk and mechanically pressed the keys of the comptometer.

*

I was drying the dishes after tea. 'I won't be home this weekend, Mum. I'm going to Foster with Steve.' I waited for the onslaught, but there was dead silence.

Then Mum said, 'Jenny, you've been forbidden to see Steve.'

'I'm twenty; you can't forbid me to see anyone.'

'Your father won't allow you to go.'

'I don't intend on telling him. Mum, I'm going!' Dishes finished, I went to my room.

On Thursday night I packed a small suitcase. I had never been away with a man, and doing so without my parents' blessing added to the excitement. The next day I rushed home from work, grabbed my case and after saying goodbye to my unhappy mother, I met Steve at his place.

The train left Spencer Street at six o'clock, and during the three-hour journey Steve enjoyed a couple of beers. After a short walk in the dark, we arrived at the small country house of Steve's brother-in-law. It was dirty and untidy with a tiny kitchen, where the combustion stove was providing the heat for the house. Frank lived with his only daughter, as Steve's sister had died a few years previously. He showed us to a bedroom that had a double bed, and I looked incredulously at Steve. 'I'm not sleeping here; you know that.'

With a foxy grin Steve said, 'Well, where are you going to sleep?'

'You told me I would be staying at the Collises' place.'

'Did I? Well they're probably in bed now.'

Frank, standing quietly, said nothing.

'Well I'm not staying here,' I glared.

'Jenny, you're an idiot. Frank, would the Collises mind?'

'No, she can sleep with the kids.'

'Can you organise it?' Steve went to the fridge and opened a bottle of beer.

He was his old self the next morning, and we went for a walk around Foster, finishing at the pub. That night, we went with a few of his mates to do some net fishing at Waratah Bay, but Steve got drunk and abused me for being there and not giving him time with his mates.

The next morning, he wouldn't speak, and went off with his mates. I waited. Frank mentioned Steve would probably be at the hotel, because on a Sunday it opened for lunches. So I set off for the pub. I went into the lounge and beckoned Steve from the bar window. He ignored me. I ordered myself a gin, followed by another and another. Eventually, Pete, one of Steve's mates, took me, more than a little drunk, back to Frank's. Steve didn't return. That evening, Pete called into Frank's on his way to the pub. I had been violently ill all afternoon and could barely lift my head.

'What you need is some more of the same: another gin. It'll fix you right up,' Pete said with a smile.

'Oh, no, never,' I moaned, feeling acutely ill again.

'No, I'm serious. At least come and have a beer, it'll make you feel better.'

'Where's Steve?'

'He's at the pub.'

'Okay, I'll just get dressed.'

The beer helped and I began to feel better, but Steve still ignored me.

'Don't worry. He'll be okay, once he's slept it off. You're off home tomorrow aren't you?'

'Yes,' I said glumly.

Not only were Steve and I at cross-purposes all weekend, but we argued on the way home. It was many years before I enjoyed another gin.

I was quite unhappy with the relationship at that point, and perhaps it might have ended there if Steve hadn't been barred from the hotel and I hadn't been forbidden to see him. I didn't want to admit to my parents that I had made a mistake, especially considering the reasons that led me to go out with Steve. I felt so miserable after Bart, and Steve seemed the only one interested in me. I was angry with my father and I just wanted to get back at him. I had grown to care for Steve, and foolishly thought it was love. At times we did have a lot of fun together, and he was caring, but he could also be very cruel. It seems strange now, but at the time it was the only life I knew, and I just accepted it as it was.

9

My father opened the bottom drawer of his desk and pulled out a bottle of whisky. He took a large swig, replaced the stopper in the bottle, and put it back in the drawer. His concentration was low as he pored over his books and wrote some cheques. It had been a disastrous week. The takings were down and quite a few outstanding accounts were due to be paid. He realised barring Steve was not the brightest thing he'd done, because now a large number of his regular drinkers were frequenting the Robert Peel. He was losing money in the bar, and the counter lunches were down. If things didn't improve he would have to cut Sheila's hours and he didn't want to do that—she had children to feed.

Throughout his life my father had worked hard to make something of himself. He was only twelve when he commenced working in the mines in Western Australia, and by the time he was eighteen he had his own bus with a route from Carnegie to St Kilda. He had killer selling instincts and was more than successful at selling insurance. His expertise in buying a run-down business and building it up was obvious with both the florist shop and the general store. That was his plan for the hotel. However, it was thwarted by too many rules and regulations implemented by the licensing board. The customers, especially those in the bar and the back parlour, didn't like change either.

As my father was reaching into the drawer for the whisky bottle again, there was a loud knock at the residence door. My mother opened it to find two policemen.

'Come in … I guess you're doing a check?'

'Well no, Mrs Wilding … actually it's your son.'

Worried, Mum asked, 'Is he okay?'

'Yes … he's down at the station. We received a radio call asking us to drop in. Either you or Mr Wilding is required at the station.'

'But what's wrong?'

'Mrs Wilding, if you'll get your husband we'll speak to you both.'

Shaken, Mum went to the back room. 'Ray, there's two policemen at the door … It's David … he's at the police station. He went out after lunch—I don't know where. Never know what he's doing these days. The police want to speak to us both.'

'What's the problem, fellas? My wife says David's at the station.' My father, still a handsome man, looked frail. His body was wasting away due to his drinking and poor appetite. Twitching his shoulders, he looked up at the burly policeman.

'Mr Wilding, your son has been apprehended driving a stolen vehicle. He knocked down three shop verandahs in Smith Street. Done a fair bit of damage to the car too.'

'You're mistaken … my son can't drive …'

'Well I guess that may be why the verandahs were knocked down. He's facing a few charges. You need to come down to the station, to be present while he's questioned.'

'Sure, of course.'

Dad turned to Mum. 'You stay here. Have this fixed up in

a jiffy.' Turning back to the police, he said, 'I'll take my car … be there shortly.'

My father mentioned later that as he drove to the police station, he remembered the drive home from Seymour and what his son had said: 'They're neat police. One of them showed me how to start a car with silver paper.' He also remembered the policeman's comment: 'Your son's an adventurous kid … if this escapade is the worst thing he gets up to, you'll have no worries.' He said, at that moment, his heart sank.

When David was born, my father had been overjoyed: after four daughters, finally a son. His previous marriage had produced three daughters, and then his first wife had a son— the only problem was that it wasn't his. He couldn't forgive her betrayal. They separated and eventually divorced. He was bitter after his failed marriage, and vowed never to trust another woman.

He had a car accident while he was working in Albury, and met Mum in the hospital. He got to know her while she nursed him back to health. She was a small, quiet woman with sparkling eyes, who was always cheerful, and he found himself attracted to her. He asked her out and eventually married her. However, his first wife's betrayal haunted him and it seeped into his new marriage. Dad found it impossible to trust Mum. He was haunted by the thought that she was betraying him while he was away working. He probably knew this was unreasonable, but just couldn't stop himself. In the early days of their marriage, after he'd been drinking he would accuse and abuse her verbally, but soon it became physical. He would look at her the next morning; she would be bruised and battered, and he'd feel disgusted, but he couldn't bring himself to say sorry. When they discovered a few months after they were married that Mum was expecting a baby, he hoped it would be a boy. He was blessed with me, but finally, four years later, the son he had longed for arrived.

But now his son was off the rails. His interest in school had waned, even though academically he was second in his year. Dad had noticed David idolised the hotel barmen and that he spent time talking to them about racing—something my father detested. Many of the customers, Steve among them, talked incessantly about which horse should be backed, and Steve sometimes took David to the races. My father guessed that the barmen and Steve were sometimes placing bets with the bookmakers on David's behalf. Dad had never been interested in gambling, and it was the last thing he wanted for his son. Mum had mentioned to Dad that now Steve was barred, David was meeting him elsewhere, but she didn't know where.

My father spent a long time at the police station trying to convince the police not to charge his son. Although he could sell just about anything to anyone, his powers of persuasion seemed useless with the police. They made it clear that the significant damage to the shop verandahs and car was a serious offence, and the boy had to realise that he must be responsible for his actions. However, my father would not give up, and argued that his son should be given another chance. He said he would pay for the repair of the verandahs and the damage to the car. After consideration, the police told Dad to bring David back to the station the next day, and the senior officer would carry out a formal warning regarding the consequences if David reoffended. It would be made clear that any further antisocial behaviour would not be tolerated. If David showed remorse, and my father paid for the damages, they would give David another chance. It seemed that police often favoured the option of giving first offenders a second chance, rather than entrenching them into the penal system.

My father attempted to talk to his son when they got home, but David ignored him and went up to his room, banging the door shut. Dad was at a loss, but realised how far removed from his son he was. For much of David's life, my father had been managing businesses, and when he looked back, he realised they had spent little time together. He favoured David over me. He had spoilt him and allowed him to be irresponsible. If David wanted money, he got it. But on the other hand, my father believed he had disciplined David. For example, he had dealt with the situation when my brother tried smoking as a youngster. He believed he didn't stand any nonsense. The problem was that David was mixing with the wrong types: kids at school, the youngsters at the Police Boys' Club, the barmen. Dad regretted buying the hotel. He felt David was a good kid; he was creative—his sketching and paintings were fantastic—and like his father, he loved animals. Dad vowed to himself he'd spend more time with him.

The next day my father took David back to the police station. He looked at his son sitting in the foyer. David was scared, jiggling his foot and twisting his hands together. Dad wanted to comfort him and give him a hug, but instead he did nothing. My father didn't feel that comfortable himself. They waited about five minutes and then a policeman asked David to follow him. Dad rose to accompany his son, but was told to wait in the foyer. He slumped back into his chair.

It was half an hour before David returned, looking pale and contrite. He shook hands with the senior officer who had returned with him, and thanked him politely. My father tried to strike up a conversation with the officer, but he was quickly dismissed.

Dad and my brother left the police station, and when they were in the car Dad asked, 'What did the officer say?'

'Aw, I dunno. Told me I'd better not get into any more trouble. I had to tell him how it happened all over again.'

'What else?'

'He hauled me over the coals … what do you think? I don't want to talk about it.'

My father could not get anything else out of his son. David sat back in the front seat and looked straight ahead.

*

After dinner that night, Dad sat with Mum in front of the TV. This was unusual, because he normally retired to the back room each evening. They didn't speak, but it was a comfortable silence. He pulled out his pipe and slowly filled it with tobacco. It took him an inordinate amount of time, and all the while Dobie the cat paced round and round the chair, watching him. Finally Dad crossed his legs, and immediately the cat jumped up and settled himself, stretched out on Dad's lap. He absentmindedly stroked the cat. He had been doing a lot of thinking the last couple of days, and had come to realise that the concerns he and Mum had for David and I probably would not have eventuated if they had bought a business elsewhere. Dad thought Mum looked so tired and he didn't know why he lost his temper so often with this good woman. He had noticed that David was tending to do the same; he didn't respect his mother.

My father realised he had to ensure David's escapades didn't escalate into something much bigger. He had started with small incidents—smoking, wagging school, running away from home—but now he was stealing cars. Each time it was becoming more serious. He had to ensure the cycle was broken, but how?

David refused to return to school after completing year nine. Mum suggested to Dad that with David's flair for sketching, a career in advertising or display might be suitable. My father disagreed and found David a position at Motor Spares in the city. He felt that with David's love for cars, working with car spare parts would interest him. But David hated working indoors, and soon gave the job away. He tried several labouring jobs, but nothing lasted.

Once David started working, my father felt his son should be more responsible and repay some of the costs of the stolen car escapade. He told David he expected him to repay five pounds a week. David did pay each week, but the outstanding account did not reduce. David's gambling debts increased and other costly scrapes continued. Although Dad realised that the payment plan he had set up for David was ineffectual, he continued to loan his son money. My father also realised that David had come to expect that his father would just foot the bill. Each time, he told his son this was the last time, but when the boy got into financial trouble again, he would buckle and pay the debt.

10

My relationship with Steve continued, and I usually met him at his place. Sometimes he was there, but often he was not. I waited in his room, or in the lounge with the family, rather than return home and have my parents realise I'd been stood up.

'You here again? Well Steve isn't.' Steve's mother, Alice Stillwell, was a tall, unsympathetic woman, with a long, wide nose and straight grey hair caught up in a bun. She barely tolerated me. 'Haven't you got the message yet?' she asked.

'He asked me to meet him here,' I replied. Clearly she didn't approve.

Two of Steve's seven siblings lived at home. His eldest sister Iris, an eccentric, bitter woman, stomped around the house but at least was civil to me. Keith—or Redder, as he was known—was rarely seen. He came home drunk each night, heading straight upstairs to the room he shared with his son, Alan.

'Iris, out of my way, I have to take Keith his dinner,' Mrs Stillwell said.

'Bugger Keith! You're just his slave.'

'He at least pays board—no-one else does.' Armed with a tray, Mrs Stillwell clambered the steep stairs, panting as she went.

At weekends, Redder never ventured downstairs but

remained in his room, and each mealtime, his mother tramped up the stairs.

Freeloaders, extended family, cousins, nephews and grandchildren abounded at mealtimes. It was difficult for Steve's mother, a pensioner, to cater for these uninvited guests, but she always made the meal go round, never turning anyone away. Sometimes I would find a single piece of meat amongst the carrot and parsnip in the stew; there would be mashed potato to mop up the plate, which was covered in thin gravy. Everyone took advantage of the soft spot beneath the strong-minded woman's hard exterior, ignoring her caustic tongue.

Flossie, another sister, was married with several children. I always felt welcome in her Maidstone home. I never met Eve or Claude, who were estranged from the family. And Joyce, the wife of Frank who lived in Foster, was dead, while Steve's youngest brother Bill had died from tuberculosis (TB) years before.

After Bill died, Steve went to work in the butter factory at Foster. It was while he was living in Foster that he discovered he too had TB. He believed it was from the milk; however, prior to Bill's death they had shared a room. Steve spent twelve months in the sanatorium, and once cured, avoided getting a chill. He was required to have yearly check-ups in case there was a recurrence, but rarely kept the appointment. He never bothered to tell me he'd been sick, and it was several years after I met him before I found out.

I sat in the tiny, cluttered lounge room with the others, waiting patiently for Steve's return, but as the family always retired early, I soon found myself on my own. In the dimly lit room I watched television, and once the house was silent, the other inhabitants of the house emerged from the old fireplace and the cracks in the skirting boards. I stifled a scream as a six-legged creature walked across the floor followed by an army. I had a violent abhorrence of cockroaches, and the varieties inhabiting this old run-down house were huge, black and ugly. I became used to the creatures encroaching late at night; however, I made a habit of keeping my legs curled up on the decrepit couch.

The front door banged, followed by footsteps down the dark, narrow hall.

'Hi Jen, been waiting long? Sorry I'm late—needed to help a mate out.'

'Who?'

'You don't know him… he's in a bit of strife. Are we washing hair tonight?' Steve grinned broadly. 'I'll just get a sandwich. Mum won't have kept tea. It'd be different if it was Redder coming in late.'

'She wasn't too happy about me being here. Basically said you didn't care. I feel an idiot sitting with them all while I wait for you.'

'Come on Jen, they're all jealous that I have such a great girl.'

I smiled and went up to him. He put his arm around me and bent down to give me a kiss. I smelled the stale odour, but didn't comment. Steve started to fill the concrete trough that was the kitchen sink, and placed a chair in front of it while I gave my hair a brush.

'Did you bring your shampoo and stuff?'

'Yes, here 'tis.' I sat on the chair and put my head back.

Steve dipped a small saucepan into the water, poured it over my long hair until it was quite wet, and then he commenced to gently massage in the shampoo. Slowly he kneaded my scalp.

His long, slim fingers were extraordinarily sensual.

'That's wonderful'.

'It's meant to be.' He continued massaging and then rinsed my hair with tepid water from the saucepan.

I relaxed, enjoying the experience.

This was the Steve I was attracted to. When sober he was caring, kind, zany and full of fun, but totally without responsibility. Because I'd experienced a good deal of trauma and little laughter throughout my life, I relished the fun Steve created. A simple man from humble beginnings, he fundamentally brought himself up, while his family struggled to cope with the basics of living. I wanted him to have what I felt he'd missed, but I didn't understand that he was happy with his simple life.

'Can you reach the towel?' Steve asked. He squeezed as much water from my hair as he could while I stretched my hand out to the other chair and grabbed the towel. He wrapped the towel around my head and stood in front of me, drying my hair.

Steve didn't care how he looked, and he wasn't interested in material things. To supplement his gambling, he pawned the clothes and gifts I bought him. He promised to stop gambling and cut his drinking. Naïvely I believed him; I wanted to believe him because I wanted our relationship to work. I hoped eventually I could leave home. In the sixties it was rare that a girl would leave home before marriage, because it was virtually impossible to survive with the salaries paid to women—only sixty-five percent of the salary a man would receive in the same job.

*

Stan, Steve's boss, lived on the premises where Steve worked, but went away at weekends. He suggested Steve and I might like to use the premises to allow us some privacy. We took him up on the offer, and I relished the time we spent there.

'Like a beer, Jen?'

'Have you got lemonade?'

'Have I got lemonade? Course I have.' Steve smiled. He was always sober, good-humoured, loving and caring when we were at Stan's. I curled up on the old lounge and sipped my lemonade with a little beer added.

'Tonight we're having crumbed cutlets, grilled tomatoes, boiled spuds and peas. How's that sound?' He skipped and kicked one long leg back till it hit his bum as he threw his hands in the air.

'Great. What can I do?'

'Sit and look beautiful,' he laughed.

He got the electric frypan out of the cupboard and lightly beat a couple of eggs, put flour on a plate and breadcrumbs on another.

'Can I help with the crumbing?' I got up and walked over to Steve, putting my arms around his waist. He turned around, gave me a hug and a peck, and pushed me gently away.

'Jen, I like doing this. I'm not welcome in the kitchen at home … well, really I'm not welcome at home at all. No, you sit down … let me do it … I want it to be special.'

'I like being here; we can just be ourselves.' I returned to the couch.

'Yep.' Steve rolled the cutlet in the flour, dipped it in the egg and then patted the breadcrumbs on. I watched him and thought how happy he looked.

After dinner we watched TV, then he walked me to the

corner of my street and said goodnight.

During the next twelve months, our relationship oscillated between being great, and upheavals that would cause a breakup. We always got back together. I was desperate to leave the hotel and Collingwood, and began thinking more about marriage. I felt sure that once Steve left his environment, our relationship would be all it should be. Initially, happy with his aimless lifestyle, he wasn't interested; however, an offer of a new job helped change his outlook, and he contemplated settling down.

Mobile doughnut wagons that went to the Victoria Market, the Melbourne Show, Moomba, country shows and various other venues, were garaged not far from Steve's home. Steve knew the owners, who were settled, married and running a successful business—a different calibre from the mates he knocked around with. They offered him a job, which meant starting at three o'clock in the morning on the days that he worked. The dough was mixed the night before in a large trough, where it was left to rise overnight. The next morning it was divided into sections, kneaded and left to rise again. Then it was rolled out; the doughnuts were cut out, placed on a board and put in a rack to rise once more. Once a few boards of doughnuts were prepared, they set off to market to commence cooking and selling. Steve's day finished mid-afternoon, and after the long day he enjoyed relaxing in the pub. I was still in a nine-to-five job, and continued to meet him after work.

'How was the market today?' I asked as I stood on tip-toes to give him a kiss.

'Really busy, completely sold out. Ernie gave me a bonus when I got paid.'

'Great, are you going to bank it?'

'Well that's what I want to talk to you about. Jack, my other boss, has bought a new Jaguar. He's selling his old one. Thought we might buy it.'

'How much? They're expensive.' I screwed up my face.

'It's pretty old, but it's got spoke wheels and the "big cat" mounted on the bonnet.' Steve's face lit up. 'It's cool. We could get away from here at weekends, go to the beach … go for picnics …'

'But how much?'

'A hundred.'

'Is that all?'

'Jenny, it's pretty old … not in great condition, but we'd be able to get around.'

'You really want it, don't you?'

'I've never had a car.' Steve gave me a pensive look.

'What the heck.'

Steve's eyes lit up.

Once he bought the car, weekend driving excursions took precedence, and Steve didn't drink or see his mates.

*

It had been a memorable year of parties, as most of my friends celebrated their twenty-first birthday. Now this special birthday loomed for me too.

'Mum, I'd like to have a party,' I told her one morning as I ate breakfast in the hotel's kitchen.

'Well I'm sure that can be arranged, Jenny. I'll talk to your father. We'd have to get a special licence for the night to have it here.'

'It's so unfair. This is our home … other people don't have to get a licence.'

'Yes, but this is also a hotel.'

'Mum, what about Steve? I don't want a party without him. Will you talk to Dad?

'No, Jenny … I'm not getting involved … you know how I feel about Steve. If you want him at your party, you'll have to talk to your father.' Mum turned to the sink and gave a sigh.

That night, after I had cleaned up in the bar, I found my father in the back room.

'Well Jenny, Mum tells me you want a party. Hard to believe my little girl is turning twenty-one!' He smiled.

'Mmm.'

'I've given it some thought. We could set up a jukebox in the back lounge for dancing … the food and drink could be served in the dining room. We'll have some cocktails … perhaps brandy crustas. How would that be?'

'Sounds great!' I wondered if I should raise the issue of Steve, since Dad seemed to be in a good mood.

'Dad, I want Steve to come,' I said quietly.

'No … definitely not.'

I didn't know what to say after my father's response. 'Dad, he's my boyfriend; we've been going together for eighteen months.'

'And I'm far from happy about that.'

'He's fun, he makes me happy.' *Most times.*

'Does he really? Are you sure about that?'

I didn't answer. 'I don't want a party if he can't come.' I looked unwaveringly at my father.

There was a deathly silence. He fiddled, but I held my gaze.

After a very long silence, he said, 'He can come … it's your birthday … but you tell him from me, he'd better behave or I'll turn him out—party or no party.'

I put my arms around my father and kissed him on the

cheek. 'Thanks, Dad! Really, thanks!'

Jubilant, I rushed into the kitchen. 'Mum, Steve can come!'

'That's good, dear; must make you happy.'

Mum's face told a different story. It was obvious her views about Steve had not changed. But at least she was keeping it to herself.

'I've a friend who makes speciality cakes, so I'll organise that,' she said. 'We'll need to go shopping for a dress.'

'Yes. Can we go Saturday?' I asked excitedly.

'I'll check with Dad if he can do without me. But I think it'll be okay.'

I bought a rich red flowing chiffon dress with a throw-over. I felt quite grown up.

*

The party was a huge success. Dad remained sober, served brandy crustas to my friends and made an appropriate speech, while the jukebox in the back room encouraged dancing. Ken, the barman, was the master of ceremonies, and hinted that an engagement might be announced. This was the only time my father's face betrayed his true feelings. I squirmed. I'd successfully convinced Dad to let Steve come, and I knew making that announcement would be a disaster. Anyway, at that stage we had no definite plans, except that we might marry the following year.

After the party, Steve and I talked about it and decided to get engaged in November. I was determined to buy a house before we married, so I discussed a savings plan with Steve. He agreed to bank a regular amount each week and I decided to find myself a second job.

Rita, my friend from Kraft, had announced her engagement and also wanted a second job, so we both applied for a waitress position at Stacy's in St Kilda Road. It was a unique restaurant. Patrons sat in booths and used the telephones provided to phone their orders through to the kitchen. Rita and I worked hard two nights a week: a six to ten o'clock early shift, and a late shift that didn't finish until two o'clock in the morning. I waited on tables or took the orders on the phone in the kitchen, and sometimes I served in the adjoining shop. I also had to take my turn at the dishwasher, a job I detested. It was like being in gaol. The dishwasher was surrounded by benches where the dirty dishes were dumped. As soon as one lot of dishes were cleared, more replaced them. I dreaded this role when I was on the late shift, with the only break being half an hour for tea. I was paid ten shillings per hour.

One particularly busy night, I found myself looking after six tables. As a table vacated, I was expected to clear it, re-set it and attend to the new patrons immediately. The popularity of Stacy's meant there was always a queue. I was always hurrying.

The empty table cleared and re-set, I rushed to the centre counter to make up the entrées for table three. They were all having oysters. Rita was there preparing entrées for one of her tables. I smiled at her as I placed rock ice on the plates, arranging the oysters on top, with the dipping sauce and lemon on the side, and quickly delivered them. Another table needed clearing; I took the dirty dishes to the kitchen.

'Jenny, entrées table five!' Jane, on the phone in the kitchen, brandished an order sheet at me, while at the same time passing the order for the main meal to the chef. I grabbed the entrée order as I rushed through the kitchen door. *Hell, more entrées.*

'One ham steak, steak & kidney, mixed grill and special hamburger, table three!' yelled the chef.

'Oh damn, that's me,' I said to no-one in particular. I scurried and organised the table five entrées and delivered them, picked up the empty entrée plates from table three, and dashed back to the kitchen. After grabbing three of the meals, the fourth wouldn't fit on the tray; I rushed the three meals to the table and returned for the fourth. Tray in hand, I turned tail, charged back out into the restaurant and slammed into another waitress. The tray fell from my hands, the plate smashed and the meal splattered across the floor. I picked up the ham steak, pineapple, vegetables and pieces of plate and returned to the kitchen.

'Chef, I was bumped. Sorry, I'll need another ham steak.'

'Plate broken, eh? Don't worry.' The chef grabbed the ham steak from my tray.

'On a clean plate it goes, add a few fresh vegies, a piece of freshly grilled pineapple and out you go.'

I gaped at him. 'That steak's been on the floor. I can't take that out!'

'If you're not taking it out, see the manager. I'm not cooking another—there's nothing wrong with that one.'

Jane nudged me. 'Just do as he says. If you make a fuss they'll tell you to go.'

I looked at her, picked up the tray and delivered the ham steak to the unknowing patron.

On another occasion I was just as appalled. The daily special was a Hawaiian chicken dish that was served in a pineapple case. When returning the dirty dishes to the kitchen, the waitresses were told to put the pineapple cases to one side to be used again. That day taught me to be careful what I ordered in a restaurant.

As well as the restaurant job, I also worked in the doughnut wagons, either at night or during the weekends. There were endless work opportunities: regular shows at the Exhibition Buildings, the Royal Melbourne Show, Moomba and various country shows. It was the hardest work I've ever done. Sometimes as many as ten people worked in the small van, kneading the dough, cutting out, cooking, jamming and serving. The conditions were terrible, but it was certainly an experience! At one Bendigo Easter Show, the crowd, intent on getting their doughnuts, pushed so hard against the van that it was dislodged from its chocks and started to roll backwards down the road. The surprised looks on the faces of both the crowd and the workers in the van was comical.

After working in the van, I needed to put all my clothes to the wash. The odour of stale fat permeated through to my underwear. I was often too tired to shower when I arrived home, and once I was in bed, the smell of my hair made me feel ill.

*

'Aw, I love that one.' With my arm through Steve's, I pointed to a ring in the window. For the last couple of months, each time I'd been shopping, I paused in front of jewellers' shop windows. I decided Paul Bramm had the best range.

'Yeah, it looks okay, but there's no price.'

'They never put prices in the window. I want gold, and I like it because it's a solitaire. The two diamonds down each side just finish it off.'

'Still … depends on the price.'

'Well, let's go in and see.'

Last Sunday, as Steve was saying goodnight, he had suggested we look for a ring the following Saturday. I was very excited and kept trying on ring after ring.

'Steve, do you like this one?'

'Yeah, it looks good, but do you like it?' He smiled at me.

'I think so, but I'll try on some others.' I looked at the pad of rings. With so many beautiful rings, I was confused. I picked another, put it on and turned to Steve. 'What about this one?' I looked up at him with a smile.

'Yeah, it's good too.'

As I turned back to the rings, Steve pulled out the rolled up newspaper from under his arm and turned to the sports page at the back.

I pored over the rings then turned again to Steve. 'What do you think?'

'Hmm … it's okay,' he said, without raising his head from the paper.

The smile left my face. I was acutely embarrassed; what must the shop assistant think?

'The second one you tried on looks beautiful … it really suits your hand.' The shop assistant's voice invaded my thoughts.

'Yes, Jenny … you should get that one.' Steve folded his newspaper and sidled up to the counter. I agreed, and once it was paid for, Steve carefully put it in his pocket.

I'd already told my parents that we intended to get engaged, and after I did, David overheard them talking. They thought I was ruining my life. But they felt since I was determined to continue with this man, the only hope they had to bring me to my senses was to accept the engagement and allow Steve in the hotel. He had still been barred after my party. David said they thought by bringing the relationship into the open I might realise my mistake. My father had begrudgingly said that now I was twenty-one they had no control over the situation, and Mum had said that she guessed the best thing they could do was support me.

'I haven't made a mistake … but I'm glad they've relented,' I replied to David when he told me.

Before I left that morning, my mother had suggested I bring Steve home once we had chosen the ring.

I excitedly showed my parents. They acknowledged Steve, admired the ring and suggested it be kept in the hotel safe until the engagement was announced the following week. They hid their feelings well. I knew they weren't happy, but really had no perception of how devastated they must have felt.

I saw less of Steve now I was working the extra jobs. I saved all the money from my part-time work, and arranged for a regular amount to be deducted and banked by the pay office at Kraft. I assumed Steve was saving too. We intended buying a block of land. On one of my nights off from the restaurant I arranged to meet him at his place, but when I arrived, he wasn't there.

'Mrs Stillwell, I'll wait for Steve in his room.'

'As you like, but you're quite welcome to sit and watch telly, you know.'

'No, it's okay, I've got a book to read.' I never went anywhere without a book.

Mrs Stillwell had softened remarkably towards me since Steve and I had become engaged. Just after the engagement, she had cornered me and said, 'Jenny, I'm glad you're marrying Steve. You'll be good for him. Never thought he'd get married … but one never knows. When Steve told me, he said to me, "Ma, I won't always have you to look after me, so I've had to look for someone else."' She had laughed.

I wasn't sure if she made it up, or if Steve really said it. Either way, I didn't like it. Perhaps Mrs Stillwell was just making mischief.

Sitting on Steve's bed, I looked around the room. *He's never had a chance.* His bare room with peeling wallpaper and a torn curtain was at the front of the house. It contained an old wardrobe with a door that wouldn't shut properly, and a sagging bed with thin blankets.

Mulling over where he was and how different life would be once we married and he was away from Collingwood and his mates, I noticed his bankbook on the bedside table. I opened it and a chill ran through me; the balance was five pounds, three shillings and four pence. *He's supposed to have around £700!* The land we'd been looking at was around £1300. *He must have another bankbook*, I thought.

I waited. Ten o'clock, eleven o'clock ... Finally the front door banged and he walked in.

'What ya doing here?' he asked.

'What do you think I'm doing here? We were supposed to meet at seven.'

'Oh shit!' He slumped onto the bed.

'Where have you been?'

'None of your business.'

'Where have you been?'

'Out with a beautiful blonde with big, erect tits— sensational.'

'Stop it.'

'Hey! What're ya doing with my bankbook?' It was still lying in my lap.

'Steve, where's all the money?'

'I've lent it.'

'Who to?'

'Go home. A man has to have some sleep.'

'Go to hell, Steve! I've had enough of your lies!' And with that, I left.

The next evening I tackled him again. After much hedging—

Steve's usual ploy—he finally admitted that rather than having savings, he was in debt. He had agreed to be guarantor for a mate for some furniture, and he'd helped him with the deposit. The mate didn't make any repayments, the company sued, and now Steve must pay up or else. I was flabbergasted.

'How could you do this? What about our block of land?'

'Jenny, I promise I'll start putting money away next pay. I'll bank it all except for a few pounds.'

'Why would you go guarantor? Making yourself a big fella … how are you going to pay?'

'Ah, well I don't know. They've given me seven days.'

'Well you know you can't.'

'I'll find it.'

'Yeah, you'll borrow or pawn something, won't you?'

Steve said nothing.

'You're impossible!' I got up and went home.

At work the next morning, the phone rang.

'Jenny, I'm really sorry about everything. Can I see you tonight?'

'Steve, nothing ever changes.'

'Jenny, give me a chance. Let's talk tonight.'

That night, he made great promises. I wanted to believe. He always made a good case, and this night was no exception. Feeling helpless, and with my self-esteem at a low ebb, I agreed to give him another chance. I even offered to loan him the money. After lamely refusing, Steve accepted.

The relationship limped along. We argued about money, my parents, and Steve's lack of interest in buying land and choosing a design for a house, to the point that I really wanted to end it.

My boss Norm had separated from his wife about six months ago, and she had returned to South Australia. Meanwhile Bev had been engaged to Ralph for nearly twelve months, and they seemed happy. But now the day-to-day flirting between Bev and Norm that had always existed had intensified. I worked closely with them, and their flirting made me feel embarrassed and uncomfortable. I felt like an outsider.

Bev and I decided to go to Adelaide the Easter following my engagement. We were excited because neither of us had ever been away without our parents, except for my fateful weekend at Foster. We planned to travel by train and stay at a guesthouse. Steve took me to Spencer Street Station, where we met Bev and Ralph. When it was time to board, I kissed Steve goodbye, and Bev kissed Ralph. Then we hopped on the train, waving goodbye to the boys as it left the station.

We explored the train from end to end, and were amazed to find the metal bowls of the toilet emptied straight onto the ground beneath the train as it sped along. No wonder we couldn't use them while the train was at a station! We found the dining car, bought a drink and started chatting to a couple of young boys, who returned with us to our carriage. Eventually they left to prowl and we settled back.

'I've got something to tell you, Jenny. Look.' Bev held out her hand

I looked at the hand, wondering what I was supposed to see.

'We've broken our engagement.'

'Don't be silly. Ralph saw you off.'

'I know. He thinks it'll all be okay when I return. But I've given the ring back and I'm not changing my mind. I didn't want to go to Adelaide engaged. I thought it was the right time to finish it.'

'It's hard to believe. You seem okay.'

'I know … I am … it's actually a relief.'

I fell silent. This was totally unexpected. Bev and Ralph had a block of land at Seaford, and already had plans drawn up for their house. I wondered if the breakup had anything to do with Norm being single.

My mind turned to my own troubles. I continued to cling to the hope that if Steve left Collingwood, his family and mates, it would give him a new start and things would be different. However, deep down something told me the relationship would never work.

I had pretty much decided to break our engagement, but didn't know how to tell my friends, and especially my family. I would have to admit that they were right. With Norm's marriage over and Bev's relationship ended, how would it look if I broke my engagement too?

11

'Sis, come outside!' David rushed into the dining room and grabbed my arm.

'I'm reading. Get lost!'

'Ah come on, Sis! Please!' David pulled me from the chair and pushed me towards the front door.

I begrudgingly opened it.

'What do you think, hey? Isn't it magnificent?'

Parked in the street was a bright red 1954 FJ Holden with chrome wheels. The suspension had been lowered so that it barely cleared the road. Proudly, David opened the passenger door. The interior was immaculate, with a wooden dashboard and black upholstered seats.

'Isn't it neat? What do you think?' David asked.

'Wow, it's great! Fantastic colour. Going to take me for a spin?'

'Do you trust me? Remember you said I was too dangerous to be on the road,' David jibed.

David had to repeat his licence test three times; whereas I had been lucky, succeeding the first time. I teased him mercilessly about this.

He pulled the bonnet knob and walked around to the front of the car. 'You need to look at this.'

'Why? An engine's just an engine.'

'Not this one.'

I looked under the bonnet. 'Wow!' The rocker cover, intake manifold, and air cleaner were all shiny chrome, and so clean. 'Gee, neat! Must've cost a packet. How did you pay for it?'

'Dad's lent me the money. I'm paying him back a bit each week.'

'You get away with murder.'

'I know. That's what happens when you're the favourite son. Hop in and we'll go to Studley Park.'

David revved the engine loudly, and with a jolt we took off up the street and screamed around the corner. At the traffic lights, he braked hard. I held on tight—seatbelts were a rarity in 1963. David's inexperience, combined with his showing off, created a hair-raising drive, and I was glad to arrive back at the hotel.

'What do think, Jen? How did she go? Great. What?'

'Yeah, the car's great. But keep driving like that and you'll be picked up for sure.'

'Not likely. I'm getting my endorsed licence … I'm sick of me job. Want to be behind the wheel … drive trucks ... it'll be cool.'

'Your driving will need to improve,' I said coolly, and walked inside.

David had tried several jobs since leaving school. None seemed to last. Working indoors was not for him. After he left Motor Spares, he drifted but eventually found a job he liked, jockeying on a truck. Even so, this didn't last, and I wondered if it was because of his inability to accept authority or responsibility. He fraternised with the barmen and the hotel customers more and more, sometimes joining them at the races. Indeed he went to either the races or the trots (or both) most weekends. David was in his element; he loved being on the edge, and his betting became riskier. When he didn't go to the races, he placed bets with a bookmaker. Steve of course enjoyed the races and trots, so I sometimes went with both of them.

I was more than envious that my father continued to enable my brother by propping him up with money. Dad never offered me money—not that I ever asked. I had no idea how much David owed, but I knew it must be a large amount. The jazzed-up car alone would have cost a tidy sum. I felt my father should encourage David to save for what he wanted, and not pay his speeding fines—what punishment was it if he didn't feel it in his hip pocket?

The boy who always wanted to know where his mother was when he came home was now a man who had little regard for her. He was rude and abusive, like a bomb ready to explode. Neither of my parents appeared able to pull him into line. Yet when things were going David's way, there was not a nicer guy, and that was the guy who showed me his car.

After the ride in David's car, I went upstairs to put on some make-up, because I was expecting Steve. Before I went to work at the restaurant, we were going to look at a block of land in East Oakleigh that I'd already seen. I was really looking forward to showing Steve. Each weekend recently I had spent time exploring options for our new home, looking at established houses, as well as new house and land packages. Sometimes Steve came with me, but most times he didn't. Recently, old market gardens had been subdivided, resulting in a large development becoming available. This was where the block of land was situated, and the subdivisions were selling fast.

When Steve arrived he insisted he must see his football

team, the Magpies, play at home, and he promised to look at the land the following day. Dejected, I went with him and his mates to the game. We went to The Commercial after the match, and after drinking a lemon squash, feeling totally bored, I left for work.

Steve had recently traded the old Jaguar for a 1958 FE Holden so we could drive to Sydney for our honeymoon. He knew the old car couldn't make the trip. The next day we drove our new car, first to the agent and then to the block of land. There were three adjacent blocks for sale in a small court, each costing £1,350. The first, on higher ground, had the best fall, and was therefore the better buy. We said we'd think about it and get back to the agent. He encouraged us to make a decision on the spot because others were interested, but I wasn't prepared to buy until I was sure.

We talked it over and decided to buy, but found the first block had indeed been sold, so we had no option but to buy the next. With little money available, we settled for a 'spec' house. The builder allowed several changes from the original design, which made it more individual. We paid cash for the land, but had to apply to the bank for a loan to pay for the house. On our income we could only borrow £3,500 from the bank, so we took out a second mortgage for £250.

Once the deposit was paid, I organised the conveyancing and was told the dimensions of the block must be checked. Bev had already done this exercise with her block at Seaford, so the next weekend, she and I set off with a builder's tape that we'd borrowed. Steve went to the football.

It had rained heavily overnight, the grass was high and the block was covered with blackberry bushes. This didn't stop us mucking around while we measured, and we ended up badly scratched and soaking wet. With the sale completed, the foundation trenches were dug. Steve and I excitedly went to inspect. We were quite disappointed, because the outline of the foundations made the house look small. However, on our next trip a few weeks later, the frame was up and the house looked much bigger. We wandered through, stepping from floor joist to floor joist, looking at each room. I was ecstatic that this was to be our house, and Steve was very enthusiastic too. I wondered how he really felt, not ever having owned much in his lifetime. He seemed happy.

*

I woke to a commotion in the hallway. I heard my brother yelling, then Ken the barman's voice, then my father's. I peeped out my door to see them all in the wide hallway, yelling and throwing their arms around.

'What's going on?' I asked, rubbing my eyes.

'Some fucking idiot's stolen me car!' David yelled, stomping up the hallway. 'Ken put his head out the window when he heard the car start up, but it was too late. They drove off.' David looked furious and ready to burst into tears.

'Oh David, have the police been called?'

'Of course. What do you take us for?' scowled my father.

'Whoever stole it will just want to joyride … it's the damage they do, though …' David lamented.

I glanced at him, wondering what he was thinking. How did he feel now that the shoe was on the other foot and it was his car? And what did he mean by 'it's the damage they do'? I wondered whether he'd ever damaged cars that he'd pinched to use for joyriding.

'Sorry, it's bad luck … but I'm going back to bed. I have to go to work in a few hours.' I returned to my room.

The car, when it was eventually found a few days later, had been thoroughly stripped: the wooden dashboard, the chrome extractors and even the wheels were all gone. David was devastated. The insurance my father had organised didn't cover the extras, and as far as David was concerned, the extras were the most important parts of the car. As it was too costly to restore, he regretfully sent it to the wreckers. Would my father ever be repaid for a car that no longer existed? I thought not. *Dad will wipe the slate clean, I bet.*

David had been working at Arnott's Biscuits for a while, and enjoyed this job. He wasn't confined, and working as a truck jockey had its perks. Biscuits regularly 'fell off' trucks. When he turned nineteen he obtained his endorsed driver's licence, and soon after secured a driving position with Murphy's Trucking Company.

Sending his pride and joy to the wreckers affected David. He seemed to always be in a foul mood, and no-one could speak to him. Now he walked or caught public transport to work. He found this especially annoying when on early morning shift, or if he was going out with his mates or on a date. He appeared to have a large following of girls. A different one seemed to ring each night. But he didn't respect them; he spoke unkindly about them and made derogatory remarks. Well, he'd had a good role model.

I was sitting reading in the lounge one night when he stormed past after work and went into the kitchen, looking for something to eat. I ignored him. This aggravated David, who started abusing me. I promptly told him to shut up. He stomped from the kitchen, stood in front of me and yelled that I was nothing but a slut. I stood up and yelled back. David suddenly turned, picked up a lounge chair and, with super strength, tossed it at me. The noise brought my father in, and he told us both to shut up or else, but ended up sticking up for David before he returned to the bar. I picked up my book and went to my room, where I stayed for the rest of the evening, missing tea.

I slept late the next morning, but when I passed my parents' room on my way to the kitchen, I was surprised to see my father still in bed.

'Dad's got another hangover,' I said as I gave Mum a peck on the cheek and grabbed a cup from the cupboard to make myself coffee.

'I suppose … but even with a hangover, he's usually up by now. I'd better check.'

Dad had suffered two heart attacks when we lived at Cheltenham, and Mum had said to me on several occasions that she was just waiting for a recurrence, especially considering the way he drank.

A few minutes later, she rushed to the phone.

'I thought he was sleeping … I think he's unconscious … could be a stroke,' Mum told the doctor.

I rushed up the stairs. Dad looked odd; his mouth was pulled up at one side and he was very pale. I stood looking at him while my mother fussed over him. When the doctor arrived I went downstairs and sat in the dining room.

The doctor was upstairs a long time, but he eventually left.

'Is he going to be alright? Was it a stroke?' I looked up at my mother as she entered the room.

'Er … yes … the doctor thinks he'll be okay.' Mum appeared distracted; she walked out to the kitchen and fiddled, making herself a cup of tea.

'Well … if he had a stroke, why isn't he in hospital?'

'N … Not sure. Your father wouldn't be happy going to hospital … the doctor felt, seeing I'm a nurse, I could look after him.' Mum avoided looking at me.

Something was fishy, but I couldn't put my finger on it. Dad often took sleeping pills, and it struck me that perhaps he might have taken too many, and that he might have had a bad reaction because he'd also been drinking alcohol. I didn't know and it was obvious I wasn't going to be told. My father recovered and was out of bed in a couple of days. I just couldn't understand what the problem had been. He had looked so awful with his disfigured face, and yet now his features were normal. Mum would not discuss it.

*

As my wedding day drew closer, I decided to give notice at Stacy's. When we moved to our new home, it would be difficult to get to and from the restaurant late at night. Normally, when I went to work direct from the hotel, I wore my uniform with a coat over the top. Without thinking, I did the same on my last night.

It had been an uneventful night, but before I rang for my taxi (the only way to get home at 2 a.m.), I went to get my pay envelope.

'You'll need to hand in your uniform before you leave.' The manager was counting the money in the till, and didn't look up as he said this.

'I can't. I came to work in my uniform, but I'll wash it and drop it in.'

'No way. Girls leaving have promised that. Never see the uniforms again.' The manager looked down his glasses at me.

'I've got nothing else to put on.'

'You got a coat.'

'Yes, but …'

'Go and get the uniform off, then I'll pay you.'

I didn't argue. The manager's voice had risen markedly during the conversation. And every word had been heard by the several girls cleaning up, Mr Stacy (the owner) and his daughter—all of whom were in the foyer. But no-one said anything. I went to the change room, took off the uniform and stood in my petticoat. *I don't have a choice and I'm in the taxi on my own.* Usually Rita and I worked the same shifts and we travelled home together, but tonight Rita was not working. I folded the uniform, placed it on the bench and put on my overcoat, buttoning it firmly from top to bottom. Nobody would know I only had a petticoat on underneath, but I felt naked.

I went back to the manager and handed him my uniform, and he in turn gave me a pay envelope. There wasn't a thankyou for the twelve months I'd worked at the restaurant. I walked out to the waiting taxi, realising another door had closed. Monday would come and nobody would give the waitress who left on Saturday a second thought.

I was pleased when the taxi stopped outside the hotel and I could escape inside. No employer had the right to put me in that position, but it wasn't until years later that I realised I had rights in the workplace. Workplaces would change during the sixties, after the unions secured improvements in workplace conditions, and raised awareness of workers' rights.

David thought it was a huge joke when I relayed what had happened. He said, 'You shouldn't let them push you around; they wouldn't get away with that with me!' He was now utterly entrenched in the truckies' world, and the main commodity transported in the large vehicles that he drove for Murphy's was sugar. It was all shift work that paid well, and he made a bit on the side selling sugar that 'fell off the truck'. With his excellent wage, he was soon able to buy a classy car. Once again he had wheels, and once again he was never home. He was picked up for speeding twice the first week after he took delivery of the new car. The fines were added to the loan. He continued to drive the car like a maniac, revving it up before taking off each morning, no matter what time it was. Mum asked him not to do it, but he ignored her pleas.

Several weeks after he bought his pride and joy, he arrived back at Murphy's yard to garage his truck for the night. A large crowd was gathered in the street and he wondered what was attracting them. David parked his truck, signed off, collected his coat from his locker and made his way to his new Fairlane, which was parked in the street.

He reached the outskirts of the crowd and saw the exterior brick wall of Murphy's was now a crumbled pile of bricks. Looking over the crowd, he was horrified to see that the crumbled pile half-buried his car—the roof was now six inches lower.

'What in the fucking hell happened to my car?' he yelled to no-one in particular.

His comments and a picture of the car made the first page in the *Sun* newspaper the next morning:

> Yesterday at Murphy's Trucking Company, a truck was accidentally reversed into a wall that then collapsed onto an employee's car. The car's owner, arriving at his car after finishing work, was somewhat upset. He commented, 'What in the f...... hell has happened to my car?' David Wilding recently bought the Fairlane that is now beyond repair.

12

I opened my eyes and stretched. At last, my wedding day. I hopped out of bed and stared at the drab scene outside my window: the brewery grain store, the factories and the brothel. Today I was leaving it all behind, along with the stench of stale beer, the squalor, and the hotel—my home for the last three years. I was leaving my controlling father, who, ever since I could remember, felt entitled to terrorise his family. Now David's behaviour seemed to be echoing my father's. Steve was a drinker, but he was not violent; he had never physically hurt me. I felt sorry for my mother, but I was glad to be leaving it all behind. I scanned the sky; it was a beautiful October day.

I tried to push my trepidations aside. What did the future hold? Would Steve be different once he left Collingwood and his mates? Surely having his own home would give him pride and purpose? I hoped so; my future depended on this. A knock on the door jolted me from my thoughts.

'Come in.'

Mum entered with a tray loaded with scrambled eggs, toast, tea and a beautiful rose.

'Breakfast in bed for my darling daughter.' Mum smiled, planting a kiss on my forehead.

'Oh wow, thank you!' I hopped back into bed.

Mum sat on the end of the bed. 'Eat up … the girls will be here soon. You've got a ten o'clock hair appointment.'

My mum had been so supportive during the wedding preparations. She had come with me to Clegs to choose the material for my dress, accompanied me to the reception house, helped me choose the flowers and organise the wedding cake. I knew she was trying to accept Steve but I also knew it was with a heavy heart.

I glanced at my wedding dress hanging on the wardrobe door and my veil lying on the other bed.

'It's beautiful isn't it, Mum? The poor dressmaker needed to take it in each time I went for a fitting. I hope the veil's okay … should have tried it on last night … but it arrived so late … I was so tired,' I prattled on.

'Your dress is lovely. You've lost a lot of weight, but you look amazing in it. Don't worry, the veil will be fine.' Mum smiled. 'I've a few things to do in the kitchen before Sheila arrives.'

She stood up, leaned over, and hugged me.

'Jenny, my one wish for you is that you have the greatest happiness in your life. Always remember that I love you and will always be here for you.'

Mum quickly turned and left the room.

I showered, and then went downstairs just as my bridesmaids arrived. We chattered away and then set off to catch the tram to the city to get our hair done. When we arrived home, I noticed my case was still in the hallway.

'Mum, Jim hasn't picked up my case.' It had been arranged that Steve's best man would pick it up early in the morning.

'Don't worry; I'll get Dad to organise something. You go and get ready.'

We wandered upstairs and the girls went to the bathroom

while I checked if my brother, who was our groomsman, had left for Steve's place. I returned to the bathroom and burst out laughing. In front of me were Brenda and Bev in knickers and bra, and perched on their heads was the headgear that the hairdresser had fixed in place.

When it was time to leave for the church, Bev put the veil over my face, and immediately it was obvious that it wasn't right. It was perfect with the veil back, but once it was brought over my face it was impossible to tell whether I was coming or going. The front piece was far too full, but there was no time to do anything about it, so she adjusted it as best she could and we set off. At the church Bev had plenty of time to adjust the veil again, because the groom had gone missing. It was Caulfield Cup Day and he was outside listening to the race, while some of his mates listened to the radio in the back of the church.

When we emerged as a married couple, the first person I saw was my new mother-in-law. Mrs Stillwell had refused an invitation to the wedding. She didn't feel she fitted in with the Wildings, but she came and stood outside the church to see her son on his wedding day. More photos were taken in the Fitzroy Gardens opposite, and then finally we were on our way to the reception centre opposite the St Kilda beach.

The whole day was a blur, although Bev and Brenda, both fun-loving, ensured my day was perfect. For David, being groomsman was a new experience. He felt quite dapper in his dinner suit and bow tie. My parents were the perfect hosts and my father remained sober. All I remembered was photos, photos, photos, walking down the Reception Centre's staircase to be introduced to the guests, and the cutting of the cake.

I prepared Steve's speech, but he of course didn't look at

it before the day. He stood up and read a paragraph, and then added, 'Well that's another cab off the rank!' I was acutely embarrassed. He continued in the same manner. Steve was a natural comedian and 'Well that's another cab off the rank' became the theme of a funny and enjoyable speech. The longer he spoke, the more he warmed to the occasion, but I just wished he'd shut up.

After we danced the bridal waltz and Steve had danced with Mum, he disappeared. I wandered around chatting, but after a while I went looking and found him in the back room, drinking with the waiters. He was more than a little happy. Although furious, I held my tongue—what could I say? I went to change.

With 'Auld Lang Syne' playing in the background, we went round the circle saying goodbye.

'I've got the motel keys,' said Ken the barman, smirking as he put his arms around me.

I moved on to the next person, thinking Ken was trying to be funny. When I met up with Steve, we waved goodbye and left in my father's car. A few days previously Steve had organised a service for our car, and the mechanic had discovered the head was cracked. Mum convinced Dad to lend us his beloved car.

'You've got the keys to the room, haven't you?' I said as we travelled down Queens Road.

'I thought you had them,' slurred Steve.

'Why would I have them? Either you or Jim was supposed to be organising taking the cases to the motel. One of you did pick them up, didn't you?'

'Hmm … no, I think your dad got Ken to take them. Thought he'd give you the key.'

'We'll have to go back … Ken told me he had the keys … I thought he was joking.'

We returned to the reception and once again I felt foolish. We set off with the keys in Steve's pocket, but one thing led to another, and soon we were screaming at each other. I was crying and Steve was swearing.

'Stop … let me out!' I yelled as we travelled along Flemington Road.

Steve braked hard. In a rage I jumped out, and Steve sped off. I stood there. *He'll turn around and come back,* I thought as I watched the taillights of my father's car get smaller and smaller.

With cars flashing by, I started down Flemington Road in the direction of the motel, feeling silly in my going-away outfit—a tailored suit and large hat. Dad's car was parked in bay number six of the motel, so I walked up the stairs and knocked on the door of room six. It was opened by a stranger.

'Sorry … I must have the wrong room,' I murmured. *What do I do now? We picked up the key because the office would be closed.* I wandered down the stairs and—miracle of miracles—found someone in the office. I felt foolish asking which room I was in. Dressed as I was, I felt it was obvious that I was a bride arriving after the groom. The guy grinned as he handed me a key.

I found Steve fast asleep in our room. Wiping away angry tears, I grabbed some blankets out of the cupboard and made up a bed in the bath.

I woke stiff and sore, and clambered out, tossing the blankets on the floor. I turned the shower on and stood under it for a long time, allowing the water to run across my body and face. What should I do? I finally ventured into the bedroom and saw Steve sitting up in bed drinking a glass of water. We both avoided eye contact.

I eventually broke the silence. 'How could you get so

drunk? Why didn't you come back for me last night? It was all supposed to be so special.'

He avoided looking at me and said nothing, but went to the bathroom, closing the door. I dressed in slacks and a checked shirt, and put my sponge bag in the case.

The bathroom door opened. 'Jen, I've left my shaver at home … I'll have to call in and get it. Do you want to drop in and see your mum before we set off?' It was as if the previous night had never happened.

'Suppose so,' I sullenly answered.

He moved across and hugged me. 'Jen, I'm sorry. It all got away from me. I was enjoying myself. Let's forget it and have a good time, hey?'

I shrugged and stepped away. After having breakfast without any conversation, Steve put the cases in the car and we set off. He dropped me at The Vine, saying he'd be back in a few minutes. I walked into the kitchen, where Mum was sitting at the table with a cup of tea, her head in her hands.

'Hi Mum.'

'Jenny, what's happened? Are you okay?'

'Yes, of course. Steve forgot his shaver. He's gone home to pick it up. He'll be back soon and then we'll be off. Just thought I'd say hello and thank you for everything. It was wonderful, and Dad was great.'

'Was it, darling? I hope so.' Mum rose and put her arms around me, and I returned her hug.

Steve arrived. 'Hi Ma, forgot my shaver. Really great reception. Come on Jen, we'd better get going.'

'I'll see you off.' Mum put her arm around my waist as we walked to the car.

We drove to Sydney Road and were soon on the Hume

Highway. Without any set plans, we intended to stop when it suited us. We proposed travelling along the Newell Highway, bypassing Sydney, so we left the Hume at Springhurst. It had been a late start, so at about three o'clock when we were nearing Wahgunyah, Steve suggested stopping. It was a beautiful spot, quiet and serene. Our motel room had a balcony that faced the river, which was lined with large ghost gums, their grey white trunks towering to the sky and their wide open branches swaying in the breeze. A walking track meandered amongst them.

'I won't be long … just going into town to have a look around.' Steve started towards the door.

'I thought we might walk along the river.' I was still feeling down after last night, and even though Steve had apologised, it didn't change the fact that the whole night had been spoilt. Now he was taking off and leaving me on my own. I'd hoped a walk along the river would rekindle some romance.

'Perhaps later … I'd like to see what's in town.'

'Well I'll come with you.'

'Bugger off—can't you see I want time on my own?' He slammed the door as he left.

I slumped on the bed. *I bet he's going to the pub.*

I dozed, and woke in a darkened room to the sound of the door opening.

'Jen, I've found a great place for dinner. Put your glad rags on and we'll walk into town. It's not far.'

We had a lovely evening—eating in a restaurant was very special. The few restaurants that were in Melbourne were quite expensive, and most people only ate out on birthdays or very special occasions. Very occasionally we would eat at a Chinese restaurant because they were more moderately priced.

That night was the start of the honeymoon I had expected, and the rest of the honeymoon was enjoyable and memorable. Nevertheless, Steve disappeared late each afternoon for a few ales; otherwise he was on his best behaviour, and made every effort to ensure I was happy.

We visited my relatives in Swansea, staying at the Black Swan Motel on Lake Macquarie. One of my aunts and her husband lived on tiny Coon Island on the lake, and access was via a small wooden bridge. There were only a few small cottages on the island, which is now a nature reserve, and many years later Auntie Irene was the last person to leave the island. Her cottage was small with a narrow, tiny kitchen, two minute bedrooms, and a magical lounge room that overlooked the lake. The windows of the lounge were only a metre from the water that lapped against the solid rock wall that protected the house.

I decided to try my luck fishing. I sat on the rocks in front of the lounge windows and soon felt a tug on the handline, which I excitedly started winding in. A long wriggly thing appeared, and I realised I had caught an eel. My uncle had said they lurked in abundance amongst the rocks. As I wound it in, the eel started working its way up the line. I dropped the line and ran screaming into the house to find Steve and my uncle roaring with laughter. Steve eventually went outside and untangled the eel, which had twisted itself securely in the line.

When my grandparents migrated from England, they had settled in Weston, a coalmining area near Newcastle, and initially the family had lived in a tent. I told Steve I'd like to see where my mother had lived, so we drove inland from Swansea along rough roads and through very dry areas, and eventually arrived at Sixth Street, where we found my mother's old run-down house. I sat in the car and imagined Mum as a small girl living in this hot, dusty place, and understood why she had left as soon as she had been able to. On our way back to Swansea we passed through Kurri Kurri, where Mum completed her nursing training, so of course I sought out the hospital. My mother had spoken of her life as a student nurse. She had told me that her sleeping quarters, which she shared with several other nurses, was on the verandah of the nurses' home. Mum had said it was freezing in the winter because some windows were broken. In the heat I was experiencing, I found it hard to imagine that it could ever be freezing.

We continued to Sydney and spent the rest of our honeymoon in Bondi, where we had a magnificent view of the beach from our room in the Astor Hotel. Each morning we walked along the beach, relishing the feel of the sand slipping through our toes. We swam in the warm water, or just lay on the green grass hills between the sand and the main road. Steve decided not to drive Dad's car around Sydney's one-way streets, so we caught buses into town, to other beach spots, and to Circular Quay. We visited Taronga Zoo and took several ferry trips, including one that travelled beyond the Sydney Heads. It was not a good choice; the sea was rough and we both became quite seedy. Another day we visited the Blue Mountains, where Mum had spent her honeymoon.

We had dinner one night at the Coogee Hotel, as we had heard that the Delltones were performing. I loved the Delltones—especially Pee Wee, the tall Delltone with the long face who, although not particularly handsome, had the most wonderful deep voice. To see the group in person was an experience, and I also felt particularly close to Steve. He was not used to cabarets or luxury dining, yet he was relaxed, loving, and was obviously enjoying the evening. That night I felt optimistic, and looked forward to our future together.

13

Our house wasn't due to be completed until January, so on our return from Sydney we stayed at The Vine. This was not an easy time for anyone. Mum and Dad gritted their teeth, while Steve was delighted at the bar's proximity. Each day he adjourned there around three o'clock after he finished work. I still preferred staying in the residence during the hotel's opening hours, but found myself at a loose end when I arrived home at five thirty. I would take a deep breath and join Steve in one of the lounges if I could coax him from the bar.

I was uncomfortable with the whole situation. I felt awkward living as a married person and sharing my bedroom with the person my parents were not thrilled about. Steve was spending far too much time in the bar, associating with his mates, and I wanted to be in my own home cooking meals and independent of my parents. I knew it wasn't forever, but this didn't help.

David idolised Steve, and where meal times could have been excruciating, they were mostly pleasant, with banter going back and forth between the boys. Mum, as always, tried to keep the peace, and Dad was mostly civil, but a strained atmosphere existed.

*

Finally our home was ready. I dragged Steve from room to room, chattering about my plans. It didn't matter that there was little furniture, or that only our bed was new. A small wardrobe from the hotel kept it company. The two spare bedrooms were empty. An old wooden table with a crack up the centre furnished the kitchen, while an old moth-eaten three-seater couch took pride of place in the lounge. Mum gave me some black-out material to use in the bedroom and lounge until we were able to afford curtains. It didn't matter; it was our home.

David visited most weekends, and although I'd avoided him at the hotel, his visits drew us closer. He disliked the hotel life as much as I did, although he got on well with the regulars. But David and my father didn't see eye to eye about anything. Steve worked at weekends, so when David arrived around lunch time on a Saturday, we would natter over a sandwich and a coffee, then either go for a drive in his car, lounge around the house or do some gardening—which was not David's favourite activity.

David still hero-worshipped Steve, so sometimes he stayed for dinner to see him. David's gambling had not abated and nor had Steve's, so after placing a few bets at the TAB, Saturday nights were often spent watching the trots on TV's *The Penthouse Club*. Alternatively, David and Steve might go to the trots at Moonee Valley. Sometimes Mum went with David, and even placed the occasional bet. She vainly hoped her presence might discourage him from betting too heavily.

Although the initial excitement of a new home waned, growing vegetables became a passion for Steve. He dug up a patch of the backyard, and each day after work he tended his vegetables, weeding and watering until dark. He had never grown anything before, and loved working the earth and eating the produce.

With Steve arriving home mid-afternoon and me not arriving until six o'clock, he regularly cooked tea. Sometimes his warped sense of humour came into play. I'd get a phone call at work asking me whether I needed any bread, or what was I planning for tea. 'I'll organise tea; it'll be on the table when you get home,' he'd say. When I arrived home I'd find the house empty. I'd know that he'd gone to Foster, and that he would return in a few days, contrite.

Initially Steve handed his pay cheque over each week, but after a few months it became spasmodic. He would lapse, either disappearing to Foster or gambling on the races. It didn't matter if it was the horses, trots or dogs; he would bet on any form of racing. I somehow managed to furnish our home and buy material to make curtains, but I resented his lack of responsibility, so consequently we fought. Never physically violent in the past, now he sometimes struck out when he was drunk.

One night he arrived home very late, and although wide awake, I feigned sleep. He turned on the bedroom light, sat on his side of the bed and took off one shoe. Then he stood up, said 'Fuck!', and then sat down heavily. This continued for every article of clothing he removed. I gritted my teeth and kept still. I knew he was only trying to start something. I accepted my lot—this was how my mother was treated, but it was a lonely existence.

I continued working part-time in the doughnut wagons, and the extra money bought things for the house. The Moscow Circus came to town and I worked several evenings a week with Steve. One Saturday night we set out for the circus.

'Steve, I need your pay … the house payment is due tomorrow.'

'Haven't been paid yet.'

'Payday's Thursday; it's now Saturday. I need it, Steve.'

'Get fucked! If I say I didn't get paid, I didn't get paid.'

He pushed his foot down on the accelerator.

'Steve! Slow down … we'll have an accident!' We were driving down Glenferrie Road in Hawthorn. 'Steve! Slow down or let me out.'

He slammed on the brakes, and the car screamed to an abrupt halt.

'Just get out, stupid,' Steve said. 'Get out!' He leaned over, opened the passenger door and pushed me out; then he pulled the door shut, driving off at high speed.

I stood in the gutter, watching the vanishing car, and realised my purse was still on the seat. Without money, how could I get to work, or back home? I hailed a taxi and when I arrived at the circus, asked the driver to wait while I got money from my husband. Steve was nowhere to be seen, so I asked Max where he was.

'He's not here … thought neither of you were turning up!' our boss angrily retorted. 'You go and work in Arnie's truck. I'm fed up with Steve. This is the last time he lets me down.'

'I'm … I'm sorry … I thought he'd be here. We left together. I … I had to get a taxi … I've got to pay the driver. Could you please lend … ?'

'Another blue, hey? Probably off to Foster. I reckon he starts these blues so he can get away.'

Max handed me a ten-dollar note and walked off. I paid the driver and then worked jamming and serving doughnuts in Arnie's wagon, expecting Steve to turn up. He didn't. We finally finished cleaning up around midnight.

'Like a lift home, Jenny?' Arnie was flouring the mix for the next day, prior to closing the lid of the trough to allow the dough to rise.

'Thanks, I was wondering how I was going to get home.'

Arnie nodded.

He chatted to me about football and gardening on the drive home, but never mentioned Steve. I was silently trying to work out how I'd get into the house without keys.

Arnie pulled up outside the house. 'I'll wait till you get inside, Jenny. Wait till you get the lights on.'

'I haven't got keys … they're in the car.'

'Damn … Steve would've known you couldn't get in. One o'clock … this should be fun,' Arnie said between gritted teeth. 'Any windows open?'

'No, I always lock them. Sorry. Perhaps the toilet window … it only has glass slats, but it's tiny.'

'We can try.' Arnie walked down the drive to the back of the house and I helplessly followed.

'Anything to stand on? Oh, the wheelbarrow'll do.' He wheeled it under the window, stepped onto it, pulled the window slats off, and, with difficulty, pulled himself up and struggled through the small hole.

'Hell … there's water everywhere.'

I groaned. What on earth … where could water have come from? Arnie opened the back door, and indeed the laundry and toilet floors were covered in water, which was venturing into the hallway. Water was lapping over the side of the trough, and the plug was nowhere to be seen.

'Oh no!' I turned off the dripping tap, plunged my hand into the cold water and pulled the plug.

'Well Jenny, you've got a bit of a mess. Want some help?'

'No, I'll be fine. Thanks for the lift ... and helping me get in.'

'It's okay ... I'd better be off—my wife'll wonder where I am.' He strode down the back steps and once he rounded the corner, I burst into tears, cursing Steve. I swept as much water out the door and down the steps as I could, and wiped the polished hall floor dry with a mop. Tired and miserable, I decided to leave the laundry and toilet floors until the morning.

The next morning as I passed the laundry, I was amazed to see all the water gone. It had seeped through the raw wood floorboards and drained away under the house. Steve returned a couple of days later, but it took me a week to bring myself to speak to him.

*

When my father sold the hotel six months later, my parents came to stay while they looked for a house. Now my home was cluttered with their stuff. The lounge room contained two of everything, as well as Dad's office furniture. Without the hotel, my father was lost. He would sit at his desk under the lounge room window, working at who knows what for hours, furtively having a swig from the whisky bottle hidden in the desk drawer.

Eventually they moved to East Bentleigh, and Mum enjoyed having a home again. Dad attempted to re-enter the insurance business, but was unsuccessful. In desperation, he tried several hotel bar manager's positions, but nothing lasted. Mum realised that they couldn't continue this way, and enrolled in a nursing reorientation course at the Royal Women's Hospital. A whole new world and career opened up. She joined the teaching section of the hospital as a Nurse Clinical Instructor, and this role provided happiness and peace.

My father's continued drinking prevented him from keeping a job, and he became bitter and resentful. One Sunday evening after Mum returned from the hospital, she got changed and was walking towards the kitchen to start dinner, when Dad, sitting by the fire, started an abusive monologue. When Mum told me of the incident later, she said something snapped inside her and she rushed to the fireplace, picked up the poker and stood menacingly over my father, with the end of the poker inches from his face.

'Don't ever speak to me like that again! I'll not be responsible for my actions if you do. Do you understand?'

'Go to hell! You're nothing but a prostitute!' Ray snarled his favourite abuse.

'I'm serious; I mean it. Don't try me anymore, or you'll get this across the head!' She lifted the poker.

My father cowered, and covered his head with his hands.

'You're just a weak, good-for-nothing drunkard!' Mum returned the poker to the fireplace, and standing tall, walked slowly out to the kitchen.

Things changed from then on. Although sometimes his sharp tongue got the better of him, Dad became quite meek and mild. Roles reversed; Mum was the financial provider and now the stronger partner in the union.

*

My religious beliefs had taught me that marriage was a life-long commitment, therefore I never considered leaving Steve. I wanted a baby, believing naïvely that this would cement our marriage, and soon discovered I was pregnant. I had no morning sickness; I just bloomed. Kraft allowed women to work only to the fifth month of their pregnancy, and after seven years I was sad to leave. At a farewell afternoon tea in the boardroom, I was presented with baby clothes and a bouncinette.

Steve took the car to work, often returning late, and I felt isolated at home all day. It was a hot summer, and without air-conditioning I found it trying. At night, if I couldn't sleep, I'd lie on the polished floor at the open front door to catch the cool breeze, and there I'd stay till morning. During the day, once the housework was finished, I'd watch the midday movie and have a nap, then water the garden before preparing tea. I went to doctors' appointments and hospital visits on my own. Husbands were not encouraged to accompany their wives, and anyway Steve was not interested; he never thought to ask me about my doctor's visit. I decorated the nursery, made all the baby's nighties (embroidering each one with a small design), and knitted tiny matinée jackets, singlets and bootees. Mum's knitting needles were clicking; she made a beautiful shawl and layette for the baby.

Dad obtained a barman's position at the Mountain View Hotel. Not long after he started, I received a call saying he was suffering chest pain. It was Steve's day off, so we went to the hotel together, and I stayed in the car while Steve went to get Dad. I looked up as they came through the doors, and thought how frail my father looked. Steve helped him into the car.

'I'll drive your dad's car home,' Steve said as he closed the door.

'Dad, I'm taking you to my doctor,' I said.

'I'm not going to your doctor. He knows nothing about me. I'm alright; I'll see my doctor later.'

No amount of persuading would change his mind.

'Well I'm taking you home. I've rung Mum … she's coming to our place when she finishes work.'

I put my father to bed in the spare room and went food shopping. I arrived home to find his car missing. I hurried inside and went to the spare room.

I ran down the back steps to Steve, who was busy in the garden. 'Steve, where's Dad?'

'Isn't he in bed?'

'No, the stupid idiot, I bet he's gone home. I'll ring Mum. We try to help him … he's beyond it. Couldn't get a drink here, I suppose.'

*

At tea time several weeks later, the phone rang.

'Hello,' I answered.

'Jenny, it's Mum. I've just arrived home … Dad's not very well. I'd like you to come over.'

'Now? I'm getting tea ready.'

'You could have tea here. I'd really like you and Steve to come over.'

'Okay, we'll be over soon,' I said, exasperated. I went out the back to call Steve.

'Dad's not well … Mum wants us to come over.'

'Shit. I'm fed up with your father.'

'I know … I feel sorry for Mum. Let's just go. We'll have tea there.'

When we got there, Mum opened the door. 'Hello, Jenny … hello, Steve.' She gave me a kiss on the cheek and patted Steve's arm.

'Hi, Ma.' This was Steve's term of endearment, which he'd begun to use when we married. 'Ray'd better go to the doc's this time. I'm sick of his messing everyone around.' Steve entered the hall.

'I came home … found Dad in bed. Everything … so tidy. He usually folds his clothes … puts them on the stool at the end of the bed. But he's put everything away.' Mum wiped her eye and put her arm around me. 'Jenny … Dad died sometime today.'

I pulled myself away and rushed into the bedroom. My father was lying in bed and looked like he was sleeping. I stood at the end of the bed. *He can't be dead, he can't be dead.* Tears welled.

The day before, Mum and I had sat knitting for the baby, due in six weeks, while we watched the wrestling on TV—a great favourite of hers. I could take it or leave it. I usually spent Sundays at my parents' while Steve worked. Soon after I arrived, Dad had promised to come over to my place the next day to paint a chest of drawers for the baby. As the day wore on, he kept sneaking out to the garage. Mum hadn't spoken to him for a couple of days, and I ended up arguing with him about his drinking. I had still been angry this morning, so I hadn't contacted him about coming over. Now he was dead. I joined Steve and Mum in the kitchen.

'When I came home from work … his hat … it was on the ground … in the garage. He's so particular about his hat. I came inside … no lights … so quiet.' Mum looked up. 'Are you okay, Jenny? I didn't want to tell you over the phone … didn't want to upset … the baby …'

'She'll be okay, Ma … I'll look after her.' Steve put his arm around me.

David arrived later on. He was not currently working, and was rarely home. In fact, Dad had commented the night before, when David was absent, 'That kid's up to no good. I know it. We'll have the police at our door before long.'

Steve quietly told David about his father.

'Fuck him, fuck him!' David rushed out the front door and wasn't seen again until the next morning.

Mum and I made the arrangements. The local doctor, who Mum called when she found my father, was forced to order an autopsy because Dad hadn't seen a doctor for three months. The funeral directors took him to the coroner.

It was a quiet funeral. I detested watching the coffin going into the ground, and vowed I would never watch a coffin descend again. People gathered in my mother's lounge room, paying their respects. I looked out the window and thought the whole thing was bizarre. You bury your father and then sit and have tea and sandwiches.

My brother didn't cope. Dad's health had deteriorated, and more so since leaving the hotel. David had argued frequently with him, which sometimes resulted in physical violence. David had had an excellent teacher in this regard. They'd had an argument a matter of days before Dad died, and David never had the opportunity to make it right. He felt guilty. I felt guilty too, because of my recent argument with Dad about his drinking.

It upset me that my father would never see his first grandchild, but Mum encouraged me to look forward to the baby's arrival. This I did. Now my dad was gone, I bought some blue paint and painted the chest of drawers myself. I made curtains for the baby's room, and washed the nappies in preparation for the new arrival.

A week or so before the baby was due, Steve didn't come home from work, and took off to Foster. He eventually returned, but the car didn't, because Steve had had an accident and the repairs were being done in Korumburra. Now we would have to get a taxi to the hospital, I supposed.

The baby was late, and each night I went to bed hoping this would be the night. Ten days after the due date, my doctor suggested I go to the hospital the next day. As soon as I put down the phone I felt a sharp pain in my back. I trudged to the outside toilet and soon realised I was in labour. Steve arrived home and immediately rang Mum.

'Ma, the baby's on its way. Jenny's real sick.'

With each contraction, I was vomiting and Steve was helpless. What he was thinking of I'll never know, but he decided to cook tea.

He put his head around the door and said, 'I'll make a curry.'

'Oh no!' I put my head in the bucket again.

The neighbours across the road offered to take us to hospital, and Steve wanted to go straight away, but I waited till about nine o'clock. I hopped into the back of Peter's car and was acutely embarrassed by my continual visits to the bucket. Once at the hospital, the nurses took control, settling me and ushering Steve out. Husbands were not welcome. The hospital's directive was that they go home or wait in a waiting room.

Steve went home. Periodically the nurses entered the room to check the baby's progress, but the rest of the time I was on my own. At about eleven o'clock the attending nurse said, 'Your baby will be here before midnight.' I thought, *What a great date: the sixth day of the sixth month in the year nineteen hundred and sixty-six.* Then the contractions stopped.

My cheery obstetrician arrived the next morning. 'Hello, Mrs Stillwell. What are we up to? I need to examine you and then we'll see about getting this baby into the world.' Dr Champion started to sing. '*Brown paper packages tied up with string, these are a few of my favourite things* ... went to see the Sound of Music last night, great show.'

It wasn't an easy birth, but finally the doctor held my baby up by the ankles. 'It's a girl child, it's a girl child,' he chanted.

In my groggy state, I thought it was a boy, but then realised what I could see was the cord extending from the baby. She was put on my stomach for just a minute and then whisked away to a table surrounded by nurses. I could no longer see my baby and I hadn't even held her.

'Is something wrong?' I asked.

One of the nurses, hovering over the baby with a hypodermic in her hand, looked over.

'No, we're just checking her out. A forceps-delivered baby needs to rest, so don't worry if you don't see her for a couple of feeds.' The baby was placed in a cot and wheeled out.

I lay back. I had a baby girl! Happy tears trickled down my face. It was the most wondrous feeling I have ever experienced.

Mum arrived at the commencement of visiting hours and saw the baby before Steve. I had waited all morning and most of the afternoon for him.

'How are you feeling, dear?'

'I'm fine, Mum ... but I only saw her for a minute. She's got red hair. They told me she might miss the first few feeds because she was a forceps delivery.'

'Don't worry, that's not uncommon,' Mum replied. 'She'll be tired. Red hair? I'm sure she hasn't!'

'Steve hasn't come in.'

'He'll be here soon, I'm sure. What are you going to call her?' said Mum, trying to take my mind off Steve.

'Steve and I thought we'd call her Lauren. Do you like it?'

'It's nice … and her second name?'

'Anne.'

'Lauren Anne … lovely … very feminine. I can't wait to see her.'

'It's almost viewing time for the nursery. I wish Steve would come.'

Mum visited the nursery and then returned. 'Well I never, she has got red hair! She even opened her eyes for her nanna.' Mum bent and gave me a kiss. 'She's beautiful, darling.'

Finally Steve arrived in the early evening. He'd been to the pub, boasting he had a daughter, and celebrating with a few drinks. He was on his best behaviour, and totally in awe of the little bundle he saw through the nursery window. However, during my hospital stay he rarely visited. I would sit up brightly, waiting. As more and more visitors arrived for the other patients, I'd gradually slip down into the bed.

The first morning after Lauren's birth, I woke to find a strange doctor by my bed.

'Good morning, Mrs Stillwell. My name is Dr Maddison. I'm a paediatrician. I was called in last night to attend to your baby.'

'What's wrong? Is she alright?' I anxiously asked.

'I'm a doctor, not a prophet. Until tests are completed, I can't say. She's not keeping anything down and is quite ill, although stable. When I know more I'll let you know.' The doctor left.

I couldn't comprehend what was going on. Yesterday I'd watched babies being brought to their mothers at each feed, and again early this morning. Each time I hoped my baby would arrive. She didn't. I had no idea what it all meant. Confused, I sank down in the bed.

Later on, my doctor arrived.

'Morning, Mrs Stillwell. How are we this morning?' Dr Champion cheerfully boomed.

'What's wrong with my baby? Another doctor's been here. He wouldn't tell me what's wrong. He said he's a doctor, not a prophet.' Trembling, I started to cry.

'Now, now—it's not as bad as all that. Your baby isn't well and yes, Dr Maddison was called in as a precaution. Once we get the tests back, we'll have a better idea and we'll let you know immediately.'

'I want to see her.'

'Of course you do. I'll organise for you to be taken to the nursery this morning. How's that?'

'Thank you.' I smiled and wiped my eyes.

I was wheeled into the nursery that contained three long rows of cots, with nurses busily attending each in turn. I was manoeuvred to the end of one line, where a nurse was sitting by a tilted cot. Lauren was dressed only in singlet and nappy.

'Hello, Mrs Stillwell, I'm Nurse Helen ... I'm specialling your baby. She looks a little pale but she's really doing quite well. We're pleased with her. Unfortunately I can't let you nurse her, but you can touch her and hold her hand.'

I leaned over the cot and held the tiny hand. The little fingers curled instantly around my index finger and a warm, sharp sensation swept through me. She was so perfect: her red hair, tiny face, minute ears and pointed chin. She stretched. The tiny toes wriggled and curled over a finger of my other hand. I gently stroked the bottom of Lauren's feet.

'You're beautiful ... so tiny ... Just get well, little one.' I stroked her arm.

In no time the ward nurse returned, and I placed a kiss on Lauren's forehead before I left. Back in the ward, the image of my baby in the tilted cot stayed with me.

A couple of days passed, and still no-one spoke to me regarding my baby. I was now allowed to go to the nursery to feed her under supervision. Lauren was being kept in a semi-vertical position to relieve the vomiting, and I needed to feed her in this position.

I stepped through the nursery doors. 'I've come to feed my baby,' I said to the nurse standing near the door.

'Oh, you're the mum with the baby with a hiatus hernia.'

'Is that what's wrong with her?' I looked at the nurse.

'Haven't you been told? Please don't tell anyone I told you! I'll get into trouble. The doctor must intend to tell you soon.'

The nurse refused to answer any more questions. I fed Lauren and returned to the ward. Later Dr Champion sat on the bed and explained her problems. After a feed, her stomach would protrude into the oesophagus, which caused the projectile vomiting. He said that handled correctly, the problem would eventually right itself. He recommended that Lauren be kept as upright as possible, and said that although she would be an easy vomiter until she was about seven, the condition would settle.

'So the news is not that bad, is it, Jenny?' Dr Champion patted my hand.

'I guess not. It'll be hard to keep her upright though.'

Ten days after Lauren's birth, David and Steve arrived in David's car to take me home. Our car was still in Korumburra. In the back seat I nursed my baby in an upright position. Once home, I went to the bedroom to change her nappy, putting her head on two pillows. David came in as I took off the soiled nappy.

'Gee Sis, she's so little! Her bum's only the size of my hand. I didn't think babies were so tiny.'

'Me neither. I'm scared stiff.'

Steve walked into the room and just looked. He stood watching, arms folded and one foot in front of the other. After I changed the nappy, I picked up Lauren and went to him.

'Ready for your first nurse? Here you are. Hold her for me while I change. Keep her up, don't let her lie horizontal.'

Steve awkwardly took the baby in his arms, his long fingers curling around the bundle. 'She's so tiny.' He took the small hand, and the baby immediately curled her tiny fingers around his. He smiled and started cooing.

The arrival of Lauren softened Steve, and he became very attentive. Lacking any experience with babies, I found the arrival of a sick baby stressful. Mum came each night after work and helped. Late one night after we had all gone to bed, Mum heard the baby crying continually, and met me in the hallway, where we both stood shivering in our nighties.

'Mum, I've done everything. I've fed her, burped her and changed her nappy. I've given her the medicine and still she cries. I don't know what to do.'

'You go back to bed; you need your sleep. I'll look after her.'

The baby's bassinette was in the warm lounge. Mum picked up the baby and sat in front of the glowing embers of the fire. I watched for a while as she sang softly and gently rocked Lauren. She instantly stopped crying, so I went to bed. The next day Mum said she thought Lauren had sensed my tension, because she had gone straight to sleep.

'Hi Ma, how did you sleep?' Steve was in the kitchen preparing breakfast.

'Fine after the baby settled down.'

'Yeah, Jenny was up and down to her a bit. No use me getting up. I can't feed her.'

'Jenny's very tired. Settling a baby is not all feeding, you know,' Mum replied between tight lips.

My life changed. All day I seemed to be feeding her, and everything to do with the baby required extra attention. She had to be propped up on pillows even when she was bathed. When I wasn't doing something for her, I was doing a mountain of washing created by the regular projectile vomiting and the extremely loose bowel motions. I became an obsessive nappy counter. I counted the nappies going into the washing machine, then into the washing basket, then pegging them on the line— and of course I counted them when I took them off the line and again when I folded them. Usually the count was between two and three dozen.

Nevertheless, I was content; my baby made me complete.

14

After Dad's death, David continued living with Mum, but he was rarely at home, except to sleep. However, during the year after Lauren's birth, his visits to my home became more frequent. He loved nursing the baby, and once she was crawling he adored playing with her. We became quite close, and although I knew Mum was very concerned about David's other activities, I relished his visits. I was lonely. Steve was up to his old ways, drinking and gambling, and was rarely home. The Steve that surfaced when Lauren was born had all but disappeared.

During the following year, David seemed to be continually in trouble. He was arrested several times for minor offences, which successively became more serious. Each time bail had to be raised. Mum found the ordeal quite stressful, so it fell to me to organise his release. The visits to barristers, magistrates and county courts that followed become familiar, but the subsequent anxiety for both Mum and me never became easier.

David lost his licence and, being a truck driver, this meant he lost his job. He made no effort to find an alternative job. Instead he sat in front of the television all day, with the heater on, smoking and flicking ash on the floor for Mum to clean it up when she returned from work. Most evenings he'd disappear, arriving home in the early hours. Mum was beside herself. She knew he was up to no good, but if she said anything, David abused her. Their relationship was strained; gone was her violent husband, only to be replaced by an abusive son.

David regained his driving licence after six months and found a new job, but he mixed with the wrong crowd, frequented the wrong places, and spent his money on cars, or girls for whom he had little respect. One weekend, he went to Adelaide with a mate named Rodney. When my brother returned, he told Mum he was moving into his mate's flat. Mum told me this man troubled her. He was much older than David and she didn't trust him, but part of her was relieved that David was moving out. She had found living with him and being aware of his comings and goings impossible to deal with. On the other hand she was fearful for her son, who was indeed her favourite child.

Several weeks after David moved, the ringing phone jolted me awake. Steve was asleep beside me; heaven knows when he had arrived home. Phone calls at two in the morning, like telegrams, usually meant trouble. Heart racing, I clambered out of bed, praying the baby didn't wake.

'Hello.'

'Jenny, it's Mum. David's in trouble,' Mum sniffed.

'What now, Mum?'

'It's … it's serious this time … aggravated break and … and enter. Bail's a thousand dollars.'

I could barely understand her. 'Wow, that's high. I guess you want me to bail him again?'

'Will you?'

'Not in the middle of the night, Mum. Let him stew. I'll go tomorrow afternoon.'

'Jenny, I'd rather you go in the morning.'

Exasperated, I raised my voice. 'It's the afternoon or nothing, Mum. I've got things to do!'

'Alright, I'll mind Lauren. Jenny, where did I go wrong?'

'You didn't.' My newfound fondness for David was fast diminishing. 'You should wash your hands of him. He's leading his own life … making his own choices.'

'It's easy for you to say … but he's my son … he's my son, Jenny,' she sobbed.

'Mum, make a cup of tea and try to get some sleep.'

Shivering in my flimsy nightie, I slid down the wall and sat on the hard wooden floor. *Damn him!* I rubbed my hands up and down my thin arms and drew my knees to my chin. *Mum blames the hotel, Dad's drinking … the physical abuse. David mixing with Collingwood's lowlife … and I guess the six o'clock swill wasn't great either. The hotel wasn't good for either of us. I met Steve. I hated the sordid life. Now I'm married to a carbon copy of my father. David needs to man up. He's twenty-two.* I crawled into bed next to my still-sleeping husband.

My eyes were watering from lack of sleep. My father had often described them as 'Just like a little Jap's' when I was little. Dressed in jeans and shirt, my dark hair tied in a ponytail, I drove to Mum's. Lauren's whinging in the back seat further increased the anxiety I was feeling.

Mum's short, rounded body was slouched over the kitchen table; her permed hair needed combing. I passed Lauren to her and made a cup of tea. Mum's puffy eyes glanced at my flushed face and frail frame. 'Ah Jenny, thank God I can count on you.' She smiled feebly and handed the cheque to me. 'I know you're dealing with a lot.'

'Mum, it's okay.' I hugged her.

At the Box Hill lockup, I told the desk clerk I'd come to bail David Wilding. He scanned the list.

'Van's picked him up. Be in Pentridge now.'

'I understood we could bail him up until four.' I clenched my knuckles.

'Nah, shoulda been earlier. Don't keep them long. Need ta make room for the next lot.' The policeman smirked. 'He fronts Monday. You can bail him then, if he's remanded.'

Mum will be furious, I thought, and I was right. She made it clear she was upset that her son was spending the weekend in Pentridge. I discovered I could visit the next afternoon, but because Mum and Steve were working, I'd have to take Lauren. *Damn David. I don't want my baby in that place.*

Mum said David needed clothes for court, so I rang the Ripponlea flat that David was sharing with Rodney. Rodney's girlfriend answered and curtly said that Rodney was not there.

'I need to get some things for David. Okay if I come over shortly?'

'As ya like.'

I put down the phone and looked at my mother, whose fingers constantly tapped the table. 'Well she's less than friendly,' I said.

The girl let me in, pointed to David's room, and returned to the TV. Used plates, a sauce bottle and take-away containers littered the coffee table. Dirty dishes covered the sink. I negotiated the obstacle course; there were clothes everywhere, and even worse, dog faeces left by two dogs roaming the flat. David's room stank of tobacco and stale body odour. His suit, still in the drycleaner's plastic, was in the wardrobe. *At least it's clean.* Gathering a few other things, I left.

Dark storm clouds threatened as I caught the train and

tram. I had Lauren in the pusher, and was armed with clothes, cigarettes and biscuits.

Arriving at our destination, I saw that twin turrets framed the forbidding, castle-like main entrance. The bluestone walls, razor wire, and the large sign that said 'HM Prison Pentridge' convinced me: a castle it was not. I joined the long queue leading to a heavy steel door labelled 'Remand Visitors' Entrance'.

'If I don't bring the brats to see 'im 'e'll belt me up when 'e gets out,' the woman next to me loudly exclaimed. An older couple seemed uncomfortable with the crude remarks being made by obnoxious young louts.

I was ordered to hand over anything for the prisoner and was told to sign in. After my belongings and the pusher were checked, I was ushered towards a narrow passage. An officer unlocked a heavy iron door and directed me through. It clanged shut. The bolts shot into place and the deafening noise bombarded my senses. I shuddered. My daughter and I were locked in, surrounded by foreboding stone walls.

I was told to remain in the visitors' waiting room until called. I gave Lauren some water and looked around. A haze of cigarette smoke created an eerie feeling in the sparse room. Toddlers sat on the dirty floor with broken toys. Older people, with faraway, sad faces, sat quietly opposite noisy teenagers whose conversation was peppered with expletives. A distraught woman next to me was nursing a baby. She sniffed loudly, smeared her hand across her nose and wiped it down her dress. I wanted to be anywhere but here.

'Visitor for David Wilding,' boomed the loudspeaker.

I walked quickly to the door held open by an officer.

'Down the hallway. Cubicle two.'

I carefully manoeuvred the pusher into the tiny space.

Sitting on the solitary chair, I could touch the walls on either side. In front of me were two glass screens a foot apart, each with a round hole in the centre. David's appearance startled me. His freckled face had a dirty streak down one cheek. Even with the ginger stubble, his face was ashen and his hair a tangled mess. He wore an old grey overcoat. A tin plate and cup attached to a piece of string tied around his waist also caught my eye. He looked wretched.

'Hi, Sis.' David sat, leaning his face towards the hole.

I bent forward. 'David, what's with the dirty coat, and the string?'

'The coat's what I was caught in. The string's the only way I can keep me plate for me meals. I'm bloody cold; the cops took me socks.'

'Why?'

'They were on me hands.'

'David, you're …' Lauren started crying, so I picked her up.

'No place to bring a kid,' David grunted.

'Mum and Steve are working. I had no choice. We've organised a solicitor … I've brought clothes for court. Mum sent ciggies and biscuits.'

'Thanks, Sis … good ole Mum.'

'You should think about her a bit more. She's a wreck. Were you on your own?'

'No, with Rodney.'

'He's trouble.'

'Shut up, he's me mate.'

I changed the subject. 'What's it like in here?'

'Bloody terrible. They strip-searched me … awful.' David put his face in his hands. 'We're locked up at three thirty in the arvo till eight the next morning. Then we stand around the cold yard. Plenty of fights. Have to shower in the open with cold water.' David ran his hand up through his uncombed hair. 'You'll never—.'

'Time's up.' An officer tapped David on the shoulder. David quickly stood up.

'We'll see you at court on Monday, I said.'

'Thanks, Sis.'

*

Mum and I, waiting outside the Oakleigh Magistrates' Court, saw the prison van arrive. Inside, the magistrate, sitting on an elevated wooden bench, commanded the sombre courtroom. Rodney was called first. He pleaded guilty and was sentenced to nine months' gaol. Mum groaned.

After lunch, David's case was heard, with the solicitor requesting a continuance to prepare the defence. Bail was set at $1,000 with similar surety, which would also have to be paid if David defaulted.

David hugged us both.

'David, come home for a while. You'll not be able to afford the flat now your friend's not there,' said Mum.

'I'll think about it,' David replied. 'Gotta see me girlfriend. She'll be livid—supposta meet 'er on Saturdi. Sis, could you give me a lift?'

'I guess, but I'll take Mum home first. Mum, can you look after Lauren?'

'Of course. Both of you come back for tea.'

I unlocked the car. I was tired of it all. *No housekeeping money last week, because Steve gambled the lot. I'd let David fry if not for Mum. She thinks I'm resilient—if only she knew! I'm just surviving. Steve's drinking, the violent arguments—I hope when*

Lauren grows up her choices are better than mine, I thought. I was also frustrated with Mum's continual excuses for David's behaviour, and her belief that I'd cope no matter what.

'You know, didn't get the cigs and biscuits till last night, and me clothes until I was leaving.' David lit a cigarette and started blowing smoke rings. 'Thought I was never gonna get 'em … had to change in the van.'

Cocky little so-and-so, I thought, *quite different from last Saturday.*

'I'll never go back in there. Kill meself first. Shared a cell, two strides across and three long. Locked up sixteen hours a day … it was hell.'

'You mightn't get the choice,' I snapped.

I dropped Mum and Lauren off, and drove to the radio and television repair shop where David's girlfriend worked.

'Come and meet Kerry, Sis.' David jumped out of the car without, it seemed, a care in the world.

'Kerry, meet my sister, Jenny.' David walked towards an attractive young girl with olive skin, short blonde hair and a thick, long fringe.

The girl ignored me, and proceeded to shout at David. 'Get lost! You've got a cheek …' She turned and flounced into the back room. David followed as if he owned the store.

'Ah Kerry … I've been in a bit of trouble … couldn't meet you and couldn't let you know.'

'Yeah, who do you think you're kidding?'

From the shop I heard the loud arguing, but eventually David's explanations convinced the girl he hadn't let her down. They emerged arm in arm, kissing and cuddling, to my acute embarrassment. I decided to wait in the car.

A few months later, David returned to court. With the

excellent barrister that Mum's solicitor found, he was saved from a prison sentence and put on a good behaviour bond for two years, and also received a very hefty fine. The legal bill was £3000, which Mum paid. David said he would repay her, but he never did. Mum had replaced Dad as David's financier.

David returned to live with Mum, but often disappeared at night. She never knew whether he was with Kerry or doing something illegal. He continued gambling heavily on both the horses and two-up. He drove fast in his car that was on hire purchase, and repeatedly copped speeding fines. In debt and always short of money, he didn't pay the fines. Mum propped him up, in an attempt to keep him out of trouble and gaol. Occasionally he would offer her some money, but he didn't pay board.

The relationship between Mum and David deteriorated, and he spent more and more time at Kerry's home. He was comfortable with her family, who enjoyed partying, drinking and arguing—quite different from the quiet times he spent with Mum.

Kerry discovered she was pregnant, and David initially refused to marry her. Terrible arguments ensued, and one night, in a violent temper, he drove the car at Kerry to frighten her. Her mother rang Mum, and everyone ended up on my doorstep late at night in an attempt to resolve the situation. I was now expecting my second baby, and was less than impressed. Steve stayed in bed.

Kerry's mother was different from Mum. She spoke her mind and was adamant that the two must marry, whereas Mum thought the union was doomed to fail. However, Mum also realised that Kerry must be looked after. I was aware that this was at least the second girl David had got pregnant, and felt this time he should do the right thing. The discussion went on into the early hours.

They married a month later, and settled into Mum's home. The relationship between Kerry and Mum was strained from the beginning, and the atmosphere was always tense when I visited. This was exacerbated by the fact that David decided on a career change that meant he was away during the week. He believed he could make more money as a salesman than driving a truck; hence he began working for a vacuum cleaner company, selling in country areas. Like his father, he was a born salesman. He enjoyed the door-to-door selling, which gave him freedom and a lucrative income.

*

My marriage was a replica of my parents', and although the physical abuse was not nearly as violent, it was emotionally harrowing. Steve's drinking and gambling continued, and money was always scarce. Steve socialised at the local pub, and despite the loneliness I felt every day, Lauren brightened my life.

When I was heavily pregnant with our second baby, I returned to work. Steve's escalating gambling habit meant that his pay rarely made it home. I had to get a job to survive. My friend Rita, who was now married, offered to look after Lauren. It was difficult, but each morning I left my East Oakleigh home at seven o'clock, drove to Noble Park, dropped Lauren at Rita's and then battled the traffic to arrive at work in Hawthorn by eight thirty. I was tired before I started. Unfortunately, after only a few weeks Lauren got the measles, so I had to leave the job. My mother resumed providing financial support. It was humiliating.

Steve lied continually and convincingly. Although I knew he was lying, somehow he would persuade me that he was telling the truth. On one occasion, he came home from work, parked the car in the street instead of the driveway, and came inside.

'Hi, it's good it's payday. The fridge is empty,' I said as I wiped down the sink.

Steve patted the top pocket of his overalls. 'Shit, it was in my pocket … must have fallen out in the car. I'll go and look.'

I followed him and we searched the car thoroughly. No pay envelope.

'I must have lost it. I'll ring the boss … see if it's on the ground near where the car was parked.'

My heart sank. I'd been through this before. 'You've been betting again. Steve, I can't believe you've lost it all again!'

'How can you say that, Jen? Of course I haven't,' he lied. To reinforce the lie, he went through the process of telephoning his boss and asking him to check the parking area. Of course, nothing. Mum once again provided the week's food.

Staying away from home became more frequent for Steve. When he was at home, he was often drunk, and his habits deteriorated. If he woke at night and wanted to go to the toilet, he seemed to have difficulty knowing where it was. Once he opened the linen press door and urinated over the clean linen. Another night I was in the lounge watching the TV. I heard him in the kitchen and came out to find him urinating in the kitchen sink over Lauren's bunny dish. I went back to the lounge disgusted, and slammed the door.

Steve staggered in. 'What's the problem?' he slurred.

'You're drunk … it's no use talking to you. Go to bed!'

'Get me something to eat.'

'You swept your dinner onto the floor; I'm not getting anything else. How could you wee over Lauren's dish? You disgust me!'

'Go to hell!' Steve staggered through the double doors to the hall and went to bed.

I seethed. I went into the bedroom and turned on the light. 'This drinking's got to stop. I'll leave you if it doesn't.'

'You'll never leave, especially in that condition,' he laughed, casting a glance at my pregnant belly.

Something in me snapped. I rushed over and grabbed the blanket off the bed. 'I'm not sleeping with you. I hate you!'

He jumped out of bed and lunged at me. I turned and scurried through the bedroom door, across the hall and through the lounge's glass doors, shutting them behind me. Steve followed. He still had his socks on, and in his haste, slid on the polished floor in the hall. Trying to regain his footing, he put his fist through the glass door. I had expected to be hit at any moment, but turned around at the sound of broken glass. Blood streamed down his arm as he disappeared down the hall.

I waited. Silence. I ventured down the hall and saw Steve standing over the bath, blood gushing down his arm.

'You'd better bandage that up, or you'll bleed to death.' I turned on my heel and made a bed for myself on the lounge.

Steve left early the next morning for work, and I was feeling a little guilty. The cut in his arm had looked like it needed stitches—I should have helped.

After I finished breakfast, I picked up the phone and called Steve's work. 'Hello, Max?'

'Yes. Is that you, Jenny?'

'Yes. Sorry to trouble you. Has Steve left yet?'

'No, he's still cutting out doughnuts ... seems to have hurt his elbow or something. Good thing it's not the cutting-out arm.'

'That's what I'm ringing about. I think it needs stitches and it could have glass in it. Would you try and get him to a doctor?'

'I'll get my wife to have a look at it; she's a nurse. Okay?'

'Thanks.'

'I won't ask how he got it, but I can guess.'

'Bye, Max.' I put down the phone.

A couple of weeks later I was watching the movie *I'll Cry Tomorrow* and shedding a tear, when I felt a twinge. I wondered if the baby was on its way, and soon knew it was, as the twinge became intense. I continued watching the movie, thinking I had plenty of time, but soon it was apparent that I didn't.

'Steve, I need to go to hospital. Ring Mum and let her know we'll be bringing Lauren over while I have a shower.'

'Don't have a shower. Let's just get going. Are Lauren's things packed?'

'Yes. I'm having a shower … won't be long.'

We drove to Mum's to drop off Lauren and then continued on to the hospital. I begged Steve to wait, because I knew this baby was in a hurry, but Steve left, promising to return as soon as the baby was born.

Vanessa arrived quickly, quietly and without any fuss at twenty past five in the morning. She instantly crossed her legs high in the air. A nurse running by laughed, saying, 'Hope she keeps that up when she's older!' I asked if the baby could stay with me, because my husband was returning.

'Well she should go to the nursery, but we'll let her stay a little while.'

When the shift changed, Steve had still not arrived, so the nurses insisted Vanessa go to the nursery. He arrived late in the afternoon, smelling strongly of alcohol, but this time his visits were more regular than when Lauren was born. Our neighbour was minding Lauren, and Steve brought her to see me most days. She was very excited to have a sister, and kept asking when I was bringing Vanessa home.

Steve didn't show much interest in Vanessa. He'd come home from work and make no effort to see her. I think he was bitterly disappointed she was not a boy. Being more experienced than I had been when Lauren was born, I was relaxed with this baby. Vanessa wasn't sick and she didn't cry—in fact, at times I realised it was well past her feed time. I would look into the cot and Vanessa would just look up at me with her big deep blue eyes. She was a contented baby.

My mother gave Lauren a very soft doll to be her baby, and made several sets of clothes for it. At feed times Lauren, not yet two, would sit on the lounge with me and feed her baby with a bottle. It was a lovely time with both my children. Once feeding was finished, Lauren would have her promised nurse of her baby sister.

Two months after Vanessa was born, my brother's first baby arrived. David was working out in the country at the time, but immediately came home to see his son. David was overjoyed and extremely excited at Robbie's arrival, but the next day he had to return to the country. Being the father of a newborn baby was seen as no excuse for an employee to have time off. A few days later, I picked Kerry up from the hospital. I went into her room and saw Robbie in his cot and Kerry sitting on the bed. Baby clothes were lying at the foot of the bed.

'Jenny, can you dress him?' a terrified Kerry asked.

I looked at her, thinking, *Where is the girl with all the*

bravado, the girl that is never scared of anything? She had been brought to task by a tiny little baby.

'Of course I can. It's hard when they're so little; their head is so floppy.'

'I know,' a very meek Kerry replied.

My mother enjoyed having Robbie staying with her, but his presence created a further rift between her and Kerry, and four months after Robbie's birth, David and Kerry moved into a one-bedroom flat.

Finances for me were now even more stretched with two children, and I kept trying to find ways to improve the situation. Steve was earning only the minimum wage while working in the doughnut wagons, but he had acquired a great deal of knowledge. I thought we might be able to get ahead if we had our own business instead of Steve working for a boss. He initially wasn't keen on my suggestion, but after a while warmed to the idea, so we made plans.

Firstly we had to get a wagon custom-built, find sites where we could sell, and apply for a hawker's licence. Although Steve planned the fit-out of the wagon, he left it to me to source someone to build it. I also had to apply for the hawker's licence in Steve's name, and organise the signage on the outside of the van. He did make some effort in finding sites, but of course the more lucrative ones were already taken up by his previous bosses. Finally, about eight months after my original suggestion, I proudly watched Steve drive our doughnut wagon down the drive for the first time. I again felt it was a new start.

He worked hard, but trying to make the business pay was difficult. Often he'd arrive home without any money to be banked. I couldn't understand what he did with the day's takings. I'd check the wagon, the car and his overall pockets once he'd gone to bed, but there was no money.

One night I watched from the kitchen window as he parked the wagon in the backyard. He then went to the outside toilet before coming inside.

'How did you go today? Was it busy?'

'Not bad.' He sat down to eat his tea.

'How much did you take? The wagon's payment is due tomorrow.'

'I don't know. You're always harping about money. I'll give it to you when I'm ready.' It was obvious he'd been drinking again.

He ate his tea and went to the bedroom. He didn't return.

I waited a while and then checked whether he was asleep. I searched his pockets, but there were just a few coins. I went out to the wagon with a torch and checked the till. There was just change—no notes. I searched every nook and cranny of the wagon, but found nothing. I leant back against the dough trough. *Where could it be? He came straight inside. Perhaps the car? I'll check that.* I found nothing. I was perplexed. Then I remembered he'd gone to the toilet. *Surely not?*

With a torch in hand, I went outside and opened the toilet door. *Nowhere much to hide anything here.* I shone the torch on the floor around the pan. Nothing. The beam of light moved over the walls along the rafters. Nothing. *It has to be here; he didn't go anywhere else. It couldn't be ...* I opened the lid of the pan and shone the torch into its murky depths. *Don't be stupid; it couldn't be in there.* I dropped the lid. About to give up, I saw the toilet roll and put my hand into the centre. Bingo ... my fingers closed on a roll of notes. I went inside and hid the money at the back of the linen cupboard, under the nappies.

The next morning, I gave Lauren her cereal. Vanessa was still asleep and probably wouldn't wake until about seven thirty. She was such a good sleeper. It was Steve's day off; in his dressing gown he went outside to the toilet. Very soon he wandered into the kitchen and put the electric jug on. Without a word he went to the bedroom, searched his overall pockets and his wardrobe. He returned to the kitchen, ate his breakfast, and didn't say a word. Nor did I.

I went to the bank that afternoon to make the payment due on the doughnut wagon, with Lauren, Vanessa and Robbie in tow. I now looked after Robbie while Kerry worked, and found looking after a toddler and two crawling babies challenging. Kerry and David's marriage had its problems, and Kerry would walk out on David at regular intervals, after they quarrelled. David was as physically abusive as my father had been; however, Kerry appeared to enjoy the fighting and the yelling—it was what she had grown up with. She goaded and taunted David, but then placed the blame entirely on him when she was physically hurt. I felt sorry for her and tried to help where I could. There was no excuse for what David did, but she was not blameless. David's behaviour was a re-enactment of our father's, and for both of us emotional and physical abuse was the norm. When Kerry left David, she would try to take her son with her, but I would care for Robbie when David prevented her from doing so.

That night Steve didn't come home for tea; I guessed he was probably at the midweek trots meeting. I wondered what he'd use for money, but reasoned he probably borrowed from mates. I went to bed and fell asleep. I woke hearing the key opening the front door.

'Shhh, don't wake Jenny up!' Steve said in a loud voice.

I wondered who was with him and then heard, 'Where do I sleep?' and realised it was David.

'On the lounge, I suppose,' Steve slurred.

The next morning, I went into the lounge to find David with Lauren's quilt over him.

'Hi ,Sis!' David smiled sheepishly.

'Where were you two last night?'

'Went to the trots … lost …'

'Does Kerry know where you are?'

'She'll guess.'

'You two are impossible!' I turned tail and left the room.

I fed the children, washed up, swept the floors and washed the nappies. It was Saturday; the men still hadn't risen, so with the chores completed I put the baby in the pram and Lauren on the pram seat, and walked up the unmade road to the shops to get some vegetables. Although the grocer delivered weekly, I still needed to shop most days for meat and vegetables, because I could only carry a small amount in the pram.

I was glad to get out of the house. Everything was getting me down: Steve's drinking and gambling, and the loneliness. Although the neighbours were pleasant, I kept to myself. However, Steve was friendly with the nosy neighbours at the end of the court. Sometimes after we quarrelled and I decided to get away from things, I would notice the Venetian blinds of their house flick down as they watched the car leave our driveway. I despised bringing attention to myself. Once when I decided to go to the drive-in because Steve was drunk again, I got in the car, but it wouldn't start. A friend's husband later told me that Steve had probably removed the rotor button, so I bought a spare and kept it in my handbag. The next time after a quarrel, when the car didn't start, I opened the bonnet and simply inserted the rotor button. The Venetian blinds went down again and I felt like yelling to the nosy neighbours and to Steve, 'See I've tricked you all!' as I drove off.

My dysfunctional marriage continued, but two incidents became the catalysts that encouraged me to alter my life.

Steve enjoyed watching *World of Sport* when he didn't work at the weekends. He'd sit with a beer in front of the television, and didn't like being disturbed. On this particular occasion, Lauren was playing in her bedroom with her doll's cot, while Vanessa crawled around her. Lauren loved being with her father, and after a while she went into the lounge. Steve, who usually enjoyed playing with Lauren, was intent on the football he was watching, and ignored her. She continued whinging. He lost his temper and yelled at her to get out of the room, so she sat in the hall and cried. The noise irritated Steve, and he went out and put his boot under her bottom, and pushed her up the hall. He didn't hurt her and was controlled in what he did, but it raised alarm bells for me. What would be next?

The other incident happened one evening when Steve once again was drunk. He threw his dinner across the table and went to bed. After putting the children to bed, I sat in the lounge watching television. I heard him get up, and assumed he was going to the toilet. A few minutes later, the door opened, and he came in and snarled for me to come into the hall. I thought I should humour him, so I followed. By the front door was a large pool of liquid.

'You clean that up.' Steve looked at me menacingly.

'How could you? You clean it up!' I yelled.

'That's all you're good for … do it!' he yelled back. He then stepped across the puddle, found his way into the bedroom and went to bed.

I got a mop and bucket and cleaned up the urine. Previously when Steve had urinated in the house, I had thought that he didn't know where he was because he was drunk. As I cleaned up the mess and washed the front door down, I realised that this time he'd known exactly what he was doing. He wanted to humiliate, upset and hurt me. That night I vowed my children, now one and three, would not experience the kind of childhood that I had experienced. After five years of marriage, I decided to leave.

15

'Ladies and gentlemen, please prepare for landing.' The steward's voice jolts me from my daydreaming. 'Please ensure your seatbelt is fastened, your seat back is in the upright position and your tray-table is secured. We expect to arrive at the Melbourne terminal by three o'clock.' It seems only moments since I boarded the plane in Sydney, yet I have recalled so much of my past.

I put down my notebook and quickly fasten my seatbelt as the steward moves down the aisle. I fold up the tray table and pick up the notebook, and once again look out the window at the cottonwool clouds.

When I think about it, I always carefully considered my options when making a decision. And once I made a decision, I acted upon it. I had agonised over how to leave Steve: I would decide on a course of action; then, realising it wouldn't work, I'd consider another.

The morning after I finally resolved to leave Steve, I sat at the kitchen table and did my sums. I had little money, although Bev's influence when I worked at Kraft meant I'd not lost my saving ability. I always tried to bank a little each week for a rainy day. My bankbook showed a balance of $150. To find accommodation with this meagre amount would be difficult;

I knew I'd be required to pay a bond and a month's rent in advance. Somehow I'd find a way. I wasn't sure how though, because not only did I need somewhere to live, I also needed to get a job, and to find a place where the children could be looked after while I was at work.

I needed help. Directly across the road, a brother and sister lived with their elderly mother. They were kindly and understanding, and aware of the problems in the house opposite. I got on well with them all, especially the mother, so I decided to tell Mrs Desoli my plans. She immediately suggested I come over each morning for a cup of tea so I could look in the paper for a place to live. So each morning I trotted across the road with the children. While I enjoyed a cuppa and scanned the papers, Mrs Desoli played with the girls.

When I found a flat advertised in my price range, I piled the children in the car and went to inspect it. David was now a used car salesman, and I'd recently acquired an Austin A40 after one of his customers traded it in. David had sold it to me for fifteen dollars, and I spent another fifteen dollars on a new battery. Without this car, searching for a flat would have been impossible. It was probably the catalyst that allowed me to leave.

For six weeks, I spent each day looking for somewhere to live, a suitable place for my children to be cared for, and a job to support us. Without a rental or financial history and with two small children, landlords were not interested in leasing to me. Anyway, most of the flats I inspected were either in the wrong area, unsuitable for children (with nowhere for them to play), or disgustingly dirty. Similarly, employers ruled out a woman with small children who hadn't worked for three years. I was ready to give up.

The following Saturday, Steve left early in the doughnut van to work at the local football ground.

After breakfast, Mrs Desoli rang. 'Jenny, I've just had a quick look at the "Flats Vacant" in the paper. There's one for sixteen dollars a week … might suit you. Come and have a cup of tea. Peter and Rhonda are looking forward to seeing the children.'

'Thanks for looking … they all read alright, but when you see them … I'm just about to give up.'

'Come and have a cuppa anyway. With Peter and Rhonda working, they don't get a chance to see the children often.'

'Okay.' I smiled to myself; they were such nice people. 'I'll be over in a jiffy.'

I walked across the road, with Lauren skipping along, and knocked on the door.

'Hello, Lauren!' Rhonda scooped Vanessa out of my arms. 'And how are you today?' She gave Vanessa a little tickle. Vanessa giggled.

Rhonda took Lauren's hand and wandered into the lounge. The *Age* was spread across the table in the kitchen, and Mrs Desoli pointed to the advertisement. I could hear Peter and Rhonda's voices, and the girls laughing. I looked at the paper.

'Camberwell … it's certainly the right price … only one bedroom … I'd like two, but I can't afford that.'

'Why don't you have a look? You never know, it might be alright,' Mrs Desoli encouraged.

I was scanning the paper. 'I'll probably be wasting my time, but there doesn't seem to be anything else. I guess I'll give it a try. Thanks again for looking … I'd better go this morning; if it's any good, it'll go quickly.'

I put the children in the car and drove to an address in the leafy-green suburb of Camberwell. The large old oak trees with their gnarled trunks lined each side of the street, their canopies almost touching. The large, well-preserved 1920s home behind a high thick hedge was three doors from the railway line, and close by was a park with large red canna lilies bordering it.

With my children, I walked along the path to the verandah of the redbrick house and knocked on the door.

A young woman answered. 'Hello, can I help you?' She was quietly spoken.

'I'd like to see the flat you advertised, please.'

'I'll just get the key.' She returned and with a smile asked, 'What are your children's names?'

'Lauren, and the little one is Vanessa.'

'Hello!' She looked down at the children and smiled. 'A little shy, I think.' Vanessa held on tightly to my hand. I immediately warmed to this woman, and followed her along a path around the side of the house. The flat at the end of the path was attached to the main house, but with its own private entrance.

The woman handed the key to me. 'I'll leave you to look and see if it suits. Just come to the front door to return the key when you're finished.'

I stepped into an average-sized lounge room with doors to a bedroom, kitchen, bathroom, and a locked door into the main house. The bedroom was large, and would be plenty big enough for the three of us; however, the kitchen was tiny and the bathroom not much bigger. I walked out the back door of the kitchen into a small porch that was used as a laundry. Outside was a large backyard that was completely fenced. *It would be a very safe area for the girls to play in*, I thought. A huge oak tree shaded the bottom half of the garden, and on the left was a fenced vegetable garden. To the right, beyond the high fence that separated the drive from the backyard, was a three-car garage. My car won't need to be on the street, I thought. I returned to the empty lounge room and looked around. It was dark and gloomy, but it was clean. How could I brighten it up? *Furniture will help. My blue curtains will add a bit of colour and cover the door into the main house. I could put the table in that corner; it won't fit in the kitchen. The couch could go on the other wall. At least there's a gas fire. It's better than anything else I've seen.*

I locked up, went around to the front and knocked.

'I think I'd like to take it, please.'

'Come in and meet my husband. Then we can discuss things together.'

'Thank you. I'm Jenny Stillwell.'

'Meryl Strand.'

I was surprised how accepting Meryl was of us. Landlords I'd previously come into contact with didn't want anything to do with children. We went into the kitchen, which overlooked the porch and the backyard.

'Grant, this is Jenny Stillwell … and Lauren … and Vanessa. Jenny, this is my husband Grant.'

'Hi,' I said.

'Now, Meryl says you're interested in renting the flat. Have you rented before?'

'No.'

'Well … do you have any references?'

'No, I don't, because I haven't needed to rent until now.' *This is what I'm always asked*, I thought despondently.

'Are you working?'

'No. I'm looking for somewhere to live first and then I intend to look for a job once I'm settled.'

'How are you going to pay the rent if you don't have a job?'

'I've a little saved and I'll be able to pay a month's rent in advance.'

'How about the bond?'

'I can do that at a pinch.'

Meryl and Grant went into the hall to talk. Although they didn't ask, I think they assumed I was probably leaving a relationship. They decided to take the risk and offer the flat to me, even though I had no job, no references and had not rented before.

'Jenny, if you'd like the flat, it's yours. However, if you get behind in the rent, you'll have to leave immediately.' Grant looked sternly at me.

'Oh, thank you … I won't. Is it okay if we move in next Saturday?'

'Certainly … but the money must be paid first.'

'I'll bring it along on Monday after I've been to the bank.'

I was elated—I'd finally found a place. I couldn't believe what had just taken place. Every time I'd been asked those questions previously, the outcome had always been a refusal. The couple were young and appeared very kind, but I wondered whether they had ever leased the flat before. It was actually the servant's quarters to the old home. I set off home, thinking about what to do next.

Before I could organise job interviews, I needed to arrange for the children to be cared for. When I decided I was leaving Steve, I'd spoken to the vicar of the local church I regularly attended. After chatting about attempting to salvage the marriage, he realised I was determined to leave, so decided to help. He mentioned a crèche in the city that cared for children of single parents, and suggested I talk to the matron. So with my two small children, I visited the crèche. The matron asked lots of questions, including why I was leaving my husband and where I intended to live. I felt totally intimidated by this no-nonsense, severe woman who didn't speak to the children as they sat quietly next to me. After what seemed an interminable amount of time, she suggested I could leave the children while I looked for work. She also said that until I had a position, she wouldn't charge me.

I'd started leaving the children at the crèche the week before I found the flat. This was possible because Steve left early for work and rarely came home until late. He wasn't interested in what I did. I visited employment agencies and organised interviews from advertisements in the paper. The employment agencies insisted on me doing tests, which made me quite nervous. I had to either answer written questions, or complete actual typing or comptometer tests. My typing, which I disliked, was accurate but slow, so I was hoping for a comptometer position. However, I knew I must take anything that was offered.

At the end of each day I collected my children, and the unsmiling matron would ask, 'Have you got a job yet?'

'No, but I have several interviews tomorrow,' I would reply.

The matron would sniff and walk away. I think she felt I wasn't trying hard enough, and was perhaps leaving my children with her so that I could go and have a good time.

However, towards the end of the second week, some of the interviews looked promising. When I'd got the flat, I'd asked Meryl whether I could use the address for any notification of jobs. The Friday before I was due to move, the phone rang.

'Jenny, this is Meryl Strand. Four telegrams have arrived. Would you like me to read them?'

'They're probably to do with jobs. Yes please.'

I'd been offered four positions. Over the previous fortnight

I'd found somewhere for my children to be minded, a place to live, and now had been offered four jobs. I thanked Meryl and told her I'd see her the next day, which was when I was due to move in.

Two of the jobs entailed taking a tram, as they were quite a distance from the Exhibition Street crèche, whereas it was a short walk to a position at ICI. It was a much longer walk to Cheney's, a car company, but I decided to take up their offer. The ICI job was typing, whereas Cheney's was a comptometer position and paid one dollar more per week. With the weekly wage being only forty-six dollars, every dollar counted. I rang, accepted the position, and was told to commence on Monday.

On Saturday, after Steve left in the Doughnut wagon, I started packing clothes and other things from my bedroom. I'd been quietly packing during the week, hiding cases and boxes under Lauren's bed and in Vanessa's room. Lyn, my cousin's wife, arrived and helped me pack my precious crockery and what I needed from the kitchen. I'd been to a solicitor, who advised me that I could take furniture and chattels from the house, but that I must leave a bed, linen, crockery and enough furniture for Steve to be comfortable. This meant I didn't have a bed, so I'd have to sleep on the lounge until Neil, my cousin, could transport the bed settee that Mum wasn't using.

The moving van arrived, and while furniture and boxes were packed into it, Lyn and I furiously kept packing crockery, wrapping each piece in newspaper so it would not break. The removalist was so impressed with the efficiency and speed of our packing that he offered us both a job! I had butterflies in my stomach because I was worried that Steve might arrive home unexpectedly. Once everything was in the van, Lyn piled Lauren and Vanessa into her car. She'd offered to mind the children while I went to the flat and supervised the removalist.

Once everyone had left, I wandered through the house that had been my home for five years. Now the house was almost empty. I looked out the kitchen window, through which I'd watched rabbits in fields, feeding in the early morning and at dusk; now the land was covered with homes. My thoughts returned to buying the land, building the house, and the dreams I once held. Now I was leaving it all.

I locked the front door and put the few pot plants from the verandah into the boot of my car. I turned and looked at my home. My chest tightened, and with a lump in my throat, I wondered whether I would ever enter my home again. Probably not. I was starting a new life, with new challenges. I drove away without looking back.

Fortunately the furniture removalist was extremely patient. I was accustomed to much larger rooms. I kept asking him to move the furniture from one place to another. The kitchen was so tiny that once the fridge was in position, I had to stand at the side of the oven to open the door. When the removalist left, I started unpacking. I knew it would be a big shock for the girls when they discovered they were living somewhere else and without their father. I wanted everything unpacked and in place before they arrived. I knew I would have to take care explaining why we'd moved and in helping them with their new lives.

Late in the evening, Lyn arrived. The girls were both sleepy and didn't notice their surroundings. I quickly put Vanessa in her cot and Lauren in her own bed, and they dozed off almost immediately. I settled on the couch in the lounge room. It would be a week or two before Neil could borrow a truck to transport the bed settee from Mum's, then I'd share the bedroom with the girls. I tried to sleep but couldn't. *What*

would Steve have done when he came home and found me gone?
I hoped he wouldn't find me, because if he did, I knew there'd
be ructions. What was I going to say to Lauren tomorrow?
Vanessa was too young to really understand. The lounge wasn't
meant for sleeping; I couldn't straighten my legs or turn over.
Eventually I dozed.

'Mummy, mummy!' I woke to Lauren's terrified cry. I
jumped up and ran into the bedroom. She was climbing out of
bed, but Vanessa was still sleeping.

'How's my favourite girl?' Lauren ran to me and I swept her
up in her arms, hugging her tightly.

'Where's Daddy? Where's here?'

I said nothing, just kept cuddling her.

'Mummy, I want Daddy.'

'Darling, this is our new house. There's a big backyard for
you to play in. It has a big tree in it. Daddy's going to live in
our other house, and you and Mummy and Vanessa are going
to live here.'

'But I want to live with Daddy too,' Lauren sobbed.

'I know you do, Lauren. But Mummy and Daddy can't live
together anymore.'

I continued to cuddle her. How could I make it right when
she was not going to live with her father anymore? She couldn't
understand; she was three years old. She loved her father. She
loved helping him in the garden and she loved spending time
with him in the doughnut wagon

'When will I see Daddy?'

'Soon … I'm sure it'll be soon. Let's have some brekkie.'
I put her down and led her into the kitchen. I had brought a
small table, and the toaster was sitting on it.

Lauren started to cry.

'You've taken the toaster … Daddy won't be able to cook any toast.'

I didn't know what to say. I picked her up, sat down, and nursed her. Once she settled, I organised breakfast for both the children. The move didn't appear to affect Vanessa; she sat in her high chair, happily munching her toast.

Later that morning, I took the children across the road and over a small bridge to a park. Watching them laughing and playing together, I realised Lauren, for a time, had forgotten about her father. I sat on a bench and thought about what I'd done. The girls needed a father, but if I'd stayed they would have faced a similar life to what I'd experienced: a life of uncertainty, and physical and emotional abuse, which would eventually affect them. I was not prepared for them to be exposed to the kind of experiences my brother and I had been through in our childhood. I realised I must learn to support myself financially and be the sole protector of my children. My mother would help where she could, but male support would be non-existent, because I couldn't depend on David. I didn't know what the future held, but I'd fight in every way I could to ensure my children had a better childhood than the one I'd had. I remembered when I was a little girl, and my father telling me that the grape vine must be nurtured or it will fail to thrive. If it is pruned at the wrong time, it will bleed. He never seemed to realise his children were just like the vine. My only goal now was to nurture my children so they thrived. I was determined that they would have all the opportunities possible. Somehow they would have the education they deserved, which would allow them to be who they wanted to be.

It was a new beginning, and tomorrow I was starting work, which was scary. Because I hadn't worked for so long,

I was nervous and apprehensive. The position was in the accounts division, and I knew I'd have to crank up my speed on the comptometer. But at least I didn't have to worry about remembering the conversion tables now that we had decimal currency. I sighed.

I stood up and called the girls; it was time for Vanessa's afternoon nap. Lauren enjoyed me reading her a story while Vanessa was sleeping, and it was a special time for us. I vowed I'd try to continue doing all the things I'd done with the children before we moved, so that they would experience as little disturbance as possible.

Sleep eluded me again that night, and when the alarm rang at six the next morning, I felt I hadn't gone to sleep. Slowly I rose, showered and dressed. Then I woke Lauren, who had wet the bed. Not surprising I suppose. It had been six months since she'd wet the bed, and she no longer wore a nappy at night. *Oh no, my first day*, I thought. *I'll have to bath her now; how am I going to leave here by half past seven?* I picked up a still-sleepy Lauren, and pulled the bedclothes back. *I'll have to change the bed tonight.*

'Come on sweetheart, we'll have a quick bath. Mummy has to go to work today and you're going to the crèche. You can play with the other children, and you love the sandpit.'

'I don't want to go to crèche. I want to see Daddy.'

'Sweetie, remember we talked about Mummy having to go to work? You told me you like it when you go to crèche.'

'But I don't want to go today. I want you to stay home.'

I undressed Lauren and put her in the bath. A quick wash and she was out, dried and into her clothes. She wondered what had happened; usually we played in the bath for ages.

I woke Vanessa, changed her nappy, laid her on the floor

and gave her the morning bottle while I organised breakfast. Bottle finished, I dressed her and lifted her into the high chair, and gave both the children their cereal. I grabbed a piece of toast and a cup of coffee, and put them on the mantelpiece while I did my hair in front of the mirror. I looked at my watch; it was twenty-five past seven. I couldn't be late on my first day. Quickly I hustled the girls out the door and around to the car. I had never driven along Barkers Road in peak-hour traffic, and although I'd allowed plenty of time to get to the city, I began to wonder if I'd make it. There was a car park next door to the crèche, and the charges were reasonable (eighty cents per day), so I parked the car there and took the children in.

While I'd been looking for a job, the children had been quite happy when I dropped them off at crèche. Today was different. The crèche had three rooms: the back room catered for babies to eighteen months, toddlers were in the middle room, and the big room at the front was for three to five years. First, with Lauren, I took Vanessa to the back room. The mothercraft nurse took the bottle I'd made up the previous evening, and I put Vanessa's belongings on her peg. She settled without any trouble. Lauren was holding my hand and wouldn't let go. I said nothing.

I kissed Vanessa goodbye, and Lauren and I walked back to the big front room. We went to the cloakroom and I put Lauren's things on her peg. Each child's peg had a picture on it so they could remember which was theirs.

'Lauren, this is your peg … your book is in your bag … when you want it, just look for the snail. Okay?' Lauren held on tighter. I bent down and gave her a hug. 'I'm going to work now, but I'll be back at five o'clock. That will be after rest time and during story time. Okay?' Lauren said nothing. 'Come and sit at the table with Nursie … you can do some painting.'

There was still no answer from Lauren. I led her to the table and sat her down. The nurse came up, sat next to Lauren and started to talk to her. I kissed Lauren, said goodbye and walked to the door. As I reached it, there was an awful scream.

'Mummy, mummy!' she cried. 'Mummy, mummy, don't go!'

Matron had already laid down the law to me about what to do if my children were upset. 'You kiss them goodbye, tell them what time you will return, and then keep going out the door without turning back.' She told all the mothers that if they left without making a fuss, the upset children settled much quicker. She also said, 'Make sure you are back when you say—no excuses.'

I continued walking out the door, my heart pounding. All I wanted to do was turn back and comfort my daughter. I walked the full length of Exhibition Street to Flinders Lane, where Cheney's was located, with the sound of my daughter's voice in my ears. I was a mess, and certainly not in the right frame of mind for commencing a new job. The office was dark and shabby, the desks old and rough, the toilets disgusting, and the girls were afraid to speak for fear the supervisor would reprimand them. It was a dreadful atmosphere—so different from Kraft, where the office had been spacious and bright, and the girls could talk and have a little joke as they worked. During lunch, as I walked along Flinders Street, I decided I couldn't return. I'd chosen Cheney's because of the extra money, and I hadn't rung the other places to say I wasn't taking the positions. I had intended to do it in my lunch hour that day. The job at ICI was typing, but it was quite close to the crèche. I found a phone box and rang to accept the position. This was quite acceptable, given the telegram had only been sent on the Friday. I was asked to commence the next day.

I returned to the crèche, where Matron, with a severe expression, asked what I was doing back at lunch time. I explained, but it was clear that either she didn't approve, or didn't believe me. I picked up the children, much to Lauren's delight, and we went home and spent the afternoon together.

The next day, when I left the crèche for my first day at ICI, it was a repeat of the day before. It tore at my heart to hear Lauren's distraught sobs as I went out the door. I walked up the hill to my new job, with a heavy heart and misty eyes. I was quite apprehensive. Would the position be better than Cheney's? Would I be capable?

I found out that my position as a teleprinter operator and clerk was in Commercial Services. The company was split into independent groups and monitored by Corporate Management to ensure the company's policies, rules and ideals were adhered too. I'd never seen a teleprinter, and at my interview I had said I could type but didn't have a lot of speed. The interviewer had said accuracy was more important than speed.

I was introduced to my boss, Ken Carey, whose office was on the seventh floor. He was a pleasant man, and quickly put me at ease. After explaining the requirements of the job, he took me to the second floor, where the teleprinter was located. There were two full-time operators but the section was being expanded, Ken explained. Two extra people were being employed, and they would divide their time between clerical duties and operating the teleprinter. The teleprinter transmitted customers' orders from the different ICI groups to the factories at Deer Park, Ascot Vale and Laverton.

Ken introduced me to Mary Roades, my supervisor. This prim and proper older woman with greying red hair had high expectations, and her word was law. Judy, the other operator, was quiet and just kept working. Val—a shy, unassuming girl—had also commenced that day, in the same role as me. She was returning to work after several years at home looking after her little boy. Val needed to work, as her husband had recently been gaoled for culpable driving. She found the changes in her life difficult to cope with. We formed a close bond, not only because we worked together, but also because we had both recently become single parents.

Val and I spent each morning doing clerical duties, while Mary and Judy operated the teleprinters. In the afternoon, Val and I used Judy's teleprinter, taking it in turns while she worked in the mailroom. On my first day, Mary asked me to come and type some orders. I was quite nervous; I knew my typing skills weren't great. I hadn't typed for several years, and only had minimal experience.

Mary explained how to put the teleprinter online to a particular factory and then gave me a pile of orders to send. I plodded along, making quite a few mistakes, and broke out in a sweat when I felt Mary's eyes upon me. At five o'clock, she stood up and looked severely at me.

'Well, all I can say is you're very slow and you'll need to improve quickly.' She packed up her desk and left.

Val looked at me and grimaced.

'Heaven knows what she'll say to me tomorrow,' I said.

'You'll be okay ... she's a bit of a tyrant though ...'

I was in a cold sweat. 'I can't afford to lose this job. Hope she doesn't say anything to Mr Carey.'

'She's tough. I don't think she's happy about us,' Val said.

'I don't think so either. See you tomorrow ... got to go!'

I hurried down the hill to pick up my children. I'd missed them terribly, and the memory of Lauren's cries that morning had haunted me. I arrived to find her happily playing in the sandpit. She had loved her sandpit in our old home, and I was glad there was one here for her. When she saw me, she ran over and grabbed my hand.

'Come and see what I've built! Nursie helped me.' Smiling, she dragged me to the sandpit. I couldn't believe the change in my little girl from this morning.

'How long did it take her to settle?' I asked the mothercraft nurse.

'A little while, but it'll get easier each day. Once she settled, she was fine. She's played with the other children quite contently, and she also had a good sleep this afternoon.'

'Thanks, I really appreciate it.' I smiled at the nurse and turned back to the sandpit, where Lauren was squatting in the sand, 'Come on Lauren, let's go and get Vanessa and we'll go home.'

Nevertheless, the ritual was the same the next morning. Lauren screamed as I left, and once again it wrenched me. The last thing I wanted to do was leave her so upset. It took three weeks before Lauren happily waved goodbye to me, confident that I would return.

In one week, Lauren had lost her father and the only home she had ever known. She was now living in new surroundings, she was in a crèche with unfamiliar children and with strangers looking after her, and her mother was gone during the day. It was too much for a three-year-old to cope with. If I could have done it any other way, I would have.

I gradually settled into my new life. It took some time before I was comfortable with my job, my surroundings, driving to the crèche each day, and the hardest thing—leaving my children. But slowly things came together and I began to relish my freedom. I no longer had to worry about what would happen when Steve came home. I had a job, which provided money I could control, which in turn allowed me to support my children. I had routine and was not constantly under stress. I was a better mum. I was fortunate that my mum supported me wholeheartedly and helped where she could. She made clothes for the girls, who always looked neat and tidy.

I purposely had not told my mother my new address, because I hoped if she didn't know it, she wouldn't be abused by Steve. I kept in touch by phone but didn't visit her, because I thought Steve might watch her place. After about six weeks I felt it was safe to visit. The children were excited that we were going to Nanna's, and we had a great time together. After dinner I drove home and put the children to bed. The next morning there was a knock on the door, and looking through the window, I saw Steve. The children of course wanted to see their dad, but I wouldn't let him in. I was afraid he would grab them and take off. Once before, he'd taken off with Lauren when she was six months old. When I sought police help, they told me that Lauren was Steve's child too, and that they couldn't do anything unless I had a custody order. As I still didn't have a custody order, I wasn't going to take the risk of Steve taking off with the children. He spoke to Lauren and Vanessa through the window, telling them their cat Tammy was missing them. Very thoughtful of him!

I asked Steve how he had found me, and he said my brother had been staking out Mum's place since I had left home. My brother had said to Steve, 'She'll turn up at Mum's; nothing's surer … then we'll find out where she lives.' I was appalled at my brother's lack of loyalty. Steve eventually left after we agreed that he could see the children on a regular basis. I knew this would be good for the girls, but I wondered whether he would really turn up. What he said and what he did were two different things.

A couple of months later, I experienced my first Christmas as a single mum, and it is a memory I have treasured ever since. Money was scarce, but my children were young and quite happy with simple things. During the lunch hours leading up to Christmas, I had a wonderful time searching for small toys the children would enjoy. We had arranged to have Christmas lunch at Mum's. Ever since I'd been married, we had always had it at my place. I had felt Mum had been doing Christmas long enough, and I enjoyed the preparation and organisation. But that year, I couldn't do it because the flat was too small, and I just couldn't afford to pay for everything I would need to host Christmas.

On Christmas Eve, Lauren and I left some cake—which I'd baked especially—and a soft drink for Santa on the kitchen table.

'Mummy, how's Santa going to get in? There's no chimney.' Lauren looked puzzled as she placed the drink on the Christmas placemat.

'Mrs Strand's leaving the porch door open. He'll come in that way and he can visit her children too. I'll leave the kitchen door ajar as well.'

Lauren was satisfied. The children hung their stockings up on the mantelpiece and put their pillowcases at the end of their beds. Lauren said her prayers and then hopped into bed. Vanessa fell asleep quickly, but Lauren was excited—I could hear her singing while I sat in the lounge room. As a child, I used to sing to myself and rock to and fro in bed because I found it hard to settle. I was always waiting for the loud voices and the horrible noises. Eventually Lauren drifted off. A couple of my girlfriends lived close by, and they called in for a drink and to help me fill the pillowcases. They didn't have children and were keen to be involved. They brought surprises of their own and popped them into the pillowcases, and for this I was very grateful. As we piled the toys into the pillowcases and filled the stockings with lollies, we reminisced about Santa visiting us when we were small children.

On Christmas morning I woke early and lay in bed, watching my two daughters sleeping. Vanessa lay on her back, in her cot, arms and legs stretched to the sides. Lauren looked ever so tiny in her bed, lying on her side with her knees near her tummy. The sun's rays patterned the wall above Lauren's bed, and I felt totally at peace lying there, as I eagerly waited for my children to wake. I willed the children to open their eyes and discover their bulging pillowcases. They slept on. After a while I couldn't wait any longer, and gently called Lauren. She turned on to her back and stretched. I waited. All of a sudden, she sat up abruptly. The look of amazement and wonder on her face was something I'd never forget. This first reaction, when a child wakes on Christmas morning, is something few parents experience. I knew I would treasure this early morning wonder for the rest of my life. I felt extremely privileged and very happy.

'Vanessa, wake up! Santa's been!' cried Lauren. She then crawled to the end of her bed and pulled at the bulging pillowcase. The look of wonder continued as she pulled out a baby doll. 'Mummy, Santa brought me the doll I wanted!' Lauren hugged the doll and then continued emptying the pillowcase.

Vanessa had crawled to the end of the cot and was emptying her pillowcase. I sat enthralled. Lauren came across, dragging the pillowcase with a few things still in it, and hopped into my bed. Standing in her cot, Vanessa made it plain she wanted to join us. I clambered out of bed, picked up my youngest and her still-full pillowcase, and sat her next to Lauren on the end of the bed. I hopped back into bed and helped the children explore their presents. Very excited, they spent the next hour playing with the pillowcases' contents.

We had breakfast and then I put the new dress that Santa had brought on Vanessa, while Lauren put on her new dress with minimal assistance. We went to Mum's for lunch. Everyone was there: my aunt and uncle; David, Kerry and Robbie; and of course Mum. It was a wonderful day, and brought back memories of my childhood Christmases. I remembered my mother working so hard and no-one helping her. This Christmas we all helped with the dishing up and washing up. Mum was a lot happier than the Mum I remembered from my childhood Christmases. Robbie, Lauren and Vanessa played with their toys, and were boisterous as they ran around the house. At lunch everyone pulled bon-bons, and put on the Christmas hats that were found inside. The family was together, and we were at peace with each other. Steve was the only one missing. I had tried several times to arrange for him to see the children, but he either made excuses or just didn't turn up. Lauren would wait at the front gate, swinging back and forth on it. She just couldn't understand why her daddy didn't come. It broke my heart. Today she didn't seem to miss her father; she didn't even ask why he wasn't there.

16

The plane lurches to the right as its wheels hit the tarmac. *That'll be the crosswinds the captain mentioned.*

The steward's voice comes over the intercom: 'Please keep your seatbelts fastened until we have come to a complete stop. Thank you.'

I close my notebook, where I have been making a few jottings about Mum. What I've written seems clinical, and possibly the start of a eulogy, but it is the only way I can handle what is happening. I cannot comprehend life without her. She is the one person who has always thought I was okay. Brushing a hand across my face, I look out the window.

Mark moves quickly towards me as I enter the gate lounge. He puts his arms around me, squeezing me tight. I look at him, my husband of nearly twenty years: so supportive, and yet, over the last few years, so distant.

'How is she?' I whisper. I seem to have lost my voice.

'Failing, love … she hasn't got much time.'

'What happened? Last night you all said she was alright.'

'She was. It's been quite sudden. Lauren went to the hospital this morning and realised she was sliding away.' Mark leads me along the walkway and down the escalator.

We wait for what seems like an age, until finally Mark grabs the bag off the carousel and we make our way to the car. After driving along the freeway, we turn off, but seem to be travelling forever.

Agitated, I ask, 'Where are we? This isn't the usual way.'

'I thought this'd be quicker.'

'Well, it isn't. How much longer?' I retort.

'Not long,' Mark replies quietly.

'Has anyone let David know?'

'Yes. Lauren rang him this morning, at the same time we were organising to get you home.

'Well I guess he's already at the hospital.'

'Maybe.'

David and I used to be so close, but we have grown completely apart over the last twenty years. I miss the times we had together when our children were little. I always supported him, even when I felt he was not treating Kerry right. But let's face it, Kerry enjoyed creating a situation. Where has the David gone who visited me every weekend after Lauren was born? What dramas Mum and I experienced with those two …

*

'Sis, she's left me. I've been everywhere. She's not at her Mum's … that's where she usually goes. Normally I just grovel a bit and she comes home. She's taken Robbie. I don't care about her, but I've got to get him back.'

'You've spoken to her Mum?'

'Yeah … she's saying nothing.'

David drove to Dromana over the following days and kept watch on Kerry's Mum's house. He expected Kerry would turn up, but she didn't. However, one day he saw the postie deliver the mail, and it dawned on him that if Kerry wasn't visiting her Mum, perhaps they were contacting each other by letter. That night he returned to the Dromana house and searched the rubbish bin.

He arrived at my place late, with a letter torn into small pieces. We stayed up until the early hours piecing it together. Eventually we had enough pieces in place to realise Kerry was staying with relatives in Broadbeach. David left immediately and drove to Queensland. He decided he'd get there quicker if he didn't stop to sleep. Each time he stopped for petrol, he'd wet a towel and put it around his neck to keep him awake. Once he took time to have a shower. However, lack of sleep took its toll, and close to his destination, he had an accident that left his car undrivable.

David made his way to the address he'd discovered in the letter. In the front garden he found his toddler son playing with a bucket of water. Without thinking, David grabbed him and took off, catching a train back to Melbourne. He returned to live with Mum and realised that although he was now solely responsible for his son, he still had to work. Mum did what she could, but she was working full-time, so David sought my help.

I was in two minds. I was struggling, coping with life on my own, and David hadn't been supportive when I most needed it—in fact quite the opposite. So I wasn't really predisposed to helping him.

On the other hand, Kerry was young and irresponsible, and I feared for Robbie's wellbeing. Mum made it clear she felt Robbie would be better off with David and being supported by our family, so I agreed to help. My children had been at the crèche for six months, and I'd come to know Matron quite well. In fact, she lived close to me and I was now giving her a lift in the mornings. I approached her and she agreed to enrol Robbie at the crèche. David started work early, so he asked me if I'd take Robbie to crèche, pick him up at night and bring him to his work. There seemed to be no alternative; I agreed, but this just made my life more difficult. David would get Robbie out of his cot and drive to my place. Now I had an extra child to dress and feed before I left at seven thirty. It wasn't easy, as I couldn't be late for work—Mary would not tolerate it.

At crèche, I'd settle all three children; Robbie was in the same room as Vanessa, so they were company for each other. At night I picked them up and drove along Victoria Parade to David's workplace in Richmond.

'Dadda! Dadda!' Robbie would excitedly yell and point when he saw the 'Skipping Girl' neon sign that stood above the vinegar factory. He knew he would soon see his father. I'd hand Robbie over to David and continue the drive home.

David took the role of being a sole parent seriously, and when he wasn't working, he spent all his time with his son. There was never any expectation that Mum or I would mind Robbie while David socialised. Often he would arrive at my place with Robbie in tow, and the children would all play together while we had a coffee. The flat was small, so we often walked to the nearby park. The children would rush around playing hide and seek while we talked. David and I became quite close. Sometimes he stayed for dinner, but would return to Mum's soon after to put Robbie to bed.

David wasn't sure what he was going to do, and sought legal advice. He discussed at length with me the options suggested by the solicitors. He wanted to keep Robbie, but knew this would be difficult. Of course he still had money troubles, and legal advice was expensive. Once again Mum financed him. She still worked at the Royal Women's Hospital and was now a full-time clinical teacher. She loved her job, and it provided the security she'd sought for so many years. Now she controlled her own money and spent it as she wished. She enjoyed travelling, and this was where most of her money had been channelled—but now she had to pay legal fees for her son. She loved her grandson dearly, and this was the catalyst for her agreeing to pay. My mother replaced my father and became my brother's financier, which in the long run did not help him.

Robbie settled into the routine of going to the crèche each day, and he and Vanessa were inseparable. They continually got into mischief together, but had lots of fun. Kerry continued to live with her mother.

Every Saturday during the next few months, David and I drove Robbie to Dromana to see his mother. We dropped him off, returned to Melbourne, and then drove back the same day to pick the child up. My Austin A40 had only lasted three months, and I needed a car to get the children to crèche. My solicitor organised a loan, and I bought an old Morris Minor for $400. I didn't want to be travelling back and forth to Dromana each weekend wearing it out, but David's car was still in Queensland.

Clearly we needed to get his car returned to Melbourne and repaired. The company I worked for regularly shipped containers from Queensland to Melbourne. I was able to arrange for David's car to be picked up from where it was stored, then have it put into a container and shipped to Melbourne. This took quite a bit of organising, and it was over a month before it arrived. It was a costly exercise, with Mum once again footing the bill. David never had any money in reserve.

Kerry's and David's respective solicitors continued their dialogue, because each parent wanted custody of Robbie. He was such a cute little boy, and both parents and their families loved him dearly, but a decision had to be made about who would look after him on a full-time basis. Consideration was given to shared custody, but with Kerry living in Dromana, this wasn't practical. Kerry and David both wanted their son on a full-time basis, but finally it was agreed that Robbie would live with his mother and see David on weekends. David was devastated, but understood that if they didn't agree and it went to court, Kerry, being the mother, would most probably get custody. This was the usual outcome at that time. The solicitors documented the agreement between Kerry and David, and David handed Robbie over.

Each week, with David's car still not repaired, we picked up Robbie from Dromana and returned him the same day. Kerry refused to let David have Robbie overnight, and David couldn't afford more legal fees. David felt he had been duped.

The next step was for Kerry to apply for maintenance. Mum and I had no idea how David was going to be able to pay maintenance for both Kerry and the little boy, because he continued to be in a great deal of debt. Mum realised she would never see the money she had lent David for the legal fees. He just didn't have the ability to pay, what with all his other debts. David set off to Dromana for the hearing in the Magistrates' Court.

Late that evening, when David returned full of beans, we were flabbergasted to discover that he and Kerry had decided to give their marriage another go. They had got together before the hearing and had a long, animated discussion while their solicitors stood by. What was the deciding factor for Kerry to agree to return? I will never know. I'm guessing David would have used his powers of persuasion, convincing her he was cash-poor. Also she probably didn't want to remain in Dromana with her mother indefinitely.

Supporting David over the last six months had been stressful for everyone, and now he was returning to the person that he had said—so many times—he despised and didn't respect. Mum washed her hands of them. Kerry continued to goad David with her immature attitude, and David returned to drinking. The marriage remained dysfunctional.

David's career was a different matter. He had stopped driving trucks not long after he met Kerry, and had become a salesman. He was selling sewing machines door to door in the country when Robbie was born, and later moved on to selling cars. David inherited our father's and grandfather's entrepreneurial skills, and like Dad, was exceptionally good at selling. He soon had his own car yard, and before long a second. His main obsession was to make money, and this was achieved in any way he could manage. He often cheerfully referred to the 'wood-ducks': the people he took advantage of when they were buying a car. Clients would come into his yard and David immediately sensed whether he could rip them off—and rip them off he did. They would pay way in excess of the real value, and because of David's 'salesmanship', they left thinking they had a good deal.

He continued gambling heavily, which sometimes boosted his pockets. One day he arrived on my doorstep.

'Hi Sis, what do you think of it? Pretty cool, hey?'

'Where did that come from?'

'Won it in a card game.'

'A Rolls-Royce, in a card game … I'm not buying that!'

'Believe me, I did … it was an all-nighter … the guy was stupid … kept losing but wouldn't give up. Come for a spin?'

Before me was this shiny navy-and-beige limousine. I had never driven in anything so luxurious, but it really wasn't my scene. I was more comfortable with simple things, and still didn't think I deserved anything out of the ordinary. I hopped in, and David accelerated at great speed along Stanhope Grove.

'David, slow down!'

'Gotta show you what it can do … amazing.' He was ecstatic, boasting continually as he drove the streets of Camberwell.

However, he lost nearly as often as he won, and indeed sometime later he lost the Rolls in another card game. One day, an agitated Kerry arrived to say David had lost their bedroom furniture that Mum had given them. The first she had known about it was when a removalist's van arrived.

The income from the two car yards allowed David to build a large two-storey home with all the trimmings. Kerry was now in her element, and felt superior to everyone. Her supposed higher status did not change her rudeness or vulgar language. They had lived in less than ideal conditions throughout their marriage, moving constantly from flat to flat. Now they were financially stable, but they didn't know how to deal with it. Kerry threw money around, buying expensive jewellery, and I became quite envious of the things she bought for her children and her home. I was struggling month to month, but owed money to no-one and paid my bills on time. Kerry and David still accrued debts and avoided paying. Although now financially well-off, David never repaid Mum the accumulated debts of the past.

David managed the car yard at Richmond, and a so-called mate managed the yard at Sunshine. Unfortunately David trusted the Sunshine manager and gave him autonomy. The business went into receivership after a couple of years, and David was once again in financial trouble. His house was sold.

Fortunately, after his business debts were resolved, he still had some equity. David had become known in the car business, and realised he needed to look for another enterprise.

Although he had always lived in the city, he enjoyed the relaxed lifestyle that he experienced when he was selling sewing machines in the country, and when he went to Foster with Steve. This prompted him to look for a business away from Melbourne, and he came up with the idea of buying a motel. Kerry wasn't keen, but David was determined, and decided to buy the Coach House Motel in Bairnsdale. It was weatherboard, small and run-down. Because it was the first motel in town and was over three hours from Melbourne, it had potential. Kerry was on the verge of leaving David once again, but finally decided to give it a go. Now that they had a second child who was nine months old, she knew she wouldn't be able to cope on her own.

David took over the motel and immediately set about improving it. He created a new façade with a large, modern, brick restaurant hiding the weatherboard units. The motel immediately took on a modern look. Good, classy restaurants were pretty much non-existent in Bairnsdale, and David saw the possibilities. Not only did the restaurant bring in clientele from the town and surrounds, but now the motel presented well, and the units started to be booked out each night. David continued improving the property. He landscaped, painted, built extra units and was in his element. He loved the outdoors, and like his father he was quite a handyman and enjoyed working with tools. However, he was not a paperwork man, and managing the books fell to Kerry. She had worked in an office, but only as a receptionist; she didn't know much about bookkeeping, but learned the hard way, making mistakes along the way.

The motel thrived, with David continually inventing ways

of making more money. He decided he wanted to promote his restaurant as a seafood restaurant, so a few weeks before Christmas he had 500 live lobsters flown in from Western Australia. David felt that the lobsters would be a winner for the office Christmas parties and Christmas Day lunch and dinner. He ordered a large tank to hold some of the lobsters and installed it in the restaurant. The plan was that people would be given the opportunity to choose the lobster they wanted for their meal. The waiter would extract the lobster from the tank and take it to the kitchen to be prepared. In reality a lobster from the freezer would be cooked, while the live lobster wandered around the kitchen until it was returned to the tank later.

The lobsters, very much alive, arrived in three huge chaff bags that were left on the floor of the restaurant kitchen. The bags were not secured, and lobsters started to wander everywhere, with the chefs side-stepping the critters as they worked at preparing elaborate food. It was a comical scene: lobsters like mechanical robots, walking backwards around the crowded kitchen, and kitchen staff skipping around to avoid them. The kitchen was large but full of equipment, stainless steel benches, shelves and cupboards, so there was little wasted space. David had ordered the tank for the restaurant, but had forgotten to get a freezer to store the lobsters. Chaos reigned. The motel's handyman was promptly sent to pick up a rented freezer. Unfortunately the project didn't have the expected success. The cost of the lobster meal was prohibitive to the country folk, and most of the lobsters sat in the freezer until they spoiled and had to be thrown away.

The Coach House was the first of many motels for David, mostly situated interstate. He had the knack of visualising what could be done with a run-down motel. He would renovate it, work in it for a while, and sell it at a hefty profit. He continued to have little respect for his wife, or any woman, and became more like my father as the years rolled on. He drank to excess, threw his money around, and anyone who got in his way would be abused both emotionally and physically. Although Kerry gave back as good as she got, I felt sorry for her. Her life was far from easy and, to an extent, it was a replica of Mum's. Living the life he was and being interstate, David drifted away, and we rarely had any contact. Mum missed him terribly, and never ceased to give up hope, or love, for her son.

My memories of David are sad. I believe that the little boy became the man he is because of the childhood trauma he experienced, and because he followed my father's example of what it means to be a man.

17

Parking is always a problem outside the hospital, and today is no exception. Mark keeps circling the streets; I just want to go inside. Usually he lets me out while he parks, but today he wants to be with me. Finally we find a spot and I breathe a sigh of relief. The path leading to the hospital entrance is flanked on either side by colourful shrubs and perennials. A large number of people—some patients, some visitors—are congregated outside. A few are sitting or standing forlornly, staring into space, while groups of others appear to be in animated conversation, cigarette smoke wafting around them.

The floor-to-ceiling sliding doors open, and we walk down the busy hallway to the lifts—something I have done so often during the last three months. *This'll be my last time.* When we arrive at nine-west ward, Mark leads me to a different room from the one my mother was in before I left for Sydney.

I enter the room and see the green hat covering my mother's head. *Why that awful thing? Where's her navy hat?* At the foot of the bed are my two adult daughters and a beautiful array of flowers. Vanessa has thoughtfully placed them where her nanna can see them. During the last month, from her hospital bed, Mum has basically seen only grey and white. No green trees, blue sky, flowerbeds, or all the magnificent things nature provides. The room is neither bright nor pleasant. The white, clinical walls are bare, with cracks running down from the ceiling, and the paint is peeling. My mother is in this room to allow the family privacy, and so that other patients are not in the vicinity of someone dying.

I slowly make my way to the bed. Mum's eyes are closed. My throat is tight, as if I'm about to choke. I bend down. 'Mum, I'm here; it's Jenny.'

She opens her eyes. She looks at Vanessa and Lauren at the end of the bed, and Mark and me beside her. 'I love you all … I love you very much.' As her eyes close, it is as if a blind is drawn across her face.

The doctor enters and beckons me outside.

'I believe you're Mrs Wilding's daughter?'

'Yes, I'm Jenny Yates.'

'I'm Dr Stroud, the registrar. I'd like to update you on your mother's condition. As well as her other problems, she's now developed a clot on the lung. It won't be long.' The doctor pauses and then says, 'Have you any questions?'

That's pretty cold-blooded. 'No,' I reply.

'If you need me, I'll be at the ward desk.'

'Thank you,' I murmur, and return to my mother's room. 'Where's David? Thought you said you called him early this morning, Mark?'

'We rang him, Mum,' Vanessa replies. 'He said he'd come. We thought he'd fly … he must be driving.'

'If you rang this morning he should be here. It's six o'clock, and it's only five hours' drive from Wagga.'

How will David cope if he misses Mum? I remember when Dad died, David took off and we didn't see him for twenty-four hours. For all his bravado, aggressiveness and bad temper, he has never been able to cope with feelings. He just buries them, puts them out of sight, and fills his life with money and drink. He can't help but feel guilty about the way he's treated Mum—he's hardly communicated with her these last few years.

I sit close to the bed. My mother is slightly elevated on crisp white pillows, and her once rounded and bosomy frame looks tiny. Her expressionless face, with its fine wrinkled skin, is pale and seems naked without her large round glasses framing her tiny eyes. The few wisps of hair escaping from that ridiculous hat are no longer fair but grey. She is tapping her index and middle fingers on the bed. Over the years, the constant tapping on tables and other surfaces used to drive me mad, but now the tapping on the bed is a comfort. She tries to say something, but it is garbled. The nurse mentions that another dose of morphine is sometimes helpful, and can allow the patient to say what they need to say. However, it can also hasten death. I'm desperate to know what my mother is trying to tell me, so agree for the nurse to administer another dose.

I wait. My mother watches me for a while, but says nothing and then closes her eyes. I hold her hand and she occasionally faintly squeezes mine. I put my mouth close to her ear, and whisper how much I love her and how lucky I am to have her. She doesn't speak. I keep talking, as I have heard that hearing is the last sense to go. An hour or so later my mother dies. I'm still holding her hand.

At that moment I feel a presence rise up, like a wisp of smoke, and instantly it is gone.

The others leave the room, but I stay. She seems to be sleeping, and certainly looks at peace. I cuddle her, whisper things to her that I wish I had said when she was alive, and tears slowly trickle down. My mother grew up in the Great

Depression, worked at any job she could find, studied and became a competent nurse, raised my brother and myself, lived with an alcoholic and abusive husband, and then lived on her own for twenty years as an independent woman. She returned to nursing and became a well-regarded clinical teacher at the Royal Women's Hospital. Once retired, she travelled extensively on her own, became passionately involved in lawn bowls, and helped many charities. I look at her and think she cannot just stop existing. The body before me is a shell; it's like the butterfly has left her cocoon and flown on to a new beginning. Eventually I rise and leave the room, knowing I will now be parted from my mother forever.

'Are you ready to go, Mum?' Lauren cuddles me. 'There's no hurry.'

'Yes, I want to go home.'

A man walks by as we make our way slowly towards the lift, and I smell hot chips. The doors open, and there is David. I haven't seen him for more than twelve months, although he has visited Mum once during her three-month hospital stay. My heart lurches. His fair, thinning hair is tousled as if he has been running his fingers through it. He gives me a half-hearted smile.

'Hi Sis. Where's Mum?'

'She's gone mate, about a half an hour ago.' Mark puts his arm protectively around me as David steps out of the lift.

'Aw fuck.' He brushes his hand across his forehead and looks distraught.

'David, you can see her; I'll come with you.' I put my hand out towards David, who immediately backs off.

'Don't know if I want to do that.'

'She's at peace, David. She looks like she is sleeping.' I

take his arm and guide him towards the room. We go in. He just stands dejectedly at the end of the bed, with his hands in his pockets. He reminds me of the little boy he once was. I wonder what he is thinking as he gazes at our mother. She was the strong support that kept our family together … the glue that protected us, nurtured us and guided us. Is this what he's thinking?

'I'll wait outside. Don't hurry,' I say. I sit on the seat in the hall with the family. The door to the corridor continually slides open and shut as people walk by. A few minutes later, a forlorn David joins us. He stands motionless, his head bent, looking at his shoes.

'Well I guess I'll make my way home, Sis.'

'Don't be an ass, David! Come home with us and at least stay the night. You can't drive all the way back now. You're tired and everything.' I put my arm around David but he doesn't respond.

'Come on mate, it's not a good idea to drive home tonight,' says Mark.

After a little more persuasion, David agrees to follow Mark home. Lauren and Vanessa no longer live with us, but have their own apartments, and had caught public transport to the hospital. They have decided between them that they will come home and spend the night. We pile into Mark's car and he waits for David to catch up before setting off.

'You okay, Mum?' Vanessa leans forward from the back seat and places her hand on my shoulder.

'Yes, love … it must be awful for David … not getting here before Mum …'

'You know, Mum … Nanna waited for you. We told her you were coming. She waited.'

'Why didn't she wait a little longer for David?'

'Mum, you know why. Uncle David wouldn't have coped. Nanna knew it.' Vanessa rubs my shoulder. 'Anyway, we told Auntie Kerry that she didn't have long. She inferred that we were dramatising … they didn't take it seriously.'

'Well that must make him feel worse.'

Now there is just David and I left from my family of origin, and we no longer have any relationship. I dearly wish things were different, but I know that my brother really doesn't care or, more probably, doesn't know how to care. He is damaged goods, damaged by my father just as I have been, but David won't face up to it. He just lets it sink deeper and deeper. Like my father, when David loses his temper, everyone around him is frightened. I certainly am. I'm not sure how he will handle not seeing Mum before she died.

The rest of the trip is silent; everyone is lost in their own thoughts. The girls put on a brave face for me, because their loss is great too. Their nanna was special. Vanessa is a nurse, and while her nanna was sick, Vanessa was regularly at her side, bringing soup and meals, and spending time with her to brighten her nanna's day. Lauren is a doctor, and she liaised with the medical team and interacted with the oncologist.

My mind wanders to the recent changes in my family. Mark has distanced himself from me with his own problems. Lauren moved out after her medical studies finished and is planning to travel overseas to further her study and research. The always-supportive Vanessa stayed and worked as a nurse in a local hospital. She and her boyfriend Luke, who I was particularly fond of, had planned to marry. However, Luke's mother died, and although he had graduated as a chemical engineer, he couldn't find a job. He decided to travel, and while he was away in America, the relationship waned. This upset me, because Luke was like a son. Soon after, Vanessa decided to move into a flat with friends. I was shattered.

I became even closer to my mother as she aged, and although she had leukaemia for some years, she was quite active. In the last year she had been unwell. I travelled frequently for my company, and the first inkling of Mum being seriously ill came when I received a message in New Zealand. I spent as much time as I could with her, and she seemed to improve, but before long became ill again. The phone call delivering the cruel message that Mum had liver cancer was like a sword being driven into my heart. Vanessa and I went to the hospital to be with Mum when she received the news.

When Professor Hattam told Mum it was an aggressive cancer, and offered either aggressive chemo treatment or palliative care, she said, 'Well there's no option then, because I want another couple of years. I'll have the treatment.'

My mother's body couldn't take the treatment. The doctor explained it was like a leaky pipe: as you plugged up one hole, another appeared. Throughout the illness, my daughters remained distant but supportive. They were finding their way in the world and their careers. I didn't know what to expect, and continued my day-to-day routine mechanically. Because Lauren was the one interacting with the oncologist, I didn't get to ask the questions I needed answered.

When Mum was hospitalised, I cancelled my planned trip to South Africa, and I never regretted doing so. She was able to come home for about three weeks, and this allowed us to be together. Each morning I would take her breakfast in to her and sit on the end of the bed. This was a very special time. We had wonderful chats; we laughed and reminisced, but avoided matters that we should have discussed. Mum had become quite frail and was using a walking stick; it was all a struggle. I wanted to do everything for her but Vanessa, the nurse, stressed that it was better for Nanna to do what she could for herself.

I sigh. In one short year it appears that my husband has drifted away from me, both my daughters have left home, and my mother has died. My black hole is getting deeper.

As soon as we arrive home, Vanessa puts the kettle on and makes coffee. David leans on the island bar and remains silent.

I wonder whether he regrets distancing himself over the years. I used to believe Kerry had a lot to do with it, but David is his own man—it was his choice. Money was a greater priority. He seemed to be able to smell it; he thrived on taking risks, in being ruthless—and this fostered his success. He never took to Mark either, and I have always felt that was another reason David faded out of our lives. David once said to me, 'Why would any man take on another man's kids?'

My mother loved David so much; he was the apple of her eye, and I guess I was envious. A few years ago, when David was living in Bairnsdale, Mum had to have an operation. I contacted him and said she would dearly love to see him, and—wonder of wonders—he did visit her in hospital. That night when I went in to see Mum, as I did every night, all she could talk about was my brother's visit. 'Jenny, it was so lovely to have him here,' she said. 'He lay on the end of the bed and we just chatted away about everything. It has been a wonderful day.'

I stand up. 'David, tomorrow we'll talk about what's got to be done … not tonight.'

'Sis, I think I'll go home; can't leave Kerry on her own, you know.'

As if he cares about leaving Kerry on her own! She's no shrinking

violet, and can look after herself. Anyway, when did he start caring
so much about Kerry, after the way he has treated her over the years?
He has been just as violent with her as my father was with my
mother. Although it's a little different now: Kerry can certainly stick
up for herself, and he hasn't got so much of a hold over her anymore.

'You've got staff, David; the motel runs itself … you've told
me that heaps of times. Isn't it more important to organise
things for Mum?'

'You can do that, Sis. I'll agree to anything you organise.'

'David, I'd like us to do it together.'

David drains his cup and pushes it across the bench. 'How
about another cuppa for you uncle?' He grins at Vanessa. 'Sis,
you're better at doing this sort of thing.'

I say nothing. He is a businessman; he buys, renovates and
sells motels and hotels right along the east coast. If he can do
that, he can help me arrange our mother's funeral. I'm disgusted.

We move into the lounge and sit down. I feel drained. The
girls are quiet, but David starts talking to Mark as if nothing
has happened. All of a sudden he stands up. 'Have to go … be
in touch.'

'David, you can't drive back now. It's 1 a.m.' says Mark.

'I'm going … I'm used to driving.' He moves to the door
and is gone.

The next day, Mark commences the daunting task of
notifying family and friends of Mum's death, and arranges
for the funeral directors to come to the house. He sits at the
table, phone to his ear, rubbing his index finger across his
mouth and moustache. This is something he has done when
he is engrossed, ever since I met him. He and the girls want
to organise the arrangements to spare me, but I insist on being
involved, welcoming their input. We sit in the lounge and the

funeral director gives me a book containing photos of coffins. The choosing of a coffin from a photo brings home to me the finality of it all. I choose white; I've always disliked the rich rose-coloured coffins, and the light pine doesn't seem right. I request yellow roses. Together we compose the notifications to be inserted into the daily paper. Remembering my father's coffin descending into the ground, I decide on a cremation. I also remember my mother's words from so long ago: 'When I die, don't put me in with your father.' He had organised a double grave when he was alive. I keep in contact with David and ask him if he would speak at the funeral.

'No, Sis … don't think so … whatever you organise is okay by me.'

I'm cross with David that he won't be involved with the funeral arrangements. Then I remember the time my father died. He just disappeared and left it all to Mum and I. I realise he just can't cope and he probably feels guilty. I try to understand.

I'm determined to speak at Mum's funeral; it is the final thing I can do for her. I research my mother's younger life by talking to my aunts and looking at photos. Over the next couple of days I sit at the computer and, using the notes I penned on the plane, commence putting a eulogy together. It is not easy, because I want to relay my mother's extremely difficult life and provide an understanding of why she sometimes appeared obstinate or inflexible.

Finally it is done.

'Mark, could you read this and tell what you think?'

He reads it, then reads it again.

'It's good, Jenny. Would you like me to read it for you at the funeral?'

'No. I want to do it myself. I'll be alright.' Then I say quietly,

'But if I'm not, perhaps you could take over.'

'Sure, love.'

Lauren and Vanessa are concerned when they hear that I'm going to read the eulogy. They try to encourage Mark to persuade me to let him read it. They want to spare me, but it's something I want to do.

*

It is very cold as I walk up the path to the entrance of the funeral home. People are standing in small groups in the foyer, and some are writing in the memorial book. I nod and speak to some as I move towards the chapel, where I enter on my own and see the coffin. It is covered in pink roses. Why? I sit there for a while, looking at the coffin, the pink roses that should be yellow, and wish she was still here. I return to the foyer and speak to people, but it is all a haze. I see David and Kerry with their children, and ask David yet again if he would like to speak. I show him the service I have organised, and he appears not interested, but I realise he is not coping.

Lauren reads from Kahlil Gibran's *The Prophet*, and then I stand and turn around. I am amazed—the chapel is overflowing, with a large number of people standing. I just didn't realise Mum had so many acquaintances and friends. Why didn't I know this? My chest is tight and my throat constricted, but I find an inner strength, and read with a strong voice and a sad heart. My seventeen-year-old goddaughter is quite overcome.

David and his family come back to the house and Lauren makes coffee.

'Well I think everything was okay … David?'

'I suppose.'

'David reckons you shouldn't have said some of the things

you did about your father,' Kerry snarls as she slumps into a chair.

'Everything I said was true.'

'That's not what David said coming back in the car. He was furious!'

'Leave it, Kerry.' David puts down his cup and stands. 'Let's go.'

'Don't rush away, David. I'm sorry if you didn't like what I said.'

'What I didn't like was having my mother cremated. How could you do that?'

'David, I asked for your input. I didn't know you didn't want that. You should have said.'

'Kerry, get the kids; we're going.' With that David charges out the door.

I cry.

'Mum, don't—they're not worth it,' says Lauren. She is standing by the fireplace.

I wander into my room, shut the door and lie on the bed. The girls let me be. What was that all about? My brother was at the mercy of my father's blustering rants—doesn't he remember? Perhaps it was not as often as the rest of us, but David still suffered. *Who does he think he is? I'd tried to include him in all the arrangements, but he wasn't interested. Look at the man he has become—is he proud of himself?* Then I remember a recent *Dr. Phil* segment I watched, which was about abusive relationships. Doctor Phil said research has shown, among other things, that boys who grow up with abuse are four times more likely to abuse in their own relationships. *Well my brother's living proof of that; he has abused Kerry from the early days of their relationship. Can't he see he is living proof that my father was a bully to all of us?*

Why would he want to defend our father? I turn my head to the pillow and sob.

*

Phone calls from friends diminish, the girls and Mark resume their lives, and I return to work, operating on automatic pilot. Depression raises its ugly head. It's something that I have fought since I was a young girl lying under the tree in the school ground, pretending to be asleep. I visit Mum's place, look in her wardrobe and shut the door—it is too hard to dispose of her things. It is difficult enough dealing with banks and the processing of the will. I keep my brother informed when decisions need to be made, aware that he is trying to find problems in everything I do. His actions irritate me.

Two weeks after Mum's death, I am home alone washing the dishes, when I suddenly feel a cold rush of air around me. I instantly think of her, and I feel her presence. Is she finally saying goodbye as she leaves to continue her journey? I will never know; nevertheless, it comforts me.

18

Three weeks after the funeral, I'm in the kitchen sipping coffee and thinking of Mum, when the front door bell rings.

'Kerry! What are you doing here? Where's David?'

'Hello, Auntie Jenny.' Dale, the kid who never stops eating and looks like a sumo wrestler, squeezes past his mother and charges down the hall.

'I've left him; I've had it.' Kerry brushes past carrying several plastic bags filled with clothes, and one containing food.

This I can do without. I sigh and close the door. 'Like a cup of coffee?'

'Yeah. I'm not putting up with the stuff he dishes out … his temper. Jenny, you have no idea.'

'I guess I don't, but he's just lost his mother.'

'I couldn't care less about his mother.' Kerry adjusts her dress to reveal even more of her ample cleavage. 'I'm doing what I want. How it affects him—or anyone else, for that matter—is not my problem,' Kerry scoffs. She pulls out a loaf of bread from one of the bags, grabs my bread knife and starts slicing bread on the kitchen bench. I hand her the cutting board.

Dale has slumped onto the lounge in the family room and is intently playing with his new hand-held Nintendo.

'Does David know you're here?'

'Doesn't even know I'm in Melbourne, but he'll guess.'

'Kerry, I don't want any upsets; I'm just not up for it at the moment.'

'Don't worry, I'll just tell him to go to hell.'

I escape to the bedroom.

At the far end of the house and facing the street, my bedroom is a peaceful retreat from the ruckus, as Kerry yells at her son to stop whinging, and he reciprocates. I sit on the bed, gazing out of the floor-to-ceiling window at the garden, filled with camellias in full bloom and a rockery that falls to the street below. I try to gather my scattered thoughts and to regain my composure. She is brusque and difficult at the best of times, but since Mum's death, Kerry has revelled in the unfolding drama. She has been on the phone several times telling me about her troubles. Her family, according to her, has been in turmoil. David's been drinking heavily, leaving the running of the motel to her, while Robbie, their eighteen-year-old son, has enjoyed egging his father on. I sigh. I know this is only one side of the story. Not being able to say goodbye to Mum must have been hard for David, although he never seemed to worry about her while she was alive. He's grieving, as we all are, but that's no excuse.

I hear the phone ring, and Mark answers it. There is a long pause, followed by 'Don't you threaten me!' and the sound of the phone being slammed onto its cradle. Now that Mark's home, I return to the kitchen.

'Hello, love,' Mark says as he cleans up the mess on the bench. 'What's going on? David wanted to speak to Kerry. She's not staying … is she?' he asks as Kerry stomps into the room, dumping her wet bath towel on the sofa.

'Was that David?' Kerry asks.

'Yes, he's fuming—wants you back pronto,' Mark replies.

'No way!' She flings herself onto the sofa. 'Jenny, while I'm here I'll help you go through your mum's things. There're a few things I'd like.'

'Are there? I've not been able to bring myself to do any of that yet.'

'It's got to be done. We'll go tomorrow and start sorting it out.'

Dale switches on the TV and lies on the floor, switching channels with the remote. I set about getting dinner ready. Mark, sitting on the stool at the kitchen bench, looks at Kerry, raises his eyebrows, then resumes poring over the newspaper.

*

The next morning, Kerry is adamant that she wants to go to Mum's. It's the last thing I want to do.

My mother's hall cupboard overflows with linen, gifts, and paraphernalia. I commence the painstaking task of sorting and packing. As soon as we arrive, Kerry makes a bee-line for the display cabinet, and is now selecting the crockery she fancies.

'I think I'll take this; you wouldn't want it,' she says, holding up an English china sandwich plate. It's pretty and I like it, but I can't be bothered arguing about it.

'No, that's fine.'

Kerry chats continuously, reiterating that her marriage is over and that she's not returning to Wagga. I say little, wishing she would be silent, and wonder how much longer she intends to stay. Our household is quite tense with Kerry's presence and the continual calls from David since she arrived. Last night, each time she spoke to him she deliberately aggravated him, and the abuse that followed was deeply disturbing. Sorting Mum's things is stressful for me, but Kerry is having a ball.

'Gee, this coffee set's cute; I think I'll take it.'

I look up and see the tiny cream coffee cup with little blue, pink and yellow sprays of flowers around its rim. The coffee pot has the sprays of flowers around the lid and body, and has a blue handle. I instantly remember our Sunday lunches when I was a little girl. At the end of the meal we always had coffee made with coffee essence. Mum would pour from the pot, and pass the little cups and saucers around the table. We would drop brown sugar cubes into the coffee. Drinking from these cups was a special treat.

'No,' I retort a little too loudly.

'What would you do with it?' she snaps.

'Kerry, that coffee set has special memories … there's plenty of other things you can take.'

'Alright then.' Her face set, she returns the coffee set to the cabinet.

We continue going through Mum's things during succeeding days. Once she has determined what she wants, Kerry crams Mum's treasured possessions into her Mercedes. What she intends to do with them I have no idea, but treasured they will not be. In fact I expect they will be sold—all except the orchids. Kerry collects orchids with a passion, and has numerous varieties back in Wagga. She took all the orchids except for two that she kindly left for me.

That night when everyone is asleep, the phone rings. I lean over and pick it up from the bedside table.

'Get Kerry now!' snarls David.

'She's asleep, David. Ring back in the morning.'

'Get her now or there will be trouble, you bloody idiot.'

'Don't, David … What's wrong with you?'

'You're what's wrong!' The phone is slammed down.

Five minutes later the phone rings again, but we let it go to the answering machine. This continues for about an hour, and then there is silence. Kerry must have heard the phone, but she stays in her room.

David rings the next day, and he and Kerry argue and yell at each other. There are more abusive phone calls during the evening and throughout the following day. I decide to go shopping to get away from it all.

On my return, I drive the car through the carport into the backyard and, carrying shopping bags, walk into the kitchen. Kerry is smirking, while her son is crying. My husband, standing immovable with hands on hips, appears like he is about to explode.

Glaring, Mark says, 'Kerry, this stops now.'

'I'm not going back. It's not only David I have to contend with; there's Robbie too. He's like his father. Just as abusive … at least he doesn't touch me.' Kerry flicks back her heavy fringe and snarls at Mark. 'You can't make me. Anyway, it's none of your business.'

'Jenny's got enough on her plate without all your drama, and that is my business. You're going today. And don't tell us where you're going. Got it?'

'Thanks, you heap of shit. You put on the *nice* act for Jenny but treat me like dirt when she's not around. Where're we supposed to go?'

'Kerry, that's unfair; we can't deal with David's calls any longer.' I place my hand gently on her shoulder.

She roughly pushes me away. 'Ah, you're turning on me now. You're just like him. I know when I'm not wanted.'

'No, I'm not turning on you. But let's face it: you and David haven't been concerned about us or Mum for a very long time.

We only hear from you when there's a problem. Some support from you both while Mum was sick would have been good.'

'She wasn't my mother.'

'No, she wasn't.'

'Anyway, I didn't get on with her, and David didn't have much time for her either.'

'I don't believe that; but I think with David, it is out of sight, out of mind.'

'Think what you like.'

With that, Kerry storms to her room, yelling further abuse. She packs her bag, drags the little one down the hall and into the car, and is gone.

We look at each other and collapse onto the sofa. Mark wraps his arm around me and I let out a sob, which builds until my whole body is heaving. Mark pours a brandy. I sip and feel the warmth sweep across me.

'It's over, love.' He strokes my arm.

*

I wake to the sun streaming through the drapes, and a brilliant blue sky. I cook scrambled eggs and toast for us, which we eat while sitting on the patio. The sound of the water winding its way down the stream that wanders through our garden and then cascades into the pond is soothing. The tall gum trees are still, the shrubs of varying shades of green are a backdrop for the vivid white impatiens that border the path. It is quiet, but just as we are finishing our coffee, the phone rings.

'That will be one of the girls.' Mark looks up from his paper. 'She'll want to talk to you.'

I go inside. The phone's ring still generates a feeling of unease, but I answer with a bright 'Hello'.

'Get my fuckin' wife.'

My stomach heaves. 'Kerry's not here, David. She left at tea-time yesterday. Leave us alone.'

'Jenny, you'd better tell me where she is.'

'I don't know; we told her to go. David, you have to stop this.'

'Don't bloody lie; you two are as thick as thieves! If I have to come to Melbourne you'll be sorry.'

'David, she's not here and we don't know where she's gone.'

'Bloody liar!' He hangs up.

My legs shake and I lean against the bench for support, unable to move. I've witnessed David's violence over the years. Like our father, he was and is physically abusive, and from what Kerry says Robbie is following in his father and grandfather's footsteps. *What a shame. I've always had a soft spot for him. I remember looking after him five days a week when he was little—he was just like one of my own.*

'Was it Vanessa or Lauren?' Mark walks in as the phone rings again.

I lift it and the voice says, 'I'm coming to fix you. You don't mess with me.'

Mark sees my face and grabs the phone. 'Leave us alone, you weak bastard, and stop threatening your sister! Your wife's gone. Do not, do not ring again!' he yells, and slams the phone down.

The phone calls continue, each more menacing than the last; we let the answering machine pick them up. Finally, in the late afternoon we hear a slurred voice: 'You can run but you can't hide. I'm on my way.'

'That does it,' Mark says as he picks up the phone, 'I'm ringing the police, then I'm disconnecting this phone.'

This can't be happening. My brother is right off the rails; I know he's drunk, but I can't believe he would do this to me. I saw his rages with Kerry early in their marriage, but I never thought they would be directed at me. Once I spent the day making Kerry a dress, which she decided to wear. I drove her home and David met us at the front gate. He put his arm through the open window, grabbed at Kerry, and ripped her new dress right down the front. I'm scared, yet I can't report him to the police. But as I look at Mark's face, I know I'll have no say.

*

Two uniformed cops, with heavy metal around their waists, fill the spacious lounge chairs. Mark and I recount the events of the past week. After listening to the answering machine, their response is unexpected.

One officer leans forward. 'Mr Yates, I agree they're threatening calls, but we can do nothing until an offence is committed.'

Mark explodes. 'What! You've got to do something; my wife's a nervous wreck!'

'I'm sorry. We could get in touch with the Wagga police. They'll talk to him.'

'What's the use of that?' I pipe up. 'He said he's on his way here.'

'Sergeant, the threats are real—very real.' Mark rubs his hand across his wrinkled forehead and then through his curly hair.

'I understand. We'll check the street now and have a car do regular patrols during the night, but I'm afraid that's all we can do.'

We exchange looks as the police leave. 'They're supposed to

protect, but apparently protection only occurs once something happens. Bloody stupid!' Mark exclaims. He closes the door and puts his arm around me. 'We'll be right. We'll look after ourselves. Let's have a cuppa, then I have a few things to do outside.'

'I'm terrified … you don't know what David's capable of.'

'I do.'

Mark thinks he does, but once David makes up his mind, nothing will stop him, especially when he's drinking. My head is aching, my stomach squirms and I feel nauseated, whereas Mark appears resolute and obviously has a plan. He tells me to lie down and he strides outside.

I thought I had left this dysfunctional life behind when I left Steve, but it seems it always comes back to haunt me. Mark and I have our problems, but at least we are civil; we argue, but we still have respect for each other. And no matter what, we support each other. Mark has been such a rock over the last few months, but I know he is not happy. I'm partly to blame. I have a trust issue with men—a legacy of my childhood, I guess—and this has created a barrier in our marriage. I've come to realise that some of the traits I despised in my father are also part of my nature, and I fight them all the time. I need to seek help, which I'll do when Mum's affairs are sorted. Heaven knows how I'm going to deal with my brother being involved in sorting Mum's stuff.

Darkness shrouds and threatens. I wonder, with the phone still off the hook, if David has tried to ring. Mark has locked and barricaded the steel gates in the driveway behind the carport, and fitted a heavy piece of wood to the side gate. He has parked the two cars close together to make access difficult. All doors including the security doors are deadlocked, the blinds are drawn and the dog has been left off the chain. Tosca wouldn't hurt a fly, but she will bark if she hears footsteps.

I move food around my plate, drain my wine and have another. Mark's curly, peppered hair is tousled, and cobwebs are lodged in his beard from scrounging under the house for wood for the barricades. The TV murmurs in the corner, and we don't talk. I'm tired, but afraid to go to bed.

Mark rises and puts the dirty dishes on the bench. 'I'm just going to check outside again … won't be long.'

I look at him but say nothing—there is nothing to say. Absentmindedly I replace the phone in its cradle, and I'm still staring at it when he returns. Whistling, he sets about scraping the plates and putting them in the dishwasher.

'What about a nightcap?' Mark smiles, feigning normality.

'I've already had two glasses.'

'Another won't hurt—you're not driving,' he laughs, emptying the bottle of red into two glasses, handing one to me, and raising the other. 'Cheers!'

'Do you think he'll come?' I whisper, looking straight ahead.

'I reckon he's bluffing, but I'm not taking chances. You never know with your brother. You look exhausted … go to bed, I'll just be a jiff.'

I spread toothpaste on my brush, and in the en-suite's mirror a small, strained face with troubled blue eyes surrounded by unruly, wild hair stares back.

Mark enters carrying a crowbar, which he puts under his side of the bed.

'What are you doing with that?' I ask with trepidation.

'Just a precaution; don't worry about it.'

The streetlights cast shadows across the wall. Lights from passing cars shine through the gap between the blind and window ledge at floor level. When the girls lived at home, I could not sleep until I saw the welcome sight of their car lights and knew they had arrived safely. Tonight I fear the lights. Is it a car passing, a car stopping, the police patrolling? I don't know. I turn over and face Mark.

'Are you asleep?' I ask tentatively.

'What do you think?' He puts his arm around me and hugs me tight. I lie there trying to feel safe in his arms, but the feeling of doom pervades. The night is long as we lie there in the foreboding darkness, waiting.

David takes the blue, yellow and green budgie out of its cage and places it on his shoulder. He coos to it, takes it from his shoulder and places the bird on his finger. Then he places the finger of his other hand in front of the bird. The bird hops on. David keeps putting one finger in front of the bird and it clambers onto it. Then the budgie flies around and David calls it to come back. It does so, and he continues to play with it. After a while he goes to the kitchen to get something to eat, and leaves the budgie on top of his cage. When he returns, the budgie is nowhere to be seen. The cat slinks by and David sees a green feather in its mouth. He rushes around looking for the bird, but it is nowhere to be found. He howls inconsolably.

I must have been dreaming. My brother was a member of the Gould League in his school days. He loves and cares for all birds and animals, and has a huge aviary back in Wagga. Pity his caring attitude doesn't extend to his family.

It's the phone that's woken me. I listen. Mark sits upright as it goes to the answering machine.

From the kitchen we hear, 'Mum! Dad! Mum, it's Vanessa. Pick up!' I lean over to pick up the extension; the clock on the dressing table displays 3.14. 'Vanessa, what's wrong?'

'Mum, are you in your bedroom?'

'Of course I'm in the bedroom.'

'Get out! Get out now! Uncle David's just rung—he woke me. He's in your street. He's got a gun. He … he said he's going to shoot you through the window. Mum, you and Dad get out!'

'A gun? He wouldn't have a gun, Vanessa. Are you sure?'

'Yes Mum, he means it—get out!' Vanessa screams into the phone.

'Alright, we'll go to the lounge—there's no windows facing the street. We're okay. Dad … Dad's secured the entire house and we've left Tosca out. Don't worry. We'll ring the police now.'

'You knew he was coming?' Vanessa is aghast.

'We've had threatening phone calls all week. Vanessa, I'll ring you back—we need to ring the police. Don't worry.'

The police arrive. They check the property perimeter, circle the block, and are confident no-one is lurking. The place is lit up like Las Vegas. After the police leave, I ring Vanessa to let her know we're okay, and then we try sleeping in the recliner chairs. No way am I returning to the bedroom. How dare David drag my daughter into all this, and terrify her so? I'll never forgive him.

I doze. Eventually dawn arrives and I watch the emergence of a new day: the gentle light spreads and the leaves sparkle as the rising sun filters through the trees. It's so peaceful, and for a time the terrors of the night are forgotten.

Mark wakes and smiles. 'Told you it would be okay.'

I struggle out of the chair; I'm not convinced, but we've got through the night. *I must ring Vanessa; bit early yet. David calling her was the last straw. No more excuses; I never want to see him again.*

We need to make a police statement sometime today. I wonder if David is still in Melbourne, and if so, where. At least the calls have stopped; maybe he has found Kerry and he'll leave us alone? What happened to the little kid I grew up with? We used to be so close. I put the kettle on and slip bread into the toaster, and realise I'm hungry just as the damn phone rings. *Probably Vanessa.*

'Hello.'

'Hi, Auntie Jenny … how ya goin'?'

'Robbie. What do you want?' is my icy response.

'Ah … just wondered how you are,' Robbie laughs loudly.

'Where are you, Robbie?' I can hear voices and background music—it could be a pub. 'With your father?'

'Yep, he's right beside me.'

'Are you in Melbourne?'

Robbie's laugh is chilling. 'Wouldn't you like to know? Scared?'

'Stop it!' I shriek.

'Get Mum.'

'She's not here. Probably back in Wagga by now.'

'Nup, she's not,' Robbie chuckles, 'because that's where we are. Dad and I have been enjoying a few drinks, playing snooker, and making a call or two. We've had an *exceptionally* entertaining night.' Robbie sniggers. 'Haven't we, Dad? Haven't had so much fun in ages. Tell Mum to get home today or it'll be for real, no kidding.' Robbie hangs up.

19

Obviously things have settled in Wagga. It's been several weeks since Robbie's phone call, and since then there's been no contact. Thank goodness. Mark's in America on a training course, so with boxes in tow, I head for Mum's. I need to get her house sorted; David wants it sold as quickly as possible, and Mark wants me to join him in America in a few weeks. He thinks a holiday will be good for me.

Mum's unit is small but adequate, although her bedroom is pokey. The single bed and dressing table leave little room to move. The built-in wardrobe, which I have decided to clear out, is crammed. I sit on the bed, next to the boxes (there is nowhere else to put them), and wonder where to start. On her bedside table are photos of all her grandchildren. Lauren looks about three and Vanessa much younger. They would have been taken about the time I started out on my own.

That was when I felt the most free, even though I had the total responsibility for my children, and huge hurdles to overcome. For one, there was the stigma associated with divorce, which seemed to attach itself more to women. Some of my married girlfriends stopped inviting me to their homes; I guess they were concerned I might flirt with their husbands. There were no flexible working hours or family leave. This created a huge problem when my children were sick, and required a lot of juggling. I had to keep my job; I had children to feed. Sometimes the depression I suffered as a child and as an adult would raise its ugly head. I felt as if I were in a deep, black well. When I grasped the top of the well to clamber out, it seemed my fingers were stomped on, and I would fall back to the bottom.

I think the hardest thing I ever did was leaving Steve when my children were so small. I'm not sure where the courage came from, but I can be tenacious when the need arises. With Steve I continued in a situation that I had really lived with all my life, until the night he forced me to clean up his filth. That was the last straw, and even though I didn't know how I was going to support myself and the girls, it gave me the courage to act.

My life now is so different. With Mark's help I have been able to achieve my goal of providing opportunities for my girls—opportunities that I had been denied. It was paramount that they receive the best possible education to allow them to be who they want to be. It would not have happened if I had stayed with Steve.

My memories of the years with Steve are painful, but they are also liberating, because I managed to escape the relationship. My parents' marriage convinced me that the treatment I experienced was all I deserved, and that it was normal. Not only did I have the emotional abuse, the money problems and the lack of support to deal with, but Steve constantly lied. I knew he was lying, yet he could convince me otherwise. He might tell me there was a block of chocolate in the refrigerator. I'd know there wasn't, yet he'd persuade me I was mistaken. I still can't understand to this day how he did it.

Being a single mother was difficult, but I wouldn't have had it any other way. There was heartache leaving my home, and Lauren blamed me for leaving her daddy. A psychiatrist explained to me once that when a trauma occurs in a three-year-old's life, the child's subconscious stores the memory exactly as the three-year-old absorbed it. That memory then stays in the subconscious in that form forever. I believe Lauren blamed me (not consciously, but subconsciously) for many years, which broke my heart.

The happiness far outweighed the difficulties. The memory of the wonderful first Christmas I had as a single parent often returns, as it has done now. I recall the peace I experienced once I was on my own. I no longer worried about Steve arriving home drunk. Money was short, but it was there every month (unlike payday with Steve), and I set a budget for the coming month. I have continued this, and it has allowed Mark and me to educate our children and travel to places we never dreamed of. It is allowing us to provide for our looming retirement.

I was luckier than many when I set out on my own, because of the wonderful friends and neighbours who stuck by me. Also lots of things fell into place; how lucky I was to get a rare place for my children in the city crèche. Most of all I had a wonderful, supportive Mum.

For the first eighteen months as a single parent, I had no desire to socialise, especially with men. I didn't trust men, and I rarely felt comfortable with them. All I wanted was to be with my children and try to replace, as best I could, what they had lost—their father. This was totally impossible of course, but by devoting all my time to them, I hoped to erase some of the sad incidents in their young lives. Perhaps this was naïve, but I still believe it helped a little. I felt free, but being the sole carer for my children was debilitating. The astute matron at the crèche noticed that I was struggling, suggested I needed a break, and organised for the children to go to a respite house for the weekend. I had become quite friendly with Judy from work, and together we went to Marysville, where we met two Chilean guys who were working on the Snowy River scheme. I enjoyed the attention they bestowed on us, and I continued to see one of them for a while, but I just never felt comfortable, and soon broke the relationship. I was happy just being with my girls.

At a work function I met Gordon, who swept me off my feet. He was attractive, kind and took me out for exotic dinners. I'd never experienced this kind of attention before. He was an ICI contractor working in the Melbourne office, and lived in Sydney. He made no secret of the fact that he had four children, but said he was separated. We went out during the week, but he was adamant that he return to Sydney each weekend to see his children. He treated my children well, including them in everything we did, and I thought I was in love—perhaps for the first time. The girls adored him. Little Vanessa would watch for him when he was expected, and as he walked down the drive she would yell out 'Mannie's here, Mannie's coming!'— 'Mannie' was her pet name for Gordon. He would pick her up, swing her around and put her on his hip, then walk through the door and give me a resounding kiss. I was smitten.

Gordon was transferred to the Sydney office and I was devastated. However, after working for twelve months, I'd saved enough for a budget holiday, so of course I went to Sydney. We caught the train at Spencer Street and I sat up all night, but I was able to make a bed of sorts for my excited children. I booked a cheap apartment in Kings Cross. Gordon met the train and spent the week showing us the sights, but always seemed unavailable at night. I was exceptionally naïve, or perhaps I just didn't want to believe that he was not separated, but as the week progressed I became more and more dubious. Finally, one afternoon over lunch with Gordon, Lauren and

Vanessa, I decided to face whatever it was. We were at a family restaurant, so after we had eaten I suggested the girls play on the equipment provided, and I'd watch them from where I was sitting. They raced off laughing.

'I'd love to meet your children while I'm here.' I smiled.

'That would be nice, but they're away at camp.'

'What, all of them?' The four children ranged in age from six to twelve. I thought it would be unusual for them all to go to camp at the same time.

Gordon didn't answer, but looked a little sheepish.

I looked at him. 'You're not separated, are you?'

He looked at me and said nothing.

'Tell me the truth; are you still married?'

'Jenny … y … yes … let me explain.'

'Let you explain? I believed you!'

'I care for you, Jenny, and I care for the girls.' He looked at them and smiled. 'But I also care for my family. Since I met you I've always tried where possible to tell you the truth.' He grinned. 'That way I don't catch myself out.'

'You didn't tell me the truth when you said you were separated,' I scoffed.

'No I didn't, but you never questioned it. I thought deep down you knew.'

I didn't know what to say. I was devastated.

I collected the children and went back to our apartment, intending not to see him again.

He arrived the next morning; I weakened and continued to spend time with him for the rest of the holiday. However, when I arrived home I came to my senses and broke contact.

*

I sigh, replace the photo and pick up a box. I look around; where to start? The dressing table drawers are filled with underwear, and this I transfer to the bottom of the box. Next, the winter woollies. I pick up a burgundy poncho that my mother crocheted and often wore. I can smell her; I rub my face into it and sit back on the bed, hugging it. After a time, I put it aside and continue the packing, commencing with her crammed wardrobe. She has hung several items on single hangers to fit it all in. I have no idea how she knew what she had. There are shoes, never worn and in their original boxes. I don't know where to start, and haphazardly put skirts, blouses and dresses in a box. I pick up her pink dress with white spots, and instantly see her coming through my family room door with a basket of homemade goodies.

As I continue to pack, and having had the memories of Gordon that are more than twenty years old return, my mind wanders to those days at ICI. I didn't enjoy being a teleprinter operator and clerk, nor having a supervisor such as Mary Roades. I wanted to better myself so I could provide for my children and give them what they deserved. Computer technology was relatively new, and programming appealed to me. Most companies only offered positions in their programming and system departments to graduates. I approached the programming department manager, who gave me an IQ test and immediately said I was not suitable. I knew the real reason was that I didn't have a degree. I discovered a school that was teaching Assembler, the rudimentary computer language. I applied and went to night school. Once again my mother helped me achieve what was at first glance impossible. Two nights a week, I would finish work at ICI and go to Hemingway's College to learn Assembler and read computer dumps. After I graduated, I approached the company, armed with a reference from my tutor. Again I was unsuccessful.

Soon after, I was shocked to find that my position was to become redundant. With new technology available, ICI decided to close the teleprinter room. Mary was found another position, and Val and I were promised something clerical. I was disillusioned. Being rejected for a programming position and not particularly interested in clerical work, I decided to look elsewhere. The company duly gave me time off to attend interviews.

I accepted a position as a secretary to the owner of a rag trade company. It was in North Melbourne, which meant travelling further than I'd had to for my old job, but it offered a much better salary. Mr Handelman and his son ran the company in an unbelievably strict fashion. If you took any more than five minutes for tea break, you were in trouble. Jodie, the lovely person I was replacing, was pregnant. Nearly every day Mr Handelman had her in tears for one reason or another. On the Friday after I commenced, the six girls in the ledger room were in tears, and Jodie and I were reprimanded for taking too long at tea. We explained we started our break late, but the owner said this was no excuse. That day I made up and distributed the staff pays, and then informed the boss that I had paid myself and wouldn't be coming back. I walked down the North Melbourne street wondering what on earth I was going to do. I had no job. How was I going to support my children?

I had applied for a comptometrist position with another company, but had missed out. However, they suggested I keep in touch, as new positions often became available. The following Monday, I rang, went for an interview in their computer department, and started the next day. Luck was definitely with me; not only did I get the position easily and quickly, but it was a position that grew. Soon I became the supervisor of the Edit Department, and my interest in computers increased. ACI's computer was enormous; the room it fitted into was nearly the size of a bowling alley.

My department's role was to edit all work processed by the computer, including payroll, accounts payable, sales, and the share register for all the offices Australia-wide. The enormous amount of data was first of all converted to punch card format, and once processed, a report was produced. This needed to be checked and reprocessed if it didn't balance. I enjoyed this position; it combined my comptometrist and mathematical skills, and gave me autonomy. I still hoped to break into the programming area, but was content for the time being.

I felt that everything was fitting into place. Then I received news about my house. I still hoped one day to return to it, or if the house was sold, buy another home with the equity.

I didn't know what I was going to do, and needed to talk to someone, so I went round to Mum's.

'Mum, the bank's threatening to foreclose because Steve hasn't been paying the mortgage. He's not even living there anymore.'

'Where is he?'

'Apparently he's living with a mate in Oakleigh.'

'Mmm … so what are you going to do?'

'There's about six months outstanding; I can't pay that from my salary. Would you be able to give me a loan? My solicitor says when the divorce goes through, the house will be divvied up. I hope one day to have a house again, but if the bank takes it, I'll lose any equity there is …'

Mum was silent. I hated asking her, and I knew David

had never repaid the money he had borrowed.

'If I loaned you this money—and it's quite a bit—how can you pay it back? Not only that, how will you continue to pay the monthly amount when you have rent to pay?'

'I'm not sure … I'll work out a way.'

'I'll have to think about it … I can't afford to make it a gift, you know,' said my mother.

'I wouldn't expect you to.' And that's how it was left.

I went home and wondered what I was going to do. A couple of days later, I was flicking through the local paper, and saw that the Pathfinder Motel in Kew was looking for a drink waitress. It was close to where I lived and waitressing I could do, but what about the children? I approached Mum again. As she was working full-time, I knew it was hardly fair asking her to look after children at night, but that is what I did. She of course agreed, so I applied for the job, and sure enough, was successful. Mum picked up the children from the crèche three times a week, brought them home to my place, fed them and put them to bed. She was my rock. I worked at the Pathfinder for six months, until I had paid my mother back the loan she provided. I rented out the house, and this covered the monthly mortgage and the rates.

I rarely saw Steve during the two years after I moved out, but he occasionally surfaced. I went to court to try and obtain maintenance, and was granted seven dollars a week for each child and four dollars for myself. He never paid. My solicitor, Mr Mackenzie, said this was good, as was Steve not paying the mortgage; it would go in my favour and help with the divorce. I was sceptical. The solicitor asked me to write down in an exercise book what had happened in our marriage—everything. He wanted to know about our sex life, the drinking, the violence, how the children were treated and the lack of financial support. I naïvely wrote it all down. I later realised he was just getting his kicks. He said he was going to argue constructive desertion—that I left the marriage for my own and the children's safety.

Mr Mackenzie went to court several times regarding lack of maintenance payments, and two years after the separation, he composed an affidavit for the divorce proceedings from the details in my exercise book.

It was my thirtieth birthday on the day of the Supreme Court hearing. I nervously entered the court, feeling full of apprehension. At the front of the court room at a high wooden bench sat the judge in his wig and robes, and my barrister sat at a table below. I was with my solicitor, and got quite a shock when Steve came through the doors. He sat at the back of the court. My barrister went through the preliminaries and then the clerk of the court read out the affidavit in full. As I listened to my marriage dissected into horrid little bits, I felt degraded and couldn't believe I had allowed it all to evolve. I took the stand and my barrister questioned me, asking if certain statements in the affidavit were true. Every now and again the judge interrupted with a question, and he also asked the barrister to verify certain aspects of the affidavit. It was nerve-racking. My legs were shaking, even though I was seated in the witness box.

The judge turned to me and asked, 'How old are your children?' This was clearly documented in the court papers.

'Five and three, sir.'

He leaned forward. 'You're not earning a great deal. I guess it isn't easy trying to pay your rent, and to buy food and clothes for the children.'

'No sir, but I manage.'

He leaned even further across the bench and with a smile

said, 'Well, let's hope you get a raise soon.'

'I hope so too.'

'Mrs Stillwell, you can resume your seat.' The judge sat upright again. 'Mr Stillwell, do you wish to say anything?' He looked across at Steve.

'No.'

The judge then solemnly stated that the marriage was forthwith dissolved and the decree nisi would take effect in three months. He ordered Steve to pay increased maintenance for the girls, but not for myself. My marriage was over. Steve left the court without speaking. My solicitor and I went for a drink to celebrate, and my girlfriend joined us. Afterwards I picked up the girls from the crèche and went home.

*

I look around the room—what chaos I've caused! Clothes are everywhere and the wardrobe is not yet half emptied. I need a break, so I wander out and look at Mum's garden. How she loved her camellias. They are not in flower at this time of the year, and the plants are looking a little sorry. Summer's hot sun has played havoc, and of course the garden is not getting watered. The roses don't seem to care though. The climbing Lorraine Lee is a mass of pink, and the perfume is a delight. I wander up the driveway to the front of the units, and an image of my mother bending over the letterbox flashes through my mind. I wonder what she thought when my divorce went through. I know she was devastated when I married Steve, but when I left him, she never once said or inferred 'I told you so'. She just supported me.

I caused her such pain. If Steve hadn't been barred from the hotel, I wouldn't have continued the relationship. It was my father who had barred Steve, although I do suspect Mum could have had a hand in it too. I just became more defiant. The more she tried to convince me that Steve was not the man for me, the more determined I became. I barely spoke to her prior to our engagement, but once it was announced, my parents tried to accept him. I wanted to break things off with Steve as our relationship deteriorated, but I stupidly didn't want to lose face.

I wander back down the drive and decide to make a cuppa. Sipping my tea in the bare lounge room, I think how different it is from when Mum was here. The crystal cabinet is empty (Kerry packed that up), there are no knick-knacks around, and the walls are bare. David took the pictures to put into his rental properties. The only thing left on the little round side table is a wedding photo of Mark and me with the girls.

I met Mark not long after my divorce was finalised. He was a computer engineer, and serviced both ICI and ACI computers, but work was not where we forged our friendship. At ICI, I became friendly with a girl from the computer department who also had a child at the crèche. We spent a great deal of time together, helping each other with child minding. Dian was renting a flat above a shop in Camberwell's main shopping strip. We often had dinner together, and one night at Dian's, her boyfriend John arrived with his mate Mark. She invited them for dinner and we had a pleasant evening. A few weeks later I received an invite to a twenty-first birthday party. I didn't have a partner.

'Why don't you ask Mark?' Dian jokingly suggested.

'I can't do that!' I laughed.

'I'll ask the boys for dinner and then I think you should ask him. He's a nice guy and hasn't got a girlfriend.'

After dinner we adjourned to the lounge and Dian kept

giving me the eye. How could I say anything in front of her boyfriend? Eventually Mark went down the long hallway to the loo and nervously I followed him. I met him in the hallway on his way back and very tentatively asked him to the party. Little did I know that Dian and John were listening behind the lounge door—until I heard them giggling. I was so embarrassed. However, Mark said he'd love to go.

At the twenty-first birthday party, we danced most of the night, and I felt relaxed as we laughed and chatted away. One thing worried me: he drank a few whiskies, and that had been the liquor my father consumed.

Mark asked me out again, and before long we were seeing quite a bit of each other. The children adored him, especially Lauren. I realised that Mark was the first man who had really paid attention to her since she'd lost her father. Gordon had been good, and Vanessa had been quite taken with him, but Mark was different. He was an only child who lost his mother when he was nine weeks old. He grew up with lots of younger cousins and spent time looking after them. Mark played with my children; he delighted in reading them bedtime stories and never quibbled about taking them on outings. We rarely did anything without them. He seemed to have an affinity with them, and for that I adored him. We were a family from the very beginning. But one thing niggled: he was seven years younger.

The girls were getting bigger and needed space to play, and I craved a room of my own. Now I was earning a better salary, I felt I could afford higher rent, so I looked for a two-bedroom flat. Again I was lucky. Lauren had commenced school at the beginning of the year, and the matron at the crèche helped me find after-school care. Kildonan, a church home for children, provided after-school care for six extra children, and was situated not far from Matron's home. She procured a place for Lauren. I found a flat in the same street, and was able to drop Lauren off on my way to work and pick her up in the evening, after I had picked Vanessa up from the crèche.

The flat had a really large bedroom, which was as big as the one I had shared with the girls initially. It also had a second, smaller bedroom, which was perfect for me. The bigger bedroom provided plenty of room for the girls' toys, and space for them to play. There was a large lounge room with a fireplace, and plenty of space for both lounge and dining furniture. However, the kitchen was quite small, old and dirty. The gas stove was thick with grease and smelt horrible. But I took it anyway, because the rest of the flat was so much better than our current cramped quarters, and the proximity to Kildonan was a bonus. I knew a mountain of cleaning would be required.

Dian helped me pack and clean up the old flat, while Mark and John loaded the furniture onto a truck and transported it to the new place. As soon as I arrived at my new flat, I made the children's beds and set up their toys and clothes. Unbeknownst to me, Dian and Mark were cleaning the kitchen while I did this. Dian washed down all the cupboards while Mark pulled the entire stove to pieces and washed it thoroughly. How lucky was I to have such caring people around me. Mark could never do enough; he was always trying to make things a little better.

When Mark's mother died, his father returned to live with his own mother. From that day Mark shared a room with his father, and was still sharing it when I met him. I found this incomprehensible, but Mark took it all in his stride. It was all he had ever known, and it didn't seem to worry him at the time. It became the norm for him to arrive after work at my place. We would have tea and spend the evening together, then he would return to his shared room in Footscray late at night. My life was comfortable, I had a job I enjoyed, my children were in a loving environment, and I had a man who seemed to care deeply about all of us. I was content.

We had been together for about eighteen months when Mark's company asked him to go to Switzerland and Germany for training. The training covered several areas, but the automated ticket vending machine training was crucial. Mark's company had secured a contract with the Victorian Government to install ticket vending machines for all Victorian rail services. It was an entirely new concept for Victoria, and held promise of advancement within the company for Mark, as he would head the department. The training was for six months, and I was unsure how I would be without him. He had been my constant companion and such a support for my children. We took him to the airport, where Mark put on a brave face. He had never been overseas and it was all an overwhelming experience. He looked very sad as he waved goodbye. The children and I cried.

Each night I wrote to Mark, and received the most amazing, loving letters in return. He spent time in both Switzerland and Germany training on equipment that was expected to change the face of travel in Victoria. Several months went by and I missed him terribly. He rang about once a week and it was so good to hear his voice—I was counting the days until he returned. At night I'd pull out one of his letters and read it before I went to sleep.

A few nights after Mark's weekly call the phone rang.

'Hi, how have you been? How are the girls?'

'Mark, this is a surprise … is there something wrong?'

'Well … things have sorta changed here.'

'What things?'

'Well the whole ticket thing with the government's not going ahead.'

'What do you mean?'

'They've pulled the plug ... the equipment's not going to be implemented. The contract's fallen through.'

'That's awful! I guess you'll be coming home. What about ...'

'Jenny, I've had a long talk with my boss. I've still got a job, but not the job I was employed for. I'm pretty upset ... no, I'm pissed off. All this training for nothing! However, my boss said I can have six weeks holidays so I can travel. He's trying to make it up to me I guess.'

'Oh,' I whispered. He'd been gone for several months and I wanted him home.

'Don't get upset ... I've got a great idea. Why don't you come over? With Lauren and Vanessa, of course. I've still got some training to do on the other stuff and then I've got to go to Germany for a couple of weeks. I'll get a car ... we can travel around Switzerland a bit while I'm working, and then Germany. Then we could go to France or Italy or whatever. It'd be good. Stop me thinking about how my potential career has evaporated. What do you think?'

I couldn't believe my ears. I had never been outside Australia and never expected to go; now I had the chance. I had a little saved—each month I always put a little aside for a rainy day. It was enough for the airfare, but not much else. I couldn't see how it would be possible, and I had my job to think about. I couldn't lose that.

'Oh Mark, I don't know ... my job ... money ... I'll have to think about it.'

'I'll have to know soon … if you're not coming, I'll come home.'

'Let me talk to my boss.'

'I'll ring you in a couple of days. Jenny, if it's money you're worried about, you won't need any once you get here.'

I approached Peter, my boss, explaining that I had the opportunity to spend nine weeks in Europe, but wasn't sure if that was long enough, and what about my job. Peter said my job would always be there for me, and that any time in Europe, no matter how short, was worthwhile, so I should go.

My mother and brother, on the other hand, were against the idea. I guess Mum was just worried about her family being out of the country. My brother urged me to go, but said I shouldn't take my children—it was not right to take them out of school for an overseas trip. He would look after them, he said. There was no way I was going to go overseas without my children. I couldn't be away from them and I would worry constantly about whether they were being looked after properly. I made the decision to go.

We left Melbourne on KLM, the Dutch airline, and flew to Frankfurt, where Mark met us. We were all chatting at once as Mark put our luggage on the trolley and started down the escalator, looking back at us. I remember so clearly what happened next: All the cases cascaded down the steps of the escalator and landed at the bottom. The children thought it was very funny. I was embarrassed.

Each day, Mark organised somewhere for us to go while he was working. Our first outing did not eventuate as Mark expected. I had arrived with a bad cough. Because I couldn't speak German, Mark wrote a note for me to take to the *Apotheke*, requesting cough medicine. He also gave me some money. I was too proud to show the note, so I ask if they had anything for a cough, and the sales assistant returned with tablets. I explained I needed cough syrup, not tablets. The lady behind the counter looked mystified. I then coughed several times and she raised her eyes, turned to the shelf and produced cough syrup. Mark explained later that 'Kopf' was 'head' in German and therefore the chemist would have interpreted my request as asking for something for a headache.

I decided I wanted to go and get a coffee, and a drink for the girls. Mark had told me to ask for cokes for the girls, as it is a universal word; so I did, but Lauren and Vanessa were given strong Dutch cocoas. At lunch I thought I'd be smart and use my phrasebook at a café, in a department store similar to Myer. I looked at the menu—it was totally foreign. I tried to communicate to the waiter using the phrasebook, but had no success. In broken English he said, 'I will give you nice lunch.' I sighed with relief. We had a delicious lunch and then went and played chess with giant chess pieces in the park. When Mark arrived home from work, it made him laugh when I told him about our day. Then he asked me how much money I had left. Nothing, I said. He looked at me and then asked the cost of lunch. When I told him, he grimaced. 'That was quite expensive—the money I gave you was supposed to last the week! Never mind, it was your first day; you'll soon learn the value of the deutschmark.'

We had varying experiences during our nine weeks in Europe. In Germany I was sharply told by a neighbour to bring in my bath towels, which I had hung out on the balcony to dry. It was quite okay to air doonas there, but considered bad manners to hang towels. We enjoyed a music festival in Salzburg, and stayed in a farmhouse in Austria where the cattle were kept under the house in the winter. In Italy we experienced rudeness from some Italian youths at the Venetian Palace, and in Holland the children delighted at their visit to the *de Efteling* amusement park.

Having our luggage stolen in Italy had a major impact on our holiday. After Mark finished his training, we drove to Italy and stayed several days in Jesolo, across the bay from Venice. We explored Venice's Grand Canal, and its intertwining canals, sitting back in style in a gondola. The children delighted in feeding the hordes of pigeons in St Mark's Square, and visiting the art galleries was a delight. We arrived in Florence late because we had been enjoying the sun at Jesolo. Accommodation was impossible. Out of the blue, a man on a motorbike pulled up beside us and asked if we were looking for somewhere to stay. 'Yes,' we said. 'Follow me,' he said. He took us to accommodation that was quite acceptable. However, it was on the fourth floor, and the lift was not working. Mark hefted one of our suitcases up the stairs, and we decided we would make do until the next day.

We freshened up and then went to a little restaurant for dinner, where Mark asked for some wine. The waiter brought a large urn woven into a basket and told us to help ourselves. At the end of the night he just looked down at the urn and said 200 *lire* would do. This was very cheap. We went back to our accommodation and to bed. The next morning, Mark and Vanessa went down to the car to get the rest of the suitcases, while I stayed with Lauren.

Vanessa came running past the service desk yelling, 'Mummy, Mummy, someone has shot the car! Mark says we have to call the police.'

The woman at the service desk was agitated at the mention

of police, and asked us what was wrong. Why did we want *police*? Mark explained that our luggage had been stolen from the car.

I interjected, 'Why did Vanessa say someone shot the car?'

Mark laughed. 'When I saw what had happened I said someone had rifled the car.'

The woman calmed down, and in broken English peppered with Italian, she said her husband would take Mark to the police station. There Mark was told there was no Australian Embassy in Florence, but the policeman, in broken English, offered to contact the British Consulate. Mark spoke to the Vice Consul, who arranged for a taxi to pick up me and the girls from our hotel.

All the children's clothes were stolen, except their pyjamas and the clothes they wore the previous night. I was much better off, because my clothes were in the case Mark had brought up.

We arrived at the Embassy, where a short, rounded woman with permed blonde hair started to fuss over us.

'Oh dear, I think you need a sherry!' she said to me as she ushered the children over to a cupboard. What's your name, dear? Mine's Elena.'

'Jenny. And this is Lauren, and the little one's name is Vanessa.'

'You must be cold, little one,' she said to Vanessa as she pulled out an adult-sized brown and bone angora sweater. 'Here, put this on her.' She handed the sweater to me while she gave Lauren another huge sweater.

The sweater nearly reached Vanessa's knees, and the sleeves hung down well below her hands. I folded them over a few times so her hands were free, and did the same to Lauren's. Meanwhile I was handed a sherry. It was ten o'clock in the morning. Elena was a motherly, old-fashioned and extremely kind lady who kept chatting, asking where we were from, and repeating that she didn't want us to think badly of Florence.

A little while later, a young chap came in and said he had left his passport on top of his car and had driven off. Needless to say, the passport was lost.

'You need a whisky,' said the little Italian woman, who fussed around us all. I learnt later that she was the British Vice Consul. We sat in a corner feeling very sorry for ourselves. As well as the children's and Mark's clothes, all our souvenirs had been in the car too. As we travelled through each country, the children had bought dolls in national dress, and other little knick-knacks that they were very proud of. While we were in Switzerland I had spent a long time choosing a chiming clock for Mum, and now it was gone. I was a little weepy, but needed to put on a brave face for the children. All of a sudden Vanessa cried out, 'The robbers have tooken my … my "tootie"!' At a carnival in Austria, Vanessa had taken a fancy to a little plastic hammer that made a tooting sound when banged on something. She had kept it with her everywhere she went, and of course it had been in the car.

Lauren chimed in, 'My teddy was in the car!' I gulped. Lauren always slept with that teddy, although she hadn't missed it last night. *Now we will have some fun at bedtime*, I thought.

Mark arrived and immediately the Vice Consul handed him a whisky.

'What happened? What did the police say?' I said.

'Oh it was just a complete carry-on. They kept talking in Italian with a little broken English in between. I couldn't understand them and they couldn't understand me. I got the gist that nothing can be done—that it's quite common here.'

'So that's it?'

'Well I made a statement, but they've typed it up in Italian, so heaven knows what it says!'

'What are we going to do? We need clothes for the children, and for you. And most of all, what about my health certificates and the airline tickets?' Fortunately we had our passports and our money.

'Rome has a Qantas office, and you can get some assistance from the Australian Embassy there for the health certificates,' Elena interjected.

'It's just awful! Why did we leave the stuff in the car?'

'You know why: I couldn't cart anything else up four flights of stairs!' said an exasperated Mark. 'The fact is we've come from Switzerland, where everyone is so honest. Remember me telling you about losing my wallet with 400 francs in it? The police rang me at work and told me to come and pick it up. When I offered a reward, they said people didn't expect rewards; it was just the right thing to return what's not theirs. Obviously in Italy it's different.'

'Well I'm afraid it happens a lot here. We have many poor people; it's hard for many to get jobs, and they resort to stealing. Things left in cars are hard for them to resist. They sell the stuff to the second-hand markets,' said Elena.

'Perhaps if we go there we might find some of the children's clothes,' I said sarcastically.

'Probably not,' she said seriously, 'they usually wait a couple of weeks because the tourists will have moved on.'

'Oh,' I said, feeling quite foolish. This woman had been so kind to us.

'You know, I don't want you to leave Florence with a bad impression of our city. It is a beautiful city and we are good people. I'd like you to come to dinner tonight and experience some real Italian hospitality. Do you like spaghetti?'

'Yes,' said Mark with enthusiasm.

'Here's my address … we'll expect you at six o'clock.'

That afternoon we walked the second-hand markets, but of course found nothing. I bought a couple of things for the girls to wear to the Vice Consul's place.

We arrived promptly at six o'clock. Large white pillars stood regally at the entrance to the beautiful home. In the large entrance hall we were introduced to Elena's husband, an equally rounded gentleman with a shining bald head. Tall but stooped, he only spoke Italian, but acknowledged us with a smile. We sat down to eat immediately, and Mark and I glanced at each other. On top of the crisp white linen cloth were several dishes with silver lids. The cutlery was silver and the glasses were crystal. To us it was a banquet. Elena's husband sat at the head of the table. Elena and her two daughters spoke excellent English, but as we spoke, the conversation was continually interrupted, because everything had to be translated for Papa. The silver lid was taken off one of the dishes and the dish was passed around for us to help ourselves to the spaghetti. Mark took a large serve and I dished up the children's. After we had finished, Elena asked Mark if he would like some more and Mark, thinking there was no more food to come, said yes. We chatted away answering questions about Australia while Mark ate his second helping. The daughters were especially interested because they wanted to visit 'the country down under'. Elena had disappeared, but soon reappeared with more silver dishes for the next course, and afterwards several more courses appeared. Mark found it very hard to do justice to the beautiful food because he had filled up on spaghetti.

When the time came for us to leave, Elena went to her cellar and brought back a bottle of wine. 'I want you to go back to Australia thinking kindly of Florence,' she said as she gave me a kiss on each cheek and handed me the bottle. Her daughters gave Lauren and Vanessa a big hug, and Papa shook our hands and smiled. It was such a memorable evening—one not to be forgotten.

The next day, we drove to Rome to seek help from the Australian Embassy to have our health certificates renewed. I had a severe reaction to the smallpox serum before I left Australia and I couldn't have another dose. I needed duplicate certificates, or I would have to spend time in quarantine when I arrived in Australia. We also needed to go to the Qantas office to get replacement airline tickets, and Mark needed to get a part for the car. Getting replacement airline tickets was easy, the part for the car a little more difficult, but how wrong we were about getting help from the Australian Embassy. All they offered were reverse-charge calls to Australia during their office hours of nine to five, which was out of business hours in Australia. We left disgusted, and made our own phone calls from our hotel. We were unable to get hold of Mum, but Mark's Auntie contacted the doctor, and the duplicate certificates were sent to Mark's friends in Switzerland. We had decided the best thing to do was to return to Switzerland and wait for the certificates, then bypass France and go on to England.

We went shopping for clothes at a large department store. The shop assistants only spoke Italian and I only spoke English, so I used sign language, but they were so incredibly rude and unhelpful that I left with only a couple of things.

'We'll go shopping in Switzerland,' I told the girls, who were bitterly disappointed.

We stayed with one of Mark's work colleagues on our return to Switzerland. The colleague's family were all incredibly kind. The wife arranged for her friends and neighbours to provide some clothes for Lauren and Vanessa. She also took us to the shops, where the assistants were helpful, and the girls' wardrobes were replenished with clothes they adored.

We drove to Holland and boarded the ferry for England. Because of the ferry's late arrival and the traffic on the roads, we arrived in Wood Green late at night. Beryl, one of the girls who had worked with me at ACI, had said she would like us to stay with her. However, when we arrived, her mother refused to have us. Beryl apologetically handed us some blankets and warned us to be careful of the police. After our very cold first night in England where we slept in the car in the back streets of Wood Green, we booked into a hotel. We stayed a few days seeing the sights with Beryl before returning to Australia.

All of this now seems such a long time ago. Mum met us at the airport and we went home to a grand celebration that she and Dian had arranged. Mum was very happy to have her brood in her clutches once more.

*

I take the last box and stack it at the front door for the Salvation Army to pick up. I wander back to the room and look around. I can picture Mum sitting up in bed having a cup of tea. She loved her tea, and it was rare for her to be without a cup in her hand. Those last months were so sad; up until then she had been so active with her bowls and other activities. I guess I shouldn't have been surprised when I saw so many people in the chapel when I stood up to speak. She belonged to so many organisations and she did a lot for charity too. The image of

Mum consumes me and as I leave, I pick up the burgundy-coloured thick woollen poncho from the bed and hug it to my chest.

20

Going through the filing cabinet in the garage is all that's left for me to do at Mum's, so with a bit of luck I'll be finished today. Mark has started on the rest of the garage, and will finish when he gets back. He rang last night. He has booked us several nights on the ferry that sails the Inside Passage of Alaska, stopping at the little ports on the way. It will be amazing exploring this part of the world, with its beautiful coastline and inner wilderness. Thank goodness everything will be finished here before I go. We've been married twenty years, but the last seven years or so have been difficult. I'm looking forward to this trip that will, I hope, cement the positive steps we have both taken to improve our marriage and keep it from disintegrating.

When we returned from Europe so long ago, we decided to marry almost immediately, and I clearly remember telling Lauren. I was soaking clothes and I sat her on the washing machine to watch. Lauren was excitedly telling me about Mark burying her in the sand when we were at the beach, so I took the opportunity.

'You like Mark being with us, don't you?' I said as I rubbed the dirty socks.

'Yes, he's fun and he reads good stories.'

'Well Mark and I are going to get married.'

Lauren immediately started to cry.

'Whatever's the matter? I thought you'd be happy.'

'I want to marry him when I grow up!'

I didn't know what to say. I put my arms around her, searching for the right words. 'Darling, it will be a long time till you grow up, so if I don't marry Mark, he'll probably go away and find someone else. Then we won't have him around at all.'

Lauren said nothing but she sobbed less. After a while I said, 'What do you think?'

In a very serious tone, she said, 'I don't want him to go away, so I suppose you can marry him.'

The girls went to Sunday school at St John's in Camberwell, and I regularly attended the church's services, so I wanted to get married there. However, because I was divorced, getting married in front of the main altar was not an option. The vicar suggested we marry quietly at the registry office to get the paperwork. Afterwards he would perform a ceremony in the chapel, and the guests would never know that it was not the official one. Mark and I were aghast, and I angrily said we would get married in a church of another denomination.

'I'm really sorry, but it's out of my hands. I can't marry a divorced person unless I get permission from the Archbishop, and that's next to impossible.'

'Archbishop Dann was my old vicar when I was young; he would remember me, I'm sure. Please ask him?' I replied.

The Archbishop did give permission, on two conditions: that the banns would be read three times in church prior to the ceremony, and that we would be married in the small chapel.

My wedding gown was a simple cream dress that I bought at Katies. The children were very excited to be my attendants. They felt special and looked pretty in their long floral patterned dresses, made by my mother, with puffed sleeves and a frill at the hemline. Lauren's was blue and Vanessa's pink. Together the children and I made small artificial bouquets of tiny flowers for them to carry. However, when we arrived at the church door, the girls froze, so I gently manoeuvred them down the side aisle to the chapel. The vicar was exceptional, and made sure the children were involved in the whole service. Afterwards at the small reception held in the home of one of the parishioners, he again included the children. Lauren was excited and wanted to be in everything, but always stayed close to me.

To allow us to have a weekend away, we arranged for a close friend to look after Lauren, while Vanessa went to Mum's. However, when we left, Lauren chased after the car screaming, so of course I went back to console her. She was anxious and I guess once again felt abandoned. I was cut in two: leave my child, or not go with my new husband. My mother came to the rescue once again and said she'd take both children. Lauren, content to be with her nanna and sister, gave me a big kiss and a hug, and one for Mark. Smiling, she waved us goodbye.

We moved into my old home, which I had left five years previously. In the divorce settlement, the judge awarded possession of the house to me because Steve had not paid maintenance, and Steve's outstanding commitments were equal to his share of the equity in the home. The rental from the house had paid the mortgage, rates and maintenance. However, the last tenants had left it in an appalling state, so Mark and his family decided they were going to renovate it before we moved in.

Each weekend Mark painted, wallpapered and cleaned. I wasn't allowed near the house—he wanted to surprise me. When we moved in as a family, it was like going to a new home—

everything was spick and span. The children had chosen their own colours and wallpapers, even though they hadn't seen their rooms. Vanessa was delighted with the large, bright, purple-flowered wallpaper she had chosen; I was less thrilled, but it was her room and she was happy. Lauren's choice was more demure, and suited the room perfectly. Mark had painted the house in a neutral colour with mission brown woodwork, which was popular at the time. To me it depicted a new start. But as the years passed, I regretted not selling the house and starting afresh, even though the house was so dear to me. Although freshly painted and decorated, it still bore dark memories in every corner. It certainly did not help our relationship. The girls, with a new father and no memory of the house, were more than content, especially when we installed a pool and Mark built an A-frame cubby house similar to the homes we had seen in Switzerland.

Mum continued to be a big part of our lives: sharing Sunday lunch most weekends; joining us on outings; and, although she was not so keen, coming along on our fishing expeditions. When we bought ourselves a boat for waterskiing she joined us, although she stayed on the shore. Often when we went away for weekends she would come along too. Mum and Mark got on well, but occasionally he annoyed her. One day, while I was plating up lunch, Mark suggested I dish up the vegetables before the meat. I always dish up the meat first, I said.

'He's always suggesting what he thinks are better ways of doing things. I wish he would just let you do it,' Mum said later on in an exasperated tone. 'He's always telling you what to do … it gets on my nerves.'

I've remembered those words so often since. Mark's

interfering irritates me. 'Leave me alone,' I say to myself. His way of helping is overpowering.

The girls settled into the local primary school. Lauren showed promise with her studies and Vanessa, similar to her father, just enjoyed having fun. I began seriously thinking about their secondary education. Because I was denied my dream to become a doctor, my goal from the day the girls were born was that they would have the best education possible, that they would go to university if that was their wish, and they would follow the career of their choice. I started researching schools. The public secondary schools in our area didn't have a good reputation; there were rumours of drug-taking, which was not common in schools at that time, and I had no desire for the children to go there. I considered private school, but felt Mark and I couldn't really afford it. Although we were both working, our salaries were only average. Nevertheless, I visited private schools in the surrounding suburbs, comparing one against the other. I considered sending the girls to a co-ed school, but decided against it. I felt they would be better able to excel and have the opportunity to be the best they could be in a girls-only school. During the many months that I researched the schools, I discussed what I was doing with Mark. The money was an issue, but his usual comment when I brought it up was, 'Whatever you want to do is okay ... we'll manage somehow. I can get a second job.'

I was particularly keen on a school in Glen Iris where a wide variety of subjects were offered, ensuring a path into any career. To get to the school, you could catch a bus from the corner of our street, and then a train. The accessibility of the school was nearly as important as what the school offered. I wanted them to be independent travellers, as we both worked and couldn't be running them to and fro.

With Mark's blessing I made an appointment with the headmistress, and the children were invited to attend. I coached them a little about what to expect, without making a big deal about the interview. Unfortunately, of all days, I had a flat tyre on the way and was late for the meeting, so was all a-fluster. We were directed into the headmistress's office by her administrative assistant, and were asked to sit. The headmistress walked in wearing her academic gown, and sat very straight in her high chair behind the desk. She looked severe. I sneaked a look at the children; they were watching her, looking a little scared. We discussed what the school had to offer, including the music programs, physical activities, languages and extra-curricular activities. Then the headmistress turned to Lauren.

'Lauren, do you think you would like to come to our school?'

Lauren quietly answered, 'Yes.'

'And what are the favourite things you like doing at your school?'

'I like reading and writing stories the most,' Lauren shyly answered.

'And what about you, Vanessa? What do you like?'

'Playing,' Vanessa giggled.

I was mortified, but a hint of a smile passed across the headmistress's face, and I relaxed. The headmistress turned to me. 'I think there will be no trouble finding a place for your two daughters when they reach year seven,' she said with a warm smile. With that, the interview was over. She stood up, said goodbye and ushered us out. Lauren was in the third grade and Vanessa in first grade, so it would be a few more years before this prestigious school became very much a part of our lives.

As the girls got older, Mark's constant advice grated on their nerves, and things became strained. He was only trying to help, but their attitude hurt him, and he believed it was because he was their stepfather. I tried to convince him otherwise. 'They're just being kids; most teenagers rebel,' I said. He wouldn't accept that, and the whole family dynamic changed. I was the meat in the sandwich. The girls at times were difficult and rebellious as teenagers can be, and Mark took it to heart, and just didn't know how to deal with it. If I stuck up for them, he would resent me. If I stuck up for him, the girls would be angry with me. It was an impossible situation.

*

All these memories surface as I busily sort through the filing cabinet. Most of the files are full of papers that I can get rid of, but a few I put aside to reconsider later. In the second drawer I find a file labelled 'Miscellaneous'. In it are two very old school reports from when I was in grade one and two. Each is a single sheet of paper, yellowing with age. They are handwritten in old-fashioned script, divided into three parts and headed up 'Ormond State School No 3074, Pupil's Report, Annual Examinations'. I was obviously a good student, as my marks for each subject are mostly nine or ten. I feel quite proud, but when I look at the top of the reports, I'm stunned. In grade one I was absent twenty-three half days in the first half of the year, and fifty-two in the second half of the year. In grade two it was similar: forty-six half days in the first half and forty-three in the second half. That is an astounding amount of time to be away from school. I can't for the life of me think why I would have been absent on such a regular basis. My mother, saddened by my childhood, had on various occasions spoken of those days to me. However, she never mentioned that I had periods of sickness or that I had many days away from school. I can't recall being sick. It is a baffling mystery.

I stand for a long time, looking down at these reports that are fifty years old. I'm trying to recall that time, but nothing comes. Then I have an image of a darkened room, raised voices and sticky pyjamas. It is vivid. I remember waking one night in Ormond to the sounds of my parents fighting, and feeling a sticky substance on my pyjamas. I thought I'd been sick, and so I got out of bed and went to the door, and saw my father dragging my mother down the hallway by her hair. I remember running back to bed and putting my head under the pillow to try and block out the awful noise.

I start to shake; this memory makes it seem like it happened yesterday. Why am I thinking about it now? It fades, and eventually I put the folded reports into my handbag, but a nagging question remains. A vague memory that my father fed me chocolate while I was asleep rises, but I'm not sure. I continue emptying the filing cabinet, wondering what else I'm going to find.

In the next drawer I discover photos dating back to the 1850s. There is a photo developed on tin instead of paper— apparently that is how photos were developed back then. It is my great-great-grandmother: a severe, angry-looking person. I have never seen these photos before, and wonder why Mum never showed them to me. Perhaps because it's my father's side of the family. It's a shame I have to find them after both my parents are dead. These people are certainly relatives, but because most of the photos are not labelled, I will never know who some of these people are—and I would dearly love to know. I pile paperwork that I still need to deal with into a box, and close the empty filing cabinet. Mark will clear out the rest of the garage when we come back from our holiday. He'll have a lovely time pottering around with the tools, deciding what he will take and what he will throw away.

I'm thrown off balance by those reports. The same question keeps running through my mind: why did I have so much time away from school? Unless I remember something, I will never know.

When I arrive home there is a letter from the State Trustees. My brother is requesting early release of the estate because he needs the money for his business. We haven't sold the house yet, and Mum didn't have much in the way of other assets—just a little money in the bank. I'm appalled. What would he have done about his business if Mum were still alive? I throw the letter on the table and make a cup of tea.

I feel miserable. The sorting of Mum's personal papers, the finding of the school report and the resultant memory have all taken their toll. I feel so alone. Lauren left for Canada two weeks ago. She will be there for at least three years, furthering her medical studies, and researching. I miss her terribly. In some ways watching her achieve so much has fulfilled my childhood dream and desire to be a doctor. I guess I'm thankful for my childhood; it fostered a determination that my children would choose their own careers. Vanessa is living in a flat, and is busy working as a nurse. And of course Mark is away. I've got into the practice of going to the Glen shopping centre, sitting in the food court with a cup of coffee and reading the newspaper, just to hear the chatter around me.

Mum's death has brought so much of my past life to the surface that I feel depressed. If I'm honest, I've probably been depressed for a large part of my life. When the volcano erupts, it takes some time for it to subside. I'm overcome with grief, my stomach churns, my throat closes and I feel I can't breathe. I despair for how life could have been. A different childhood would have created a different Jenny and David. I have found it difficult to forge quality relationships with men, whether husband, boss, colleague or friend. If I'd had a father who I was not afraid of, who I could talk to and—most of all—who I could trust, perhaps my dealings with men would be different. If my father, the man in my childhood world, had made me feel special or valuable, maybe I wouldn't have had self-esteem issues.

I grieve for my teenage years, I grieve for my first marriage and I grieve for my second marriage. Mark is a good person and an exceptional stepfather. But we grew apart while Lauren and Vanessa went through those difficult teenage years, which all parents endure. Neither of us handled it well. The girls' attitude irked Mark, and he continued to believe it was because he wasn't their biological father. I felt I was set apart from both Mark and the girls, and I couldn't find the right way to turn it around. This and other factors put a strain on our marriage.

The cost of private school was a struggle, even though Lauren won a half scholarship in year eight; however, my obsession with the girls' education paid off. It provided the stepping-stone for my daughters to achieve all I had hoped for them. Both have been able to follow their dreams, and have done so through hard work. But none of it would have been possible without Mark's willingness to help provide for them.

Mark took a night shelf-stacking position at the local supermarket to help with the finances. He also decided to change his day job in an effort to increase his income, and also because he was dissatisfied. It was a big mistake. He left a secure position, and the new organisation entertained their clients on a large scale. Mark started to drink to excess. He got into debt, was retrenched several times, and mixed with people who took advantage of his depressed state, adding further strain to our marriage. As each problem arose, neither of us dealt with it adequately.

I did not handle myself well. I expressed my built-up anger by yelling at Mark and applying the controlling behaviour I deplored in my father. This affected the whole family. Mark has been so supportive these last few months, and we are working together to get back on track. The concrete wall that rose between us is slowly being chipped away.

*

I fly to Seattle and as I come through the gates, an excited Mark waves. He puts his arms around me and holds me—it reminds me of our meeting in Frankfurt so long ago. He's certainly happy to see me, and the stress and depression I have felt since he went to America lifts.

'We need to go to the other terminal to pick up your case. It's in storage there.' Mark grabs my hand. 'Because we sent it as unaccompanied baggage, customs has opened it.'

'How do you know?'

'They contacted me because it had padlocks on it. They requested permission to break them.'

'I should have just brought it with me.'

'I didn't want you dragging two cases around,' says Mark with a smile.

We reach what looks like a lift to go to the other terminal. It opens and we enter. The doors close and all of a sudden we move sideways. Immediately I have a vision from childhood. I used to have a recurring dream that I was in a lift rushing sideways through buildings. It's uncanny—I feel as if I've been here before. The 'lift' is actually a train that takes us to the other terminal, where we pick up my case.

We board another flight to Anchorage. My first breathtaking sight of Alaska from the plane is memorable: rugged snow-capped mountains as far as the eye can see. We step down from the plane at eleven thirty at night, and it is still twilight. The airport is entirely surrounded with stark, snow-capped mountains. It's surreal.

The next day, we catch a train to Fairbanks, the largest city in the interior of Alaska, and the gateway to Denali National Park. This is to be as far north as we will venture. Denali is total wilderness, and I expected large forested areas, but because it is at such high altitude, it is quite the opposite. The terrain from Anchorage to Denali is permafrost; the top twelve inches has thawed, but the 2000 feet underneath is frozen. It is the land of the fur trapper, the moose, and of course the grizzly bear. But our time in Denali is disappointing; the wildlife we see is only from quite a distance. We return to Fairbanks and spend a little time before flying to Juneau, the capital. Here we stay a few days in a hostel where male and female segregation apply. Mark sleeps in the basement, and I share a room with an eighty-three-year-old backpacking schoolteacher who has a walking stick. I wake in the morning to find she has already gone exploring. The hostel has a lockout procedure during the day until four o'clock, and we are required to do chores on our return. The result is a very clean, well-run hostel that is a delight to stay in.

While in Juneau, we commence our exploration of the Inside Passage. We board a ferry that is aptly called the Marine Highway, and spend the day visiting Haines, where we are lucky to glimpse pods of whales and dolphins. We continue to Skagway, the pathway to the interior. Dating back to the gold rush days, the main street has been restored, with old-style shops, boardwalks and saloons.

The next day, we board a small boat that takes only ten passengers, and head for Tracy Arm. It is certainly a highlight of our trip, as the boat gets so close to the glaciers and wildlife. We see an amazing variety of animals and birdlife, but it is the baby seals and their mothers—on the many tiny icebergs floating past—that are my favourites, with the grizzly bear on the bank a close second. We are in awe as we watch the boat get so close to the glacier, which conveniently calves. The noise as the ice breaks away and slips into the sea is deafening.

We leave Juneau and head southbound on a ferry, sleeping on the back deck in a sleeping bag and enjoying food with the other backpackers, including my former roommate from the hostel. It is a wonderful experience sleeping under the stars, and we are kept warm by the overhead heaters. We leave the ferry at various ports: Petersburg, a sleepy fishing village; and Ketchikan, the totem town, where we stay to explore until the next ferry arrives. Ketchikan is a dreamy little town with oodles of tourist shops. Three cruise ships arrive mid-morning, and the town completely changes. The prices in the tourist shops and cafés increase significantly, and it's bedlam as the town's population grows. We hire a car and drive away from the town, with time to explore the countryside, because the next ferry is not arriving until one in the morning. Alaska is a land of breathtaking scenery, mighty mountains, magnificent crystal-clear lakes, and rugged and wild countryside. It is peaceful, vivid and unique.

In this magical land, Mark and I relax. We walk, we talk, we laugh and we make peace with each other. After our arrival in Vancouver, Mark returns to work in Australia. I stay to explore the magic vistas of Canada, visiting Jasper, Whistler, Banff and Lake Louise. While walking down the main street in Banff, I think I see my mother. I initially think my mind is playing tricks, but even so, I run after her. Of course, it's not her. I've been able to put aside my grief while I've been with Mark, but on my own, my memories of my mother return.

I decide there and then that I will seek professional help for my grief and anger on my return to Australia. I need to deal with all the issues that are haunting me. I've spent more than half my life being angry that my father drank, angry that he refused to let me be a doctor or a nurse, angry that he was both emotionally and physically abusive to his family, and angry that he didn't seem to care for me. Talking to someone and giving voice to the past may heal the pain. I have become angry about everything; I have to let it go.

Epilogue

It is Easter Sunday, and all my family have congregated at Lauren's for lunch. She has cooked a fabulous roast lunch, and Vanessa has brought a Pavlova. Now we've adjourned to the local park for a game of cricket.

I'm standing at the back, fielding, watching my family enjoying their time together. Now in my seventies, it is such a pleasure to experience normal family life. Vanessa is so much like Steve, and fortunately has inherited his good points. She is noisy and enjoys having fun, just as he did. Watching her fielding on the other side of the wicket takes me back to the cricket matches at The Vine. She is long and lean, and when she runs for the ball and kicks her long legs high behind her, it's as if Steve is here. Her mannerisms are similar, and the way she moves her body—it is uncanny. But Vanessa is strong, intelligent, kind and thoughtful. She chose a nursing career just like her nanna   a career I would have relished. She continued educating herself, and twenty-plus years later, she is now a nursing educator and Associate Professor. She passionately believes that nurses must follow processes, and that patient care is paramount. This is the ethos she promotes to her students.

Lauren has energy plus. She is continually on the go, filling her day to capacity. She makes me tired watching her.

She strives to excel at everything she does, whether it is coping with a sick patient, mothering her children, writing a research paper, keeping fit, or just playing a cricket match. Everything is a challenge. As I watch her now, she is determined to catch that ball, to get that extra run, and I guess that mentality has got her to where she is. She is a Professor of Medicine, and well-regarded by her peers. It is ironic that my daughters have chosen the two careers that I dreamt of, but was prevented from pursuing. I don't believe I influenced them, although perhaps there were some subliminal suggestions—who knows?

But the delights of my life are my four grandchildren; each one is so special, yet so different. They bring so much into my life: joy, love, tears and fun. When I held my eldest grandson Michael in my arms for the first time, I was so overwhelmed with a love I never knew I could experience. For me love had always been scary, yet this all-consuming feeling was so powerful, and filled me with such happiness. It was identical to the emotion I felt when I held my own babies in my arms. This powerful force has been repeated with each subsequent grandchild as I've held him or her for the first time.

Michael is now eleven. He is a quiet boy, a dreamer, but very creative and kind. As I watch him today, he is not involved with the cricket match. Vanessa, his mother, noticed this, and has left the others. Now Michael has a tennis racket and is hitting a ball to her. He is somewhat a loner, but an exceptional lad.

Michael's sister Catherine is batting. She is only nine, but tall, and looks at least twelve. She is loud like her mother, loves having fun, and is a born organiser. Vanessa calls her Miss Secretary. She does her own packing if staying overnight with us, she cooks, she checks her mother is keeping appointments, and she rings us each day to chat. I love that.

Lauren's daughter Isabelle is also nine. She is competitive and always tries hard to succeed. She is petite and has beautiful golden hair. She's also smart, and an avid reader. Like Catherine, she also likes to organise. She loves clothes and has a very eclectic taste. I don't know when I last saw her without nail polish on her fingers. When she rings me, I just love the way she says, 'Hello, Nanna!' It's like a drawl, but is so endearing. It gives me a lump in my throat.

Little Connor is Lauren's youngest, and my youngest grandchild. He is five, loves numbers and is obsessed with Lego. His hugs and kisses are rationed at the moment, but I'm hoping that will change. He has long legs and runs fast, chasing the ball, which he throws accurately to the bowler.

The two fathers take it all in their stride. What amazing men my daughters have chosen; both are caring, strong, supportive, and great fathers.

This day confirms how blessed I am. It could have been quite different for all of us. I'm glad I married Steve, because from that union came my amazing girls and my precious grandchildren. And I'm glad I left Steve, because my daughters have had opportunities that would have been impossible if I'd stayed. I'm glad I married Mark; otherwise I wouldn't have experienced the wonderful early years of our marriage, or travelled the world. He was very young to take on a family, and blended family difficulties arose, but even so, he brought us stability. Without Mark's help, private school for the girls would have been impossible.

On my return from Alaska, I sought professional help in an attempt to understand and resolve my childhood terrors and to try to recall my memory of the sticky substance on my pyjamas. I also wanted to moderate my controlling behaviour, and get help with my grieving. Seeing my mother emotionally abused and physically assaulted terrorised me, and created psychological problems. I got stuck in my development, and this permanently affected my ability to trust, especially when it comes to men. It also affected my self-confidence. A couple of years ago I read *The Bean Patch*, where the author Shirley Painter considered the question 'Where does a ruined childhood live?' She asked 'Does it slip into a pocket marked "past" and stay there? No, it doesn't. It lives in your heart and marks you.' This happened to my brother and me.

During therapy I came to understand that my past had created my present, but that I could create my future. The counsellor suggested I jot down memories as they arose, so my snippets of writing began. Once my memories were on paper, a weight seemed to lift. I went back to school and studied for my Higher School Certificate, and then I went to university, which I had to discontinue. Mark was made redundant, and with both girls at university, I needed to return to full-time employment. I took on a position that provided opportunities, and I became a project manager within an IT department. I continued to see my therapist, and this process continued for a long period of time, resulting in much being resolved.

While I was seeking professional help, I read *You Can Heal Your Life* by Louise L Hay. This book, more than anything else, taught me self-acceptance, self-worth and self-love. In her book, Hay promotes self-affirmation, modifying thought patterns, releasing the past, and forgiveness. Her philosophy is that the point of power is always in the present, and the past has no power over us. What we think of ourselves becomes the truth for us.

Her book became a bible for me, and I started to apply her

philosophy to my daily life. I continued my snippets of writing, and returned to study, choosing a part-time Professional Writing course at TAFE. This was not because I was confident writer— quite the opposite. Communication, both written and spoken, had always been a challenge for me. Study provided a much-needed outlet, as well as stimulation and social interaction. The snippets became longer, and grew into chapters of a book.

For a long time after my mother's death, I was sad and lonely; I missed her more than I had expected. So while I was studying at TAFE, I decided to volunteer in both palliative care and childcare. I commenced a palliative care course at a local hospital and on completion, started working in the unit. Volunteering and my writing continued the healing process that counselling had commenced. It was a privilege to care, in a volunteer role, for people who were nearing the end of their life, and to help their visiting relatives in small ways. Nobody, however close, understands how a daughter feels about her mother dying until it happens. I had some amazing conversations with both patients and relatives, that made me realise that life and relationships are complicated, and no two relationships are the same. Volunteering with children brightened my day. Being given the privilege to look after quadruplets was both fascinating and enjoyable. I started caring for the two boys and two girls from when they were three months old until they were about two, and it was a constant joy. This led to further roles: helping mothers who had multiple births, and those suffering from postnatal depression, as well as mothers with handicapped children.

I graduated from TAFE with a Diploma in Professional and Creative Writing, and soon after, my first grandchild arrived. He and my other grandchildren, as they arrived, took precedence, and my writing was shelved for quite a few years. However, my desire to go to university and gain a degree never ceased, so eventually I enrolled and completed an arts degree, majoring in Professional Writing. I wasn't confident; I struggled in classes, and was mortified when the class workshopped my writing. However, the workshopping and my assignments allowed me to return to and improve the chapters that I had written years ago. Thus *The Vine Bleeds* evolved. I get a deep satisfaction from writing; I also get frustrated when the words don't go on the paper the way they are in my head. Writing has been my saviour, and I'm so thankful that my counsellor, all those years ago, suggested I write down my memories.

The mystery of the absentee days and those memories of the stained pyjamas were not resolved. My counsellor suggested I should consider that I'd been sexually abused, as did a close friend and neighbour who I confided in. I can't accept this scenario. For all my father was, I can't accept that he would have hurt me in that way. Down in the depths of my memory, I believe I was told my drunken father fed me chocolate while I was asleep. This memory has not haunted me, but it puzzles me, as do the absentee days on my school reports. What did haunt me for an enormous part of my life was the memory of the physical and emotional abuse directed towards my mother, brother and myself. Fortunately it does not plague me any longer, but I can't help thinking how different our lives could have been. I am intelligent enough to have been a doctor, and I would have dearly loved the privilege of helping others get well.

I have intermittent contact with my brother, which is usually initiated by me. I am saddened by this. He lives interstate and doesn't seem to desire the relationship. We were both damaged by our past, and for many years I suffered debilitating bouts of depression, and perhaps he does too. My childhood was sad, and a major part of my adulthood was difficult. Most of my life has been a mix of vulnerability and strength. I remember reading somewhere that 'the little kid that lives inside us won't leave us alone until we give them a voice.' Dr C Cameron, in her article 'Dark Memories', said, 'the effort of confronting the past strengthened and ultimately enriched the lives of those who had found the courage to do it.' I have given the little kid a voice and I now know it is not so much what happens to us that matters—it is what we do about it. I look back at my life and there are many things I would do differently, but much that happened has made me stronger. I've been told it is true that you only have to forgive once. If you resent, you have to do it all day, every day. I have chosen to forgive my father. I have stopped being angry with him. I am at peace, and blessed with a marvellous family and grandchildren I adore.

Biography - J M Yates

Born in Melbourne, Australia in the 1940s, Jenny Yate's middle-class family was dominated by domestic violence, which had a profound influence on her life choices. She left school at fifteen but returned to study in later life, gained her Higher School Certificate and enrolled in a writing course. Jenny never planned to write a book but her yearning for education led her to university. After she obtained her Batchelor of Arts majoring in Professional writing she completed her memoir, *The Vine Bleeds*.

The Vine Bleeds

J M Yates

ISBN 9781925367003   Qty

RRP   AU$24.99   .....

Postage within Australia   AU$5.00   .....

TOTAL★ $_____

★ All prices include GST

Name:..

Address: ....

....

Phone:...

Email: ....

Payment: ❏ Money Order ❏ Cheque ❏ MasterCard ❏ Visa

Cardholder's Name:...

Credit Card Number: ....

Signature:..

Expiry Date: ....

Allow 7 days for delivery.

Payment to: Marzocco Consultancy (ABN 14 067 257 390)
PO Box 12544
A'Beckett Street, Melbourne, 8006
Victoria, Australia
admin@brolgapublishing.com.au

Be Published

Publish through a successful publisher.
Brolga Publishing is represented through:
• **National** book trade distribution, including sales,
marketing & distribution through **Macmillan Australia.**
• **International** book trade distribution to
    • The United Kingdom
    • North America
    • Sales representation in South East Asia
• Worldwide e-Book distribution

For details and inquiries, contact:
Brolga Publishing Pty Ltd
PO Box 12544
A'Beckett St VIC 8006

Phone: 0414 608 494
markzocchi@brolgapublishing.com.au
ABN: 46 063 962 443
(Email for a catalogue request)

www.ingramcontent.com/pod-product-compliance
Lightning Source LLC
Chambersburg PA
CBHW071404090426
42737CB00011B/1350